The New Orleans Program

The

New Orleans
Program

EAT, EXERCISE, AND ENJOY LIFE

David A. Newsome, M.D.
and
Chef John Besh

PELICAN PUBLISHING COMPANY
GRETNA 2006

The word "Pelican" and the depiction of a pelican are trademarks
of Pelican Publishing Company, Inc., and are registered in the
U.S. Patent and Trademark Office.

Library of Congress Cataloging-in-Publication Data

Newsome, David A.
    The New Orleans program : eat, exercise, and enjoy life / David A.
Newsome and John Besh.
        p. cm.
    Includes index.
    ISBN-13: 978-1-58980-344-2 (hardcover : alk. paper)
    1. Low-fat diet. 2. Low-fat diet—Recipes. 3. Cookery—Louisiana—New
Orleans. 4. Cookery, American—Louisiana style. 5. New Orleans (La.)—
Social life and customs. I. Besh, John. II. Title.
    RM237.7.N49 2006
    641.5'6384—dc22

                                                    2005032899

With the writing assistance of Mariann S. Regan, Ph.D., Professor of English,
Fairfield University, Fairfield, Connecticut

The contents of this book are intended for informational purposes only. No
medical or related diagnostic or therapeutic uses are intended, expressed, or
implied.

Printed in the United States of America

Published by Pelican Publishing Company, Inc.
1000 Burmaster Street, Gretna, Louisiana 70053

To Jennifer, Brendan, Jack, Bobby,
Paul, Dwight, Torrey, and Danielle

Contents

Preface

We knew a ferocious hurricane was coming but hoped desperately it wouldn't be a direct hit. That pleasantly sweet summer morning of August 28, 2005, turned sour when I glanced at the *Times-Picayune* headline: *Katrina takes aim.*

"Let's go. Pack *now.*" Those were strange words from someone who had ridden out every hurricane of the previous twenty years. The same words echoed in the home of Chef Besh and countless other New Orleanians, lifelong hurricane rider-outers. Soon, our eldest but roomiest vehicle became an ark of sorts—adults, children, and dogs all piled in together. We expected, as did most, to return in three days.

Not this time. It was as though Chicken George—feathered Panama hat, gris-gris, and all—had gotten Mother Nature to deliver a double whammy.

We began an odyssey throughout the eastern United States, occasionally stopping with relatives and friends and some fellow evacuees to exchange war stories. Everywhere we went, people's reactions echoed: "Oh my God, how horrible! You know, the last time we were in New Orleans, you wouldn't believe how much fun we had!" Tears mingled with smiles.

This book, finished in great measure before Katrina and her storm surge laid to waste our storied and beautiful and unique city, should not serve as her obituary.

Rather, we hope it demonstrates the need for the real New Orleans to survive: from Paw-Paw's gumbo joints, to married couples who pass by Auntie's or Mamma's on Mondays for that "best red beans and rice in town" spiced with stories, to Mardi Gras Indians, to seersucker-bow-tied Uptowners.

Driving through a poorer area of the city on the way to check on our house, I passed by a family barbecuing and picnicking in their recently submerged but now dry front yard. Nothing was green, just brown and gray. They came back, they said, "because it's home."

We had asked ourselves on our evacuation odyssey, "If we can't get back to New Orleans, where else would we like to live?" The unanimous answer was, "Nowhere else."

The whole country needs the New Orleans attitude, for its own health and life. The spirit of the city inheres in those who fled and will continue as they return to heal. Our book is full of hope and joy. We hope the entire nation will welcome not only the personally restorative nature of this book, but the restorative nature of our beloved New Orleans itself.

DAVID A. NEWSOME

Red beans and rice is a simple dish, the historical staple of the New Orleans diet, the traditional Monday "washday" meal, and in many ways, the city's staff of life. It takes very little effort to prepare, tend, and serve. It is fully nutritious, providing complete sustenance at very little cost. It was part of what I packed my truck to the bursting point with, in the weeks following Hurricane Katrina, on missions into the city to find and feed my staff, my neighbors, my fellow citizens: beans, rice, fresh water, and gasoline.

My recipe for red beans and rice and many other such fundamental, restorative, New Orleans dishes are here in the pages of this book—recipes for rebuilding yourself and your loved ones as we rebuild this city—together.

As I repeated these "red-beans-and-rice missions of mercy," it occurred to me that the recipe for the rebuilding of New Orleans itself is really very simple, too:

It all boils down to faith, hope, and love.

We must have faith in the people of New Orleans—a passionate, tenacious, and gifted people.

Let us build a city full of hope for all its citizens, by providing for each and every one.

We must love, respect, and nurture one another and work to heal the city's ills.

The old charm of New Orleans will be preserved through its architecture, music, food, and hospitality. Our cultural arts are our biggest resource and are what bring and keep us together, all races and all creeds. We don't need to sell our city. We need to clean it up and establish sound fundamental services. We need to keep the music playing, keep the beans and rice cookin', and it will return—better than ever.

JOHN BESH

Acknowledgments

This book, which we hope will be received as the first true postmodern diet book, achieved delivery at the hands of many midwives. We wish to thank and acknowledge the several and particular contributions of those who helped birth this baby.

Dwight Thaggard provided extensive research efforts, scouring Web sites and media archives to help assure we had the most current information. He also provided a great measure of the final production effort, so critical to realizing the project: that "no dessert until you finish your mashed potatoes" phase.

Assistant chef Eric Smith provided invaluable efforts in putting the recipes we offer into publishable form.

Catrinel Stancieu, of Louisiana State University, patiently provided answers to food-content questions.

Our dear friend Doris Shaheen and Ayako Goto Sever provided thoughtful and constructive ideas to improve the concept, and careful readings of the text to assure flow and reader friendliness.

Kent Mercier provided suggestions and information on the importance of family involvement, especially at mealtimes, in a child's future success.

Clinical investigation requires not only the discipline of a protocol, but more importantly the care and enthusiasm of a dedicated crew and their ability to keep participants engaged, interested, and coming back. Ferdette Johnson and her raconteur husband, Roland Johnson, sparked the group in a community of faith that allowed us to discover the real-world value of the New Orleans Program. Others who made the clinical trials successful included Elinne Dison, with her technical expertise, and Chauncey Packer, an internationally known opera singer, who also contributed expertise in exercise routines. Many forget that singers are also athletes. Melissa Lampkins, operating-room tech extraordinaire, captained the Lighten Up Louisiana Team utilizing the New Orleans Program. Only doctors are worse patients than nurses.

We are grateful to all who took the time to be interviewed. We particularly thank Jessica Sorgenfrei for establishing a comfort level with obese teens so that they would give revealing answers in their interviews, and agree to try the program.

Finally, we thank all our teachers.

Introduction

A STORY FOR OUR TIMES: TOWANDA

Recently one of my eye patients announced to me, "My niece has gone blind!"

Her twelve-year-old niece, Towanda, had been gaining weight for a few years. Then her grades took a sudden dive. Why? Because all at once, Towanda couldn't see the blackboard. She couldn't read. Towanda was diagnosed with high blood pressure and Type II diabetes. She was given medication and instructions about diet, and her family was told that Towanda should exercise more and eat less. Yet as the months went by, Towanda wouldn't follow the guidelines. Her vision deteriorated until she couldn't stay in school, or leave the house alone. She remained at home, inactive, with her blood pressure and diabetes growing worse.

At this point, I learned about Towanda from her aunt. When I gave Towanda an ophthalmological exam, I discovered that very dense cataracts were making her legally blind. Her family and doctors worked to improve her medical condition enough for surgery. When we removed her cataracts and discovered only a few other diabetes-related eye problems, we were able to make Towanda see almost perfectly with glasses. She agreed to catch up on her schoolwork and follow written eating and exercise plans for better health.

Towanda became one incentive for us to design and clinically test our own plan for healthy eating and age-appropriate exercise. We call it the New Orleans Program. My friend Mavis Early, a recently "graduated" city attorney now in private practice, reacted to the linking of New Orleans to a best-health program: "That's an oxymoron!" This is not true, as you will learn. This program has helped Towanda and other obese young people, along with their parents. Appendix B is a minimal sketch of our program. Our book fills out this sketch with our supporting reasons, and it expands our advice to give readers the whole picture. In this spirit, we've added delectable recipes and some cultural wisdom from New Orleans.

Now, Towanda is performing better in school. She's lost weight and finds her diabetes much easier to control. She doesn't need high-blood-pressure medication anymore. This is indeed a happy ending for Towanda.

Towanda's story is a story for our times. She is the tip of a public-health iceberg. Imagine: Towanda became ill from eating the wrong foods and not exercising. This health threat simply did not exist in the past.

Yet Towanda's story is becoming a common one. We are beginning to realize in America that our cultural patterns of eating and inactivity are a danger to us all, adults and children. It's as if we're pouring ourselves an obituary cocktail—that New Orleans term for an overindulgent drink that could put the drinker into the obituary column.

OUR OBITUARY COCKTAIL IS NOT OUR FRIEND

It may seem extravagant to claim that our food culture is luring us towards early death. Yet it's true. The facts bear us out, and we can't afford to ignore them. We are up against a formidable foe. Let's not underestimate the enemy! Our obituary cocktail of unhealthy food is pushed at us by the dominant culture, like an irresponsible bartender pushing a loaded drink: "Have just one more." We Americans are eating ourselves to death, as testified to by mounting rates of breast, colorectal, and other cancers. Our epidemic of childhood and adult obesity, diabetes, and high blood pressure has created headlines. Big business even feels the sting. A recent *Wall Street Journal* lead article revealed the financial strain that paying for employee obesity-related disease placed on profitability.

In the 1970s, Pres. Richard Nixon declared a "War on Cancer." Today, health statisticians tell us that war has been miserably lost. While cardiac fatalities have declined slightly since the 1990s, deaths from several types of cancer have continued to rise.

The richest nation on earth has become the fattest—and the sickest. Between 1996 and 2002, America's pharmaceutical bills doubled, from $75 to 150 billion. As a nation, we now let fast-food outlets set up shop in our children's school cafeterias, while we can't find the time to sit down with our families over a home-cooked meal. Only one in three Americans, according to the Surgeon General, gets enough exercise. Fewer than one in twenty maintains a nutritious diet, concludes a recent California study. Corporate influences invade our homes with targeted advertising, and corporate interests have transformed even our food supply. The technology of the food industry and the fevered pace of modern life aggravate these problems. We are under a profound threat to public health.

We are at risk.

Our children are at risk.

The authors of this book, like so many others, have been sucked into the quicksand of America's eating habits. Victims of our national obesity epidemic are everywhere. One of us has helped his own child out of this predicament. We envision an escape for us all.

Diets? Diets are part of the problem, not part of the solution. *Diets don't work. Diets create unhappiness.* We need a sustainable solution, a firmer place to stand than the latest "diet." We want meals that don't leave us feeling deprived or sick. We deserve an occasional party without drowning in anxiety. We seek healthier and more vital lives for ourselves and our loved ones.

FRIENDLY ADVICE

The New Orleans Program can help. It offers the *informed common sense* we need to stay healthy. It contains easy recipes for the Southern Louisiana food its authors love. It provides doable exercises. It supplies knowledge about our bodies that we can turn into action. In plain terms, it demonstrates how to eat well, exercise well, and nurture our spirits. Our book is a guide, but it's not some rigorous schedule that will drain away time and money. Our advice is adaptable and useful in balancing each person's lifestyle. It will help you to create the healthiest, happiest you possible, and to maintain that desirable you.

Our book is *not* a diet book.

In our book we are answering Towanda's alarming story with action. After studying the science and reading the experts, after clinically verifying our New Orleans Program, we have found an approach to food and exercise that works for adults and obese young people—even in twenty-first-century America. Sometimes revelations occur even in the depths of the bayous. We are as excited about our discovery as Jim Boudreaux must have been, one July morning in 1991, when he caught sight of a nest of alligator eggs in a swamp near Bayou Teche. One newly hatched white alligator was there among the eggs. After checking for alligator parents, Jim gathered up the eggs and the hatchling. Now white alligators, a refreshment for the eye, are thriving at the New Orleans Audubon Nature Institute.

Like Jim Boudreaux, we are transporting our discovery to a wider audience. The clinical success of the New Orleans Program has inspired us to write this book. We want to nourish our readers, by teaching simple and pleasurable food and exercise habits that work from birth through advanced age. As Albert Einstein said, "Everything should be made as simple as possible, but not one bit simpler." We mean to clarify the science behind our program, and we offer methods of resisting our society's twin addictions—fast food and diets. These addictions promise pleasure, but they do more harm than good. We believe that life is to be enjoyed, and food to be savored, all our lives long. We believe in sustained and pleasurable health.

THE NEW ORLEANS PROGRAM

I've been there. In 2001, I was trapped by fast-food eating patterns. When I rushed between offices at lunchtime, my only practical meal was fast food. Or so I thought. A hot burger with French fries and a large drink certainly hit the spot. Once or twice a week I treated myself to a New Orleans po' boy (fried "ersters," fully dressed with hot sauce and extra lettuce). Before I knew it, I had that typical post-forty waistline, creeping outwards slowly but surely. I looked down, and there it was. I checked the mirror. There it was again, under my chin.

I stopped and asked myself what I was doing. I checked my health statistics and found trouble. My Body Mass Index was 30. My waist had ballooned to thirty-nine inches. Even though I was trying (not always successfully) to exercise at least thirty minutes three times a week, I was nevertheless expanding. So I looked at what I was eating and how I was eating it. At the same time, I discovered that my older daughter had an early teenage version of my same problem.

As I worked on my eating choices, the New Orleans Program was born. I discussed it in detail with my friend, Chef Besh. We developed and refined it together. Along the way, Chef Besh had an epiphany: He was shocked to realize what his family was eating even while he was preparing healthful food professionally. "We're now on the program," he recently said.

The New Orleans Program has been clinically tested and is clinically successful. It is a guide to better health and longer life. Our program rests upon three specific pillars, as outlined below.

The Three Components of the New Orleans Program

- Healthy eating (chapters 1-8, Appendix B)
- Adequate exercise (chapter 9)
- A self-nurturing spirit (chapters 10-11)

Our third component, "a self-nurturing spirit," may seem a bit mysterious. We intend no mystery, and we'll explain further in chapter 10. We simply mean to honor the various terms by which people refer to this vital pillar of health. Self-nourishment, cultivation of spirituality, relaxation, stress reduction, prayer, meditation, quiet time, self-centering, and peace of mind are among these terms. We believe this area combines both personal nurture and connectedness with others, on both intimate and social levels. In our quest to improve health and longevity, we feel we must attend carefully to the wellbeing of the human spirit—and we use the word "spirit" in its most inclusive sense.

Our second component, "adequate exercise," is about feeling good, not about being oppressed. Without exhausting yourself, you can get real and substantial benefits from our suggested exercises. We present our recommendations in chapter 9, where we offer two phases of exercise, one for beginners and another for longer-term participants. Here's some exciting scientific news. Even if your weight loss is less than ideal, exercise can help protect you against heart problems and other diseases.

Our first component, "healthy eating," is the subject of our first eight chapters. We believe that to eat for health, we must at the same time eat for enjoyment. A family member who cultivates healthy eating is, by example, encouraging loved ones and children to do the same.

BEGINNING THE NEW ORLEANS PROGRAM

For those who choose to begin the New Orleans Program, we have done our best to include in this book what you need for "healthy eating," our first component. These are our goals, as authors:

"Healthy Eating" from the New Orleans Program

- We give you accurate information about eating choices.
- We explain why these choices can guide you to better health and longer life.
- We provide a short list of *pas bonnes,* strict no-nos, for a start.
- We guide you in preparing and reconnecting with healthful food.

You are the source of motivation and action. Before starting our program, you will probably also want to know what our clinical results are, how you can expect to feel on the program, and what foods we restrict.

CLINICAL RESULTS OF THE NEW ORLEANS PROGRAM

After three years of personal experience and individual successes on our program, we began the small family program described in chapter 1. We also shared our program with persons at a large midtown New Orleans community of faith. Altogether, we have collected results on more than one hundred patients who tried the New Orleans Program.

For the initial six-month period, our participants naturally divided themselves into two groups: those who followed our program well by using our manual, and those who did not stay on our program regularly. Here are the results from one structured adult group test for Phase I (six months). "Yes" includes fourteen who followed the program; "no" includes six who did not. Values are averages, with ranges.

	Group "Yes"		Group "No"	
	Start	End	Start	End
Age (years)	48 (30 to 59)		46 (37 to 59)	
Height (inches)	65 (63 to 70)		65 (62 to 70)	
Waist	39 (36 to 47)	37 (34 to 45)	39 (37 to 42)	No change
Weight	201 (162 to 292)	188 (152 to 280)	214 (179 to 246)	218 (182 to 251)
Blood Sugar	246 (95* to 210)	107 (83 to 130)	151 (88 to 217)	149 (91 to 221)
Blood Pressure	144/91 (112/ 80 to 164/98)	124/84 (118/ 72 to 152/92)	150/90 (132/ 86 to 160/94)	152/92 (134/ 86 to 162/96)
Cholesterol	242 (105 to 356)	194 (113 to 238)	215 (193 to 238)	221 (191 to 245)
(Total/ "bad")	189 (137 to 201)	133 (94 to 167)	169 (150 to 192)	179 (146 to 196)

*Note: 4 "yes" subjects had normal blood sugar at the start; 12 had normal blood sugar (about 120) at the end. One "no" had normal sugar both times.

Today, more than 90 percent of those who were successful in the program tell us they have stuck with it and kept the weight off. Some have even reached their ideal weights. These people are fitter and healthier, more than a year after the program has formally ended.

We find these results exciting. Clearly, the New Orleans Program can be understood, used, and maintained by people with real obesity and health concerns.

The weight lost over a six-month period averages two pounds a month. More weight is lost after the first month has passed, because the first month is spent revving up the metabolism and enabling the body to lose weight. The "yes" folks consistently reduced their blood sugar and blood pressure, even when they had lost only 10 to 15 percent of their starting weight. The cholesterol reductions were impressive, even though the numbers did not drop to the targeted blood cholesterol levels.

Participants in our structured groups documented what they ate every day. We met monthly to gather data on weight, blood pressure, blood sugar, and eating patterns from the checklist in the manual. Chef Besh provided recipes and cooking demonstrations on how to prepare quick, inexpensive, and delicious meals at home.

HOW THE NEW ORLEANS PROGRAM WILL PROBABLY AFFECT YOU

The program takes about six months to become fully established. After the first month, you may not notice much weight loss. Don't be discouraged. Unlike some radical "diets" whose early success is often driven by very low calories and water loss, the New Orleans Program is not a diet. It is for keeps. It is not—like many popular diets—dangerous. It works and keeps on working. After about a month, you will see slow but steady weight loss.

"I can't believe it!" Leatrice, a forty-eight-year-old professional lady in for an eye check excitedly told me about her twelve-pound weight loss after following the program just four months. "I saw my doctor yesterday. My blood pressure was much better. My sugars have been so good, she's taking me off insulin." Leatrice was still somewhat overweight (BMI now 27), but even a less than ideal weight loss paid off handsomely. Her experience is the rule, not the exception.

The exercise and self-nurture components of our program may show results more quickly. You may notice a lift in your spirits, even though you may be slightly sore from beginning to exercise. This is because you are relearning pleasure in moving your body. Your metabolism is improving. After the first six months, you will have lost weight, revved up your metabolism, enhanced your energy, improved your sleeping, reduced your internal stress, and discovered a change in your relationship to food, exercise, other people, and life. This change can be permanent.

Our participants found the program easy to follow, even though they were reluctant to give up favorite foods. We often heard, "How can I stop eating ice cream? I've always eaten ice cream. I love ice cream. It's a reward, and I enjoy it." We know how this feels. Yet when we see food in its true sense, as nourishment, we must admit that ice cream is not a key nutrient. When we eat a lot of it, we're exposed to an unbalanced load of high calories, sugars, and bad fats. Yet after six months on our program, with metabolism revved and weight coming down and our good connection with food reforged, we can still eat ice cream once in a while, in moderation. On the program, people look back and wonder how they ever enjoyed those globs of greasy fries and double-cheese pizza. They wonder how they ever inhaled that entire quart of ice cream. They have retaught themselves pleasure in food. They've found more interesting things to eat.

RESTRICTED FOODS ON THE NEW ORLEANS PROGRAM

We don't have a lot of restrictions. In fact, we encourage a cornucopia of foods and cuisines. But even at Jazz Fest, there must be a few rules. After all, we do live in the food climate of twenty-first-century America. So we have some no-nos. By not eating these, you'll find it easier to carry out the rest of the New Orleans Program.

Specific *Pas Bonnes* (No-nos) for the First Six Months

- No "fast food" except salads. Avoid the prepared dressings. (If you don't believe us, read the ingredients—calorie-dense, chemical gunk!) Oil and vinegar is best. Minimize salt. "Subway" products are OK but boring in repetition.
- No French fries. These are high-calorie, trans-fat city. Let fast-food fries get cold, then try to eat them. The awful flavor makes quitting easy.
- No fatty meats. Lean, trim meat, steaks, roasts, cutlets, and chops are great. A 5-oz. lean pork chop has under 200 calories; packs protein, vitamins, minerals, and some fiber; and is more digestible than chicken.
- No bread except 1 slice regular, low-nutritional, commercial bread or 2 slices true whole-grain bread a day. One pat of real butter is OK.

- No more than 1 8-oz. glass of fruit juice or sugary cold drink a day. Sugar-free brewed tea, filtered coffee, or diet drinks in small amounts are OK.
- No snack stuff, like chips, candy, or cheese puffs. Don't even ask! You need to get out of the snack habit anyway. (That's all it is—you do *not need* snacks.)
- No dessert. Eat a piece of fruit instead.
- No donuts. These are sugar and trans-fat city. One beignet once a week? OK, cher.
- No ice cream. It is too calorie dense and too easy to "pig out" on.

With this list of no-nos, which may seem to include the "favorite foods" of many people, the hardest part of our New Orleans Program is out of the bag. These foods may smile at us, but they are not our friends.

According to the Pew Research Center (www.Pewinternet.org.), 100 million Americans a year go online to search for health information. They do this not just in reaction to health problems but to prevent disease and maintain their health. Our Web site, www.theneworleansprogram.com, is regularly updated. It addresses your questions, from food choices and cooking tips to exercise formats and relaxation techniques. You may use it to personalize your own New Orleans Program.

Babies, children, young people, and adults—this book is for all Americans.

The New Orleans Program

CHAPTER 1

New Year's Day:
It All Begins with a Baby

Our first chapter begins where life begins, with a baby. It offers some nutritional advice for parents through their children's preschool years, as well as coping strategies for when their school-age children leave home and meet today's food culture. Our primary goal is to prevent obesity. Yet if a child does become obese, this chapter offers practical, workable help and hope.

PRELUDE TO A NEW LIFE: JOY, HOPE, NURTURE

New Orleans has its fireworks, parties, and Sugar Bowl crowds for New Year's Day, but our real carnival season begins on Kings' Day: January 6. Our spectacle of the Phunny Phorty Phellows in their St. Charles Avenue streetcar and of the Twelfth Night Revelers marks the twelfth day after Christmas, the sixth of January. On that day, our gift exchanges mark the visit of the three Wise Men—the Three Kings—bringing gifts to the Christ Child. Of the many cycles that New Orleans celebrates, the largest cycle moves from birth, to life, to death, and again to birth.

The presentation of the king cake is a fifteenth-century French custom adapted for New Orleans Twelfth Night parties and the carnival season. These ring-shaped cakes traditionally contained one coin or jeweled bean. Those who discovered this hidden charm in their piece of cake won a year's good luck and had to host the next year's party. New Orleans king cakes have a special charm inside: a baby, in the form of a tiny doll.

Several years ago, when my niece was trying to become pregnant and my sister yearned to be a grandmother, I bought a king cake and took it to a local voodoo priest. He blessed the cake with some special gris-gris. The cake found its way to my sister's place of business, and she received the slice with the baby. A month later, she got the good news of impending motherhood and grandmotherhood. This was our family's king cake highlight.

Our life cycles begin in the womb. Some people advocate broadcasting Mozart into the pregnant abdomen. It's true that babies in the womb, after a certain stage, respond to certain sounds and especially to voices. We know that a woman should become pregnant in a state of optimum weight and health, and that she needs supervision of her blood pressure and kidneys. Pregnancy is not a good time to lose weight, but you can avoid gaining too much with the simple advice of Dr. Edward Lazarus, a New Orleans obstetrician and gynecologist: "Eat fewer carbs, eat more protein, hold down the fat." Good prenatal care includes multivitamin mineral supplements and reasonable exercise.

What constitutes "reasonable" exercise appears to depend upon whom you ask. The respected Dr. Lazarus recommends at least three times a week for as far into the pregnancy as is comfortable to do cardio (bicycle, walking) and some resistance, emphasizing the areas important to delivery. Later in pregnancy, crunches are impossible. Leg and back strengthening remains feasible.

We'll venture to say that a Mardi Gras parade is good for the mother and the baby-to-be. There's a wonderful range of music loud enough to stimulate everyone's internal environment! There's great exercise catching beads and go cups! Maybe this is why many New Orleans babies, from the time they can toddle, make second-line dancing motions the moment they hear a Mardi Gras tune.

BIRTH TO SCHOOL AGE: SOME EASY CHOICES

The infant and preschool years can be a lyrical interlude, before society begins to surround the child with unhealthy food. With responsible parents controlling the child's food intake, there are few dangers except overfeeding or overindulgence in sweets. We offer some simple tips for this early period.

Breast or bottle? Either one. Today breast feeding is encouraged, with the familiar argument that breast milk may confer immunity before the infant's own immune system is active. Yet there's no solid reason to discourage bottle feeding. Good commercial formulas are available, and they can prepare an infant to take solid foods sooner. The mother should not feel guilty about choosing either breast feeding or bottle feeding.

Pros and Cons of Breast and Bottle Feeding

Breast Feeding

Pros:
- Bonding
- Immunity boost; fewer bacterial infections
- Reduced obesity risk
- Balanced food, plus digestive enzymes

Cons:
- Toxins
- Medicines
- Maternal infection
- Less control of intake
- Difficult scheduling
- Father may feel "left out"
- Public feeding not well accepted

Formula Feeding

Pros:
- Bonding
- Mother has more free time
- Better control of intake
- No toxins, medicines
- Father can participate
- Travel and public feeding not a problem

Cons:
- No immunity boost
- No antibodies for infection protection

Off the shelf or home prepared? Again, either one. Infant foods from the grocery shelf are better now than in the past, when they were loaded with salt, monosodium glutamate (MSG), and other additives—

to make baby foods tastier for the mother. Studies show that infants do have some innate food preferences: sweet over sour, fatty over dry, and some salt over no salt. Yet they will often accept a wide variety of foods. As a parent, I subscribed to this familiar Foodie Myth: "If I give my children a variety of foods now, they will eat a variety later on." Alas, this is not true. I tried to make that myth a reality with my own two children. I failed miserably. It doesn't take long for children to learn how to refuse certain foods. The parent is not to blame.

Off-the-shelf infant and toddler foods are a good choice, especially when the family is traveling. Check the label briefly to avoid MSG, as well as salt content higher than 100 milligrams (mg). The best foods are those with no additives.

It's easy enough to prepare infant food at home with a blender. A parent can choose a variety of foods and offer them in different combinations. Steaming, still popular among some, is not necessary. It was touted as health promoting by several authors in the 1920s and again in the 1980s, but it requires extra equipment and cleanup time. Rapid boiling is just as healthy and much easier. Fresh vegetables, potatoes, and pasta can be lightly boiled, to the first point of tenderness. The blender does the rest.

How much cooking is best? Here we need a short explanation. Cooking changes food into smaller, more easily digestible units. It breaks down fibrous structures and starches. The more a starch structure is broken down, the more available to the body its sugar becomes. Foods with high sugar availability (a high "glycemic index") are discouraged by many authors these days, but we don't think it's practical to be too concerned with an item's glycemic index when cooking.

For example, if we lightly boil a potato until it is just edible, its glycemic index will be half that of an overcooked, mealy, baked potato. If we boil pasta only until it is *al dente,* and not mushy, its glycemic index will be relatively low. We need to use informed common sense. *Al dente* pasta with a small amount of extra-virgin olive oil can be a quick and well-accepted part of children's meals, as can rapidly boiled vegetables, even carrots, which are now discouraged by some for their sugar availability. We should not let the glycemic-index police outlaw these otherwise healthy foods. When our children eat starches along with proteins, some healthy fat, and fiber, then the overall sugar availability of their meals will drop. That's all to the good.

Desirable Effects of Cooking

What Does Cooking Really Do?
- Breaks down food structure
- Food is more easily digested
- Nutrients are more available to your body
- Improves taste
- Increases enjoyment

Here's another thing. Cooking makes the micronutrients in food more available. This is a tremendous benefit for our children, which should not be overshadowed by an obsession with glycemic indexes. Cooking does remove some of the water-soluble micronutrients, such as vitamin C, but this vitamin is found in so many food sources today that its small loss in lightly cooked vegetables is little to be mourned. On the other hand, completely uncooked vegetables are lacking in some available micronutrients, so that some vegans or vegetarians must use vitamin and mineral diet supplements.

The one diet supplement that can help increase children's height and weight is zinc. The sources of dietary zinc are few, and a small amount of zinc supplementation (10-15 mg; see chapter 8) is reasonable and safe. Zinc also boosts the immune system.

Broccoli, that vegetable disdained by Bush 41, is a prime example of a vegetable that is health promoting when lightly cooked. It's full of protective antioxidants like members of the xanthene group, which are abundant in green, yellow, and red vegetables. Broccoli carries B vitamins and calcium, and it's loaded with fiber. The chemical sulforaphane in broccoli packs a killer punch for the helicobacter organisms that inhabit the stomach and contribute to ulcers and stomach cancer. This chemical can eliminate helicobacter germs even when they're hiding in the cells of the stomach itself—as many antibiotics cannot do. Cooking but not "killing" broccoli makes these good chemicals and micronutrients more available. Also, broccoli has more protein per calorie than just about any other food.

My favorite broccoli preparation for children is to take the florets, along with a small amount of tender stem, and boil them rapidly for no more than four minutes—until the color just begins to fade from that bright, first-blanched green. Without salt or any additives, broccoli cooked this way is simply delicious. A little bit of coaxing can persuade your children to try it and even ask for it next time. Below is a recipe with a little more jazz in it.

HOT WALNUT BROCCOLI

Serves 4.

2 tbsp. extra-virgin olive oil
½ tsp. unsalted butter
1 clove garlic, chopped fine
¼ cup chopped walnuts
¼ tsp. cayenne pepper
Sea salt and white pepper to taste
1 lb. fresh broccoli florets, with some stem, cut into thumb-sized
    pieces

Heat olive oil on medium-high heat; add butter. Add garlic and stir 1 minute. Add walnuts and seasonings. Toss; stir walnuts a few minutes just until they start to brown slightly.

Bring a pot of water to a rapid boil, drop in broccoli, and cook to a vivid, crispy green, just about 4 minutes. Drain immediately, as dry as possible. Toss with sautéed walnuts and serve immediately.

CHILDREN ENTER OUR FOOD CULTURE: HARDER CHOICES

Our obesity epidemic begins with school-age children, six years old and up. It's a frustrating story. We feed them carefully for years. Then we send them to school, and our society's food culture grabs them. All of a sudden, our well-nurtured children are reaching for fast food, salty fries, and sugary soft drinks. Just as bad, they don't seem to be so interested in active play—they prefer TV, DVDs, video games, and Game Boys. In 2004, government agencies announced that *one in three* of our babies who follow "the typical American lifestyle" will have diabetes and associated life-shortening diseases in their futures. When we look at New Orleans schoolchildren in the Mardi Gras parades, we can see lots of fat beneath those glittery, form-fitting costumes. My daughter Torrey recently told me this story:

A girl in my class eats two bags of Doritos for lunch and a bottle of water and insists that she's on a diet. She says that she's full from it even though no one thinks she is. She is a little bit overweight just because she's petite and she's shorter. She has a little frame. She has a potbelly. She's visibly a little overweight despite her Doritos and water diet.

A sixteen-year-old New Orleans schoolgirl said this to me:

I eat three or four Little Debbie cakes on the way to school to hold me until I can eat the school breakfast. I have candy to snack on throughout the day and after the school lunch. When I get home, I eat anything that I can find until dinner. For dinner, we usually have burgers, fries, and chicken nuggets. We don't eat healthy.

This girl was five feet tall and 210 pounds.

As shocking as these stories may be, these girls represent a problem that has spread far beyond New Orleans. True, New Orleans was rated the unhealthiest city in 2004, but that's a difference in degree, not in kind. National statistics show us that more of our American babies are growing up fat. We once thought that fat was a problem for children only in our cities, but today we know that it afflicts children in rural areas as well. We're trying to find out why. In mid-2005, the U.S. Centers for Disease Control took the unprecedented action of sending "fat investigation teams" into both a rural county and an urban area of West Virginia.

Being fat is dangerous to your health.

Childhood Obesity Facts

- Definition of childhood obesity: weight is more than 20 percent above healthful for height
- Weight "spurts" may precede height "spurts," especially in boys
- Genes do *not* cause obesity
- Obese parents have a 50-70 percent chance of raising obese children

- Familial obesity in the twenty-first century is largely lifestyle driven
- Children can eat and eat their way to obesity despite "good genes"

Being fat is easy to define. We are not raising concerns about carrying a few pounds over an "ideal" weight that various groups seem to keep ratcheting down. In fact, as we shall explore further in later chapters, being too thin may be as dangerous as being fat.

Without intervention, obese children will become obese adults. Diabetes, high blood pressure, and metabolic syndrome will remain constant threats and will kill many people before their time. How can we, the American public, fight this obesity epidemic that shadows our life cycles? We must first confront its causes. These causes are not mysterious. They are in many ways self-evident. They are as follows:

- Too many calories from the wrong kinds of food
- Too little exercise to burn those calories
- Too little knowledge of eating and exercise choices to teach to children

We have eaten ourselves into a predicament and dragged our children along with us. We need to understand how and why, if we want to create good strategies of resistance for our families.

THE WRONG FOODS: PUBLIC ENEMY NUMBER ONE

In our country, fast food has become a tradition passed from generation to generation. The food supply available to children and teens has changed radically since the 1950s. All parents today are themselves members of the fast-food generation. New parents will make fast-food choices for their children, who will become teens and parents in their turn. Some scientists, like Dr. Melinda Sothern, even speculate that the effects of fast food may have been accumulating in our bodies through the generations.

Hamburgers, fried chicken, pizza slices—fast food is wildly popular because, yes, it tastes good. Of course, the classic burger-and-fries combination has plenty of salt and fat. And since the time of the Psalms, fat has been used to make food feel good in our mouths. Fast-food tastes are also manipulated by artificial flavorings, whether addictive or not. However they've managed to do it, the fast-food makers have made their food tasty, and this golden criterion has sustained their success. Recently, almost 30 percent of the food eaten in this country was produced by fast-food outlets.

We celebrate the great American hamburger tradition. Hamburgers do not need to be fatty and additive laden (for details see *Fast Food Nation*, by Eric Schlosser). You can have your hamburger and a healthier you, too.

Chef John Besh, one of *Food and Wine*'s "Ten Best New Chefs in America" in 1999, was born on the bayou and grew up immersed in the rich culinary traditions of Southern Louisiana. After formal training at the Culinary Institute of America, John apprenticed in Europe under Chef Karl-Josef Fuchs in Germany's Black Forest and Chef Alain Assaud in St-Remy, Provence. Every year, John returns to France to the Chateau de Montcaud at Bagnols-sur-Ceze to train his fellow European chefs in the fine points of Louisiana Creole and Cajun cuisine. Chef John presides over two restaurants in New Orleans— Restaurant August, named "one of the 50 top new restaurants in the world" by *Conde Nast Traveler*, and the Besh Steakhouse, which opened July 2003 at Harrah's Casino. Chef Besh shows us how to have it all, with the following hamburger recipe.

TASTY, LOW-FAT, ALL-AMERICAN HAMBURGERS
Serves 6.

Rex Creole Mixed Seasoning is a good choice in our recipes calling for Creole spice, since it is lower in salt or even salt free.

3 lb. lean ground beef
1 tbsp. chopped garlic
1 yellow onion, chopped fine
2 tbsp. Worcestershire sauce
1 tsp. Tabasco
1 tbsp. salt

1 tsp. black pepper
2 tbsp. salt-free Creole spice

Mix ingredients and form into patties. Grill about 20 minutes, 8-10 minutes per side, depending upon thickness. Eat on buns with whatever toppings you like.

Today the fast-food outlets have slipped into our hospitals and our schools, by contributing large sums to athletic programs, bands, or the school system itself. Schools and hospitals, chronically in need of funds, are reluctant to kick out these franchises. Vending machines for snacks and soft drinks also help fund cash-strapped schools. The unspoken message to our children, loud and clear, is that it's all right, maybe even good, to consume fast foods and sugar-laden drinks.

Rationalizations for Why Fast Foods Dominate School Cafeterias

- "That's all they'll eat."
- "What's wrong with these choices? Parents feed them the same things."
- "It's all there's time for."
- "The school needs the money."
- "The cafeteria program has to make money."

Schools without these franchises feel they must offer our children food choices that "compete" with fast foods, to keep from losing money. Parents and even nutritionists, swayed by local traditions and a fast-food culture, can be resistant to change. Former New Orleans Schools Superintendent Anthony Amato weighs in on the effectiveness of the new FDA guidelines:

The people who prepare the nutrition in our schools, and I've analyzed that nutrition, offer foods extremely high in sodium, very high in fat content, even though they swear they're following the FDA guidelines and the child nutrition school guidelines. Yet as I analyze some of the food, it's very clear that it's really more culturally relevant than good-nutrition relevant.

So, I've had a number of sit-downs with the nutrition people to say you really, really need to change these menus. . . . I'll never forget this scene. I was sitting there and I said, "Bring me all the orders of the foods . . . for this month," and I'm looking at these orders and they swear that it's nutritionally balanced, but what I see is an order for 10,000 donuts and incredibly ridiculous food orders, and I'm saying, "But don't you see what I have in my hand? Here, you read this." And he said, "But you know, kids do need donuts." And I said, "OK, let's stop. You have the fat-laden ice creams, not the more nutritious ice creams now. There are ices that don't have the sugar content; they are yogurt based with less sugar." But no, they order not Häagen-Dazs but still heavy-content ice cream, laden with fat, and they just don't see it, they don't get it, it's just too culturally ingrained. So we have that battle going on.

There have been some heartening individual efforts to improve school food. Alice Waters, the chef of Restaurant La Panisse in Berkeley, California, has spearheaded one of these efforts in the Edible Schoolyard Program (see our "Resources" chapter for the Web site). But these enlightened people can affect only limited areas.

Note: In order not to slow down your reading, we have reserved a host of details for our Web site, www.theneworleansprogram.com. Please visit us. We update our site continually with further details and references to other useful sites.

WHAT CAN WE DO?

If enough adults care enough about what their children are eating, outside forces will be pressured to adapt. As Amato says, "If parents and communities started demanding [good school nutrition] from us, it would make it an easy job, but it's not happening."

Breakfast. As parents, we have direct influence over two of the three daily meals our growing children should eat for their energy needs. Breakfast can be simple on school days, with fresh fruit, oatmeal or grits, and a good-quality juice without added sugar. An egg lightly fried in canola oil, and served on whole-wheat toast, is also fine.

Cereal and milk can work well, if some forethought is given to choice. Many children lose some of their tolerance for lactose, the sugar in milk, as they reach the preteen years. Among African-Americans, lactose intolerance seems to be higher. If your child does not like milk, let it go. The idea that milk is a childhood necessity is a

Foodie Myth created by the dairy industry. There are many other good sources of calcium for developing bones. I haven't liked milk since I was ten years old and find it cloying on a hot day. But personal preference and lactose intolerance aside, skim milk is clearly the best choice, with one-third of its calories from protein and two-thirds from sugar, and it provides 30 percent of the minimum recommended daily calcium intake.

Cereals can be a danger zone. Most popular cereals are low in nutrition and fiber, while high in refined sugar, other refined sweeteners, and food additives. A quick glance at a cereal's nutrition label will tell you whether it is a highly processed and well-advertised "breakfast food" for children, like all the packaged breakfast rolls, muffins, and Pop Tarts. Resist your child's pleas for these unhealthy foods. Whole-grain cereals are best, with good fiber and protein. Sugary cereals, even the latest industry offerings with a "drop in the bucket" of whole wheat, won't do the trick. My younger daughter, who shares my opinion of milk, prefers to eat a good-quality, high-fiber cereal dry with banana or raisins. This provides a breakfast with a nice crunch and fruit flavor. It can be enhanced when fresh strawberries, blueberries, or other fresh fruits are available from the Ponchatoula area on the other side of Lake Pontchartrain.

Here is another quick, tasty, real breakfast you can try with a piece of fruit or a small glass of fruit juice.

CREOLE TOMATO FRITTATA
Serves 4.

This tasty and flavor-filled quick dish can play a main role at breakfast or a supporting part at other meals. The tomatoes add very few calories, lots of flavor, the valuable eye-supportive and cancer-risk-reducing antioxidant lycopene, and other plant-derived nutrients, minerals, and vitamins, including vitamin C.

4 large eggs
1 egg white from large egg
1 cup 2 percent shredded mozzarella or sharp cheddar

3 tsp. extra-virgin olive oil
1 cup chopped green bell pepper
1 cup chopped Vidalia or other sweet onion
⅛ tsp. cayenne pepper, or to taste
Sea salt and white pepper to taste
Cooking spray
¼ tsp. oregano
½ tsp. salt-free Creole spice
2 large tomatoes, sliced

Place eggs, egg white, and cheese into a mixing bowl. Combine with a whisk until smoothly mixed. Set aside until vegetables are ready.

Over medium heat, sauté with oil the bell pepper, onion, cayenne, salt, and white pepper. Stir constantly 4-5 minutes until vegetables are somewhat translucent. Cool somewhat, then stir vegetables into egg and cheese mixture.

Coat a 12-inch nonstick skillet with cooking spray and heat over medium heat. Spread egg mixture evenly over bottom of hot skillet. Immediately sprinkle oregano and Creole spice on top. Place tomatoes over top, and sprinkle with salt and white pepper. Cover and cook 7-8 minutes. Frittata should slide in skillet and be brown on bottom.

Immediately place under a preheated broiler and watch carefully for approximately 3 minutes until top is nicely browned. Place on serving tray and serve immediately or at room temperature. Enjoy with minimal calories!

We believe in serving a child moderate portions of fresh and not highly processed food. Try to give the child time to sit down and eat, with other children or parents if possible. A child who takes time to eat will be more likely to feel satisfied. Don't let your child run out the door to school while stuffing down a Pop Tart!

Good breakfast choices can also boost performance on critical tests such as the SATs. A child who "loads up" on low-density, highly processed carbohydrates will probably feel "let down" before the test ends. Slower-burning foods, such as proteins with relatively little fat, are a better idea. We offer a two-day run-up period before the test.

Best Breakfast Before a Major Test

Two Days Before Test

Breakfast:
    1 banana
    1 bowl whole-grain cereal with low-fat milk and fresh berries
    2 boiled eggs
Lunch:
    Salad with nonfat or vinaigrette dressing
    Roasted chicken
    Yogurt, unflavored or with a small amount of fresh fruit
Dinner:
    Grilled fish
    Broiled Parmesan Creole Tomatoes (see below)
    Yogurt, unflavored or with a small amount of fresh fruit

One Day Before Test

Breakfast:
    1 banana
    1 slice whole-grain toast with peanut butter
    1 small glass low-fat milk or juice
Lunch:
    Light Red Beans and Rice (see index)
    Salad with nonfat or vinaigrette dressing
    Roasted walnuts, pecans, almonds if desired
Dinner:
    Corn soup
    Grilled shrimp
    Sautéed spinach

Test Day

Breakfast:
    1 banana

1 3-oz. or so lean piece of beef brisket or pork filet sautéed
with nonstick spray, blended seasonings, sea salt, and pepper to taste until just cooked (about 2 minutes each side)
2 boiled eggs
1 small glass low-fat milk or no-sugar-added juice

Lunch. Preparing a lunch from home can be difficult. Yet it's worth a try, especially to nudge an obese child onto a weight-loss track. Your goal is simple—to minimize salt, sugar, and fat. You might include a piece of the child's favorite fruit, a meat sandwich with whole-wheat bread, or a leftover piece of fried chicken from a family meal (made the healthy way; see index for New Orleans Program Fried Chicken). Be realistic, though. Don't put all your hopes for the day's good nutrition in one lunch basket. In elementary school, your child can always lunch trade and may be "lucky" enough to secure some other child's corn chips. And in high school, you are competing against the school cafeteria and peers. Remember, you'll have another nutritional opportunity at dinner.

One note of caution: You may be tempted to put processed or packaged foods (like one of those vigorously advertised snacks) in your child's lunchbox, as an enticement for the child to eat *something*. We believe that yielding to this temptation will do more harm than good. These processed attractions typically contain not only salt, fat, and refined carbohydrates but high-fructose corn sweetener, food dyes, emulsifying and thickening agents, chemicals like BHT to prolong shelf life, and other additives. There are more than five thousand additives in our food supply today. They are put there not for our health but for easier distribution and sales. Experts wonder whether these additives are linked to asthma, increasing allergies, chronic fatigue syndrome, multiple sclerosis, immune-system exhaustion, or even cancer. Some are listed on the packaging, but most are not—like those chemical-plant-produced additives in McDonald's fries.

Dinner. We recommend home-cooked meals, and we've designed some quick, easy, and healthful recipes for family dinners.

We conducted a survey of fast-food outlets and did some comparison shopping at a small, family-run, full-service, neighborhood grocery store. Prices at this grocery were somewhat higher than at the chain stores. We took the price of a fast-food family meal and applied the same money to groceries for home-cooked meals. The results may surprise you. All costs are for a family of four: two adults, one adolescent, and one younger child.

Fast-Food Outlet		Neighborhood Grocery	
Adult combos (2 @ $3.95)	$7.90	Boneless, skinless chicken breasts (16 oz.)	$3.99
Child burgers (2 @ $2.39)	$4.78		
		Sweet potatoes (4 @ $.35, for baking or microwaving)	$1.40
Fries (2 small @ $.99)	$1.98		
Cold drinks (2 small @ $1.00)	$2.00	Romaine (1)	$.99
		Tomato (1 large)	$.95
Fruit/walnut salad	$2.39		
		Cucumber (1)	$.50
Total (with tax)	$20.76		
		Strawberries (fresh, 1 pt.)	$2.39
		Total (with tax)	$11.14

We *saved* $9.62! We also saved more than half the calories, saturated and trans fats, and sodium. The fresh, home-cooked meal took twenty minutes maximum. Here's what you do.

Sauté chicken in a small amount of extra-virgin olive oil, and season with blended seasonings, oregano, pepper, cayenne, and salt to taste. Microwave potatoes (they take much less time than white potatoes, about 3-4 minutes a side for 4). Wash salad vegetables and break up romaine. Toss romaine with 1-2 tbsp. extra-virgin olive oil, ½ tsp. vinegar, ½ tsp. Cajun mustard, and salt, pepper, and other spices to taste. We like tomato wedges and sliced cucumbers served on separate plates and added to romaine to taste. End the meal with strawberries and enjoy!

This head-to-head comparison shows that we'll have both more money and better nutrition if we avoid fast food. We'll also gain meaningful family time. Dinner is the one meal when the entire family can most likely be gathered. It can be fun, inventive, and informational. Parents can be in charge of the occasion, and everyone will learn to make better choices and alter their eating habits. Children can enjoy the selection of whole foods, the colors, the flavors, the preparation, the cooking—and most important, the product. The joy of eating good food is one of life's great pleasures.

Our suggested recipes arc intended for the majority of Americans, who do eat meat. However, some are perfect for vegetarian or vegan use.

BROILED PARMESAN CREOLE TOMATOES

Serves 2.

When our recipes call for "blended seasonings," you may use products such as McCormick Season All, Rex Creole Mixed Seasoning, Paul Prudhomme's brands, or any other you choose. Rex is lower in salt or even salt free.

1 large ripe Creole tomato
Extra-virgin olive oil
Blended seasonings
Sea salt and pepper to taste
Shredded Parmesan cheese

Set broiler on high, and place top oven rack close to broiler. Wash tomato and dry thoroughly. Cut off stem. Slice tomato in half crosswise. Gently squeeze out seeds. Lightly coat inside and outside of tomatoes with oil. Sprinkle cut sides with seasonings. Fold up the sides of a sheet of aluminum foil to make a foil tray. Place tomatoes on foil tray under broiler, cut sides up, and check in 6-7 minutes. When nearly done (do not overbroil), sprinkle tops with Parmesan. Return to broiler. Remove just as cheese lightly browns. Serve immediately.

PIZZA

Pizza Dough
3 cups flour
1 pkg. ($\frac{1}{4}$ oz.) quick-rise yeast

2½ tsp. salt
2 tsp. sugar
1 cup warm water (115-125 degrees)
2 tbsp. + 1 tsp. extra-virgin olive oil

Combine 2½ cups flour with yeast, salt, and sugar. Stir until well blended. Add water and 2 tbsp. olive oil to flour mixture until a rough dough forms.

Dust a work surface with remaining flour. Turn dough onto work surface and knead until smooth and no longer sticky, folding in flour as you go.

Wipe a mixing bowl with remaining oil. Put dough in bowl and cover with plastic wrap. Set aside in a warm spot to rise for about 45 minutes.

Adjust oven rack to lowest position. Preheat oven to 425 degrees. Using half the dough, shape into a 9x13-inch rectangle. Transfer onto foil-lined baking sheet.

Pizza Sauce
¼ cup extra-virgin olive oil
2 cloves garlic, smashed
8 overripe tomatoes, chopped
Salt and pepper to taste
2 sprigs basil

In a medium saucepot over medium heat, heat oil and garlic. Add tomatoes and turn heat to high. Bring to a boil and add salt and pepper. Reduce heat and simmer for 15 minutes. Then place tomatoes in an old-time food mill or a food processor with basil. Puree. Season again to taste.

Top unbaked pizza rectangle with sauce and all your favorite toppings. Bake until crust is browned, about 20 minutes. While first pizza is baking, make a second pizza out of remaining dough. This sauce may also be used on pasta.

FRESH BABY SPINACH QUICK SAUTE

Serves 4.

The availability of well-cleaned, dry, fresh, baby spinach, kitchen ready from the grocery store, makes this versatile vegetable fast to prepare. Even those who "hate spinach" will enjoy it if it is seasoned properly.

Extra-virgin olive oil
½-1 tbsp. unsalted butter
7-8-oz. ready-to-cook fresh baby spinach leaves
¼ tsp. salt-free Creole spice
Sea salt, white pepper, and garlic powder to taste

Pour enough oil to thinly coat bottom of 12-inch skillet. Over medium-high heat, melt butter in oil. Add spinach. Stir/toss (two wooden spoons work great for this) as the leaves begin to wilt. Add Creole spice, and continue to toss so that no spinach overcooks. When reduced and just cooked, about 5 minutes, add other seasonings. You can prepare ahead to this point and reheat just before serving. Do not overcook.

In this way, parents can cover at least two-thirds of the eating day, breakfast and dinner, with healthful and trouble-free meals. With this routine in place, the occasional birthday party or once-a-year Mardi Gras celebration will not harm a child who has a healthful weight and an active metabolism.

There is also some news about the effects of fish oil in obese children. Researchers at the University of Nevada announced in November 2005 that 3 grams fish oil a day significantly lowered bad blood lipids (triglycerides) and raised "good cholesterol." The study, scientifically controlled in forty-nine severely obese children, showed convincing results. The group size was small enough, though, that recommending daily fish oil for obese children is not yet warranted. What does make sense is adding moderate amounts of fish to children's meals twice weekly.

CHILDREN AND FOOD: NOTES FROM CHEF BESH

I'm the father of four beautiful boys, all of whom have different eating habits. While we were in France, Jennifer was pregnant with our first son, Brendan, and was very careful about what she ate. I love dining with my wife. She enjoys food, but she knows when to say "when." As she was going through her pregnancies, her body told her what to have, and when, and how much. She would eat more meals but in smaller portions, and her body craved a wide variety of foods. She gave birth to such healthy babies partly due to taking care of her body and soul, doing what her body told her to do. I would cook her certain meals, anything from just raw vegetables to a cup of soup to a salad, and even at times an oyster po' boy. Whatever Jennifer craved, I made sure that I would cook it for her in whatever way she needed. She enjoyed exercise, as well: moving and running, walking and swimming.

Going through the baby-food section of a French grocery would lead you to believe that every single French baby is a gourmet. You notice everything from *cuisse de canard* (the leg of duck) with ratatouille to beef jaw with *petit pois* (braised with peas, carrots, and ginger). You see the beautiful flavors of baby food. I believe it is almost law that these baby foods are all organically grown and prepared in a healthy manner. They taste great. I'm not a big proponent of baby food, but Brendan became hooked on the French version.

Later, back in the States, we noticed that after somebody gave Brendan his first chicken nugget, this was all he would eat. We explained to the doctor how nervous we were when all Brendan wanted was French fries and chicken. Yet the doctor advised us that the human body will get what it needs out of whatever it eats, and that this was just a phase. Well, this phase lasted quite some time. We finally put our foot down and said we weren't going to raise a child this way. We weren't going to go through pregnancy and birth just to have a child who won't eat anything but French fries and chicken.

So we made a commitment to ourselves and to our children that fast food was only for rare occasions. Normally, they would eat my home cooking, which is a New Orleans repertoire. So now, on Mondays, my children have red beans and rice; on Fridays they have a seafood dish. Every Sunday we cook together as a family and sit down together as a family. We pray as a family. After Mass on Sunday, we'll cheat a little bit and have some fried food—but good fried food. We'll stop at one of our favorite little places in Slidell for shrimp, oyster, or soft-shell crab po' boys. There is not much nutritional value to a po' boy other than the shredded lettuce and the slices of Creole tomatoes! I do make it a point to eat just half the po' boy and share the other half with a family member, so I can pat myself on the back and say, "Well, I've held it within moderation." Half a po' boy is at least six inches long, so it's not small by any means.

Back to the children. Sundays are days that we barbecue or make a pasta or a big paella. Making different things takes some time, some love, some action, and some enthusiasm. I have my four-year-old making gnocchi, hand rolling potato dumplings. I'll drop them into the boiling water and take them out. He loves them. Luke, who is at this moment three years old, loves rolling out any type of pasta. Andrew loves eating and Brendan likes to serve. He isn't the biggest fan of cooking, but he's been a superstar when it comes to hamburgers. He's our hamburger chef. Part of the deal is that we have an open fruit policy. We have fruit everywhere and the kids are allowed to eat as much fruit as they want. Vegetables we try to make the center of our meal. They can be anything from Jennifer's stewed okra and tomatoes to a salad, with interesting types of dressing for the kids. Brendan wants a plain salad; Andrew eats anything. Jack is into crunchy carrots, and he'll eat, eat, eat all the carrots in the world. Luke's big vegetables are tomatoes and cucumbers, which are "in season" here for six months. The kids just love if I slightly blanch some broccoli and have some dip, which is nothing more than a little vinaigrette.

They're all huge fans of milk and butter. We buy all of our milk and butter from two local dairies down here, Smith Creamery and Motase Dairy, because their products are not only natural and organic but have a lot more flavor. I want my children to enjoy sitting down to a "meal" meal. I want them to enjoy the social and the spiritual aspects of it, so we take our time, eat a proper meal, and have different courses and varied experiences. You can have something fried. You can also have something raw. You need to have something sweet, I think. You should also experience other flavors, sour and bitter. These aren't bad. This is how I was raised.

When I was a kid, we had every sweet that you can imagine, all homemade. None of us ever had any problems with overeating or with health issues. Why not have a bit of dessert? Why not have a policy of eating fruit whenever you want, as long as you fit in the other foods? It's great for a child to eat through varied ingredients with different flavors and several methods of cooking, all the while knowing there's the reward of dessert at the end. A dessert can be healthy or unhealthy as we choose. We can have gobs of store-bought ice cream with preservatives that you can't even pronounce, or we can make ice cream at home. That's as easy as it gets. We buy popsicle sticks and little cups, and the boys love mixing all these different flavors of fruit, putting them in the cups with the sticks, and freezing them. That might be a dessert.

We can do all sorts of things to make food exciting. A child should enjoy eating, but eating the right way, with an appreciation for good food. It doesn't have to be boring. It doesn't have to be raw. We don't have to be extremists. Let's eat in moderation. Let's have a hamburger, but let's not have one every day. Let's not have one every week. Let's have a piece of fried chicken, but only from time to time. Offset the fried chicken by eating many other things. In this all-or-nothing society, we'd be better off if we learned how to slow down and eat a meal.

My favorite meals as a child were at my grandmother's house, and there was course upon course of food. Everything was laden with some sort of pork fat or butter. My grandmother was an incredible Southern cook. We would have five or six different vegetables with every meal. We always had a type of rice. We always had a potato, believe it or not. We always had a meat. We always had something raw. Most of the time we had dishes that were really, really cooked. I'm talking about cornbread. I'm talking about green beans. I'm talking about crowder peas served in this rich broth called potlikker. I'm talking about big slices of tomatoes. I'm talking about white rice. I'm talking about pecan pie made with rich Allegan molasses syrup at the end of your meal. Then Grandmother would slice a piece of sweet potato and nearly fry it in a big cast-iron skillet. We would eat like this.

But you know what? We ate such a varied meal. We would have dinner, which was lunch midday, and then at night supper was a soup, a salad, maybe a small sandwich from the leftovers of lunch. That soup was made from broth, all wholesome and good. You knew where the vegetables came from. Nothing was preserved. It was all very real. I think this is the way that we were meant to eat. As a society, we do better when we sit down, slow down, and focus on each other and on our food. We never eat in front of the television; we want conversation. We want the food to be something great but not taken for granted. In short, that's how I'm trying to help my children eat. My wife and I don't serve them fast food. Jennifer shops to have everything in the house that I need, and a couple of nights a week, when I come home from cooking at my restaurant, I'll cook a variety of meals for them. Jennifer, who's managing these four boys all throughout the day, has time to actually give them the nourishment that we both want.

THE SUGAR HIGH

We believe that the "sugar high" is another Foodie Myth. This idea is firmly entrenched in stroller-pushers' lore. One recent national-magazine cartoon shows two children standing beside a stick figure with wild hair and crazy eyes. One of the children says to the other, "Oh, that's my sister. She's on candy bars and soda pop."

In science, there is little basis for the mythical sugar high. However, one controlled clinical study, several years ago, demonstrated that parents are quite ready to *believe* that sugar will make their children hyperactive. The researchers gave half the children flavored water with refined white sugar and told their parents this drink was sugar free. They gave the other children a sugar-free solution with artificial sweetener and told *their* parents the drink contained sugar. Then all the children played while all the parents watched.

You may be able to guess what happened. Parents who believed (mistakenly) that their children had consumed sugar were observed scrutinizing their children with extra vigilance. These parents labeled their children as "hyperactive," and the other parents did not so label their children. In fact, neither group of children was rated hyperactive by the researchers.

Parents are often unaware that their children respond to their unspoken messages. Silent parental expectations can affect a child dramatically, for better or for worse, so it's best to stop worrying about the mythical sugar high. If a child is excited and very active during a birthday party with cake and ice cream, other children, games, rides, and a buoyant atmosphere, we don't need to mistake this normal response to a joyous occasion for a disorder. We don't have to feel alarmed or guilty, and we don't need to interfere with our child's natural enjoyment of special days.

We recommend not eliminating desserts entirely but saving them for special times. And they do not have to be overly sugared and fat laden. Chef shows us some desserts that kids will enjoy.

MY FAVORITE CANNOLI

Makes 6.

1 pt. whipped, fat-free ricotta
1 tbsp. powdered sugar
1½ tbsp. lemon zest
1½ tbsp. orange zest
¼ tsp. cinnamon
2 tbsp. chocolate bits

6 cannoli shells
Powdered sugar and sprinkles

In a mixer, whip together the ricotta and 1 tbsp. sugar until light and fluffy. Mix in zests, cinnamon, and chocolate. Fill cannoli with the ricotta mixture using a pastry bag. Dust with more sugar and decorate with sprinkles.

LOW-FAT PANNA COTTA

Serves 6.

9 sheets gelatin
1½ qt. 2 percent milk
18 tbsp. sugar
1 vanilla bean

Bloom (Dr. Dave notes this is "chef talk" for putting gelatin in cold water until it swells up) gelatin sheets in cold water. Bring milk, sugar, and vanilla to a boil, and dissolve gelatin in boiling mixture. Pour into 6 ceramic molds and chill overnight.

RAISIN-PECAN CHILL

½ cup milk (can be reduced fat)
¾ lb. marshmallows
½ lb. finely crushed graham crackers
½ cup brown raisins
½ cup golden raisins*
2 cups pecans, chopped

In a large saucepan, heat milk slowly over medium heat, stirring. When milk warms, add marshmallows and continue stirring until they melt. Stir in graham crackers, raisins, and pecans. Pour into a loaf pan and refrigerate 1-2 hours. Slice and serve. Keep refrigerated. Freezes well.
*If you don't have golden raisins, you may replace with brown raisins.

COCOA QUICKIE

1½ cups all-purpose or cake flour
1 cup sugar
4 tbsp. cocoa powder (can omit if you wish to top with fruit)
½ tsp. salt
1 cup water
½ cup good oil (*not* canola)
1 tbsp. rice-wine or balsamic vinegar (not the good stuff, please!)
1½ tsp. vanilla

Preheat oven to 350 degrees. Mix dry ingredients well. Stir liquids together and add to dry. Mix lightly. Pour into a 9-inch cake pan. Bake 30 minutes and check for doneness. Enjoy!

INACTIVITY: PUBLIC ENEMY NUMBER TWO

Our children have so much to do! Their lives are filled not only with the ubiquitous TV but also with Game Boys, videos, cell phones that transmit voices and texts and pictures, and the Internet with its Web sites and e-mail chat rooms. The computer age has been widespread since the early 1990s—as I was reminded when a recent news broadcast prompted my daughter to turn to me with the wide-eyed question, "Daddy, what's a typewriter?" Of course, none of these high-tech "activities" help our children to be physically active. They don't keep our children's bodies healthy through exercise. In fact, there is a direct correlation between children's (in)activity rates and their obesity rates.

Why We Get Fat

- Life-sustaining (with no activity) metabolism ("basal rate") *plus*
- Activity metabolism burn additional calories every day.
  1. If you eat the *same calories* as you burn, weight stays the *same*.
  2. If you eat *more calories* than you burn, you get *fat*.
  3. If you eat *fewer calories* than you burn, you *lose weight*.

In one longitudinal study of children from age five into adulthood, researchers found that two or more hours of daily TV correlated strongly with obesity, tobacco use, and elevated cholesterol. Another Southern California study looked at the Body Mass Indices of 300 teens. One-third of them were overweight, and 20 percent were obese. The heavier teens were much more likely to watch TV for two or more hours and to consume multiple soft drinks.

Although these studies—like most such studies—cannot prove direct cause, we'd be foolish to ignore the weight of scientific evidence. We can't prove that cigarettes directly cause cancer, either, and that hasn't kept our society from taking action. Common sense tells us to pay attention to the overall scientific evidence and our own experiences. Let's not dismiss the evidence of our own eyes. These days teachers see young people at lunchtime talking about their diabetes control, checking their blood sugars, and dosing with insulin. This scene is sadly new in the twenty-first century.

WHAT CAN WE DO?

Parents need to ration their children's access to inactive electronic "activities" and encourage physical exercise in the time saved. This will take courage on the parents' part.

Consider the time an average child spends, every day, watching TV or using electronic devices. To convert even half this time to physical activity would be an enormous benefit to the average child's health. When we limit our child's electronic inactivities, we create time for them to be active. The excuse that there is "no time for exercise" disappears.

We're not discussing body-building here, or training for athletic events. We're talking about ordinary children and teens, all of our children, who need daily physical activity to maintain a healthy weight and metabolism. Most experts, including the American Academy of Pediatrics, say that exercise for kids should be varied and fun. After-school sports, both team and individual, are good exercise. At home, children can bike or walk with friends, if the neighborhood is safe enough. Walking and talking are a great alternative to the cell phone. Some kids like to dance or exercise at home to the music streaming through the earphones of their CD players.

Exercise should be age specific and should take into account the strength differences between adults and growing children. Children have their own exercise parameters. In chapter 9 we offer more specific suggestions on exercise for children and teens.

Exercise provides benefits you may not expect. Regular, moderate exercise just makes you feel better. There is something natural and positive about movement. To live is to move. There seems to be a mental wall of resistance that regular exercise breaks through. Brain-chemistry experts, who may attribute this phenomenon to endorphins and other chemicals, tell us that exercise can help alleviate depression, a controversially managed affliction of children and teens.

Our school systems used to provide regular "physical education." But now many of our public schools, with the extra pressure of No Child Left Behind, have "literally stripped away . . . a lot of the physical education time," according to Amato. "Some schools don't even get recess anymore." Amato described his approach.

So, what I've done is have some serious talks with our new physical education director. . . . We're now working to create programs, phys ed programs, that are done on a daily basis in school that have nothing to do with a formalized physical education program where you need a phys ed teacher. We're trying to formulate a daily physical education time in the classroom anywhere from twenty to twenty-five minutes guided by a video on the lines of aerobic-type exercises and upper-body-strength exercises.

You simply follow these programs that are on video. A teacher's aide comes in with a cart . . . [and] stops the class for about twenty to twenty-five minutes. You have video monitors in the class that manage the classroom, push all the furniture aside, and understand it has to be put right back to where it was originally. . . . So we push everything to the perimeter of the class. They create a space in the middle. . . . Then this person puts the TV in front, runs the program, and these programs are designed not just to do your regular exercises. Right now we're linked up to the city. The city just got a grant . . . to combat diabetes, asthma, and obesity. . . . Basically, . . . these three major child sicknesses, if you will, can be pushed back by certain exercises that are . . . scientifically created. . . .

These are exercises from planned programs that are scientifically based to eat up as many calories as possible during that twenty- to twenty-five-minute segment, to do cardiovascular exercises.

Here was a brave attempt to help young people exercise well at school. It may take some grass-roots community activism to call attention to our children's needs for physical activity, and push for adequate recess and phys ed time.

HELP FOR OBESE CHILDREN AND TEENS

In epidemiology, if we locate the starting point, patient zero or ground zero, we can ask the right questions and uncover the causes of an epidemic. Then we can devise strategies to control, treat, and finally eliminate the epidemic. This common sense about causes and cures leads us to some basic observations. Our human bodily functions have not changed for thousands of years. Yet our ways of fueling and maintaining those functions have been altered within the last century. Our food supply has been transformed drastically, and we are much less physically active.

The childhood obesity epidemic started in the 1960s. It has continued to grow. In the 1950s, it was uncommon to see an obese child. Today, obese children look to the left and look to the right and usually see company. Despite all the congressional committees, task forces, Web sites, books, and recommendations by experts, the rate of childhood obesity has been rising until it threatens our present and future national health. Informed common sense tells us the causes of childhood, teen, and adult obesity. Too many of us are eating the wrong foods, and too many of us are physically inactive. Our New Orleans Program confirmed this conclusion when we were able to reverse the processes that led teens and their parents into obesity.

Everyone's goal is to prevent obesity, and the New Orleans Program is meant to be used for prevention. Yet for the already obese child, teen, or adult, we offer here some workable steps for intervention. We have put together these steps from our experience with the New Orleans Program. We fully admit that it can require enormous sensitivity, tact, and communication skills to encourage a child or teen to talk about obesity in the first place. This communication is the biggest challenge. Otherwise, the New Orleans Program is easy to understand and simple to follow. It works. Here are our steps.

Identify the problem. Children are by nature fit, according to the American Academy of Pediatrics. Usually a doctor can tell whether a child is obese simply by looking at the child. A more exact clinical determination is straightforward. A child between the 85th and 95th percentile in Body Mass Index for that child's age is considered overweight; a child beyond the 95th percentile is defined as obese.

Almost all obese children, like obese adults, simply consume more calories than they use for energy. This is the simple but inevitable metabolic equation—calories in, calories out, and excess calories turn into fat. We cannot escape our physical natures.

Metabolism refers to burning energy to keep our life force going. Leading metabolic consumers include the brain, the major organs, and lean muscle mass. An average person of optimal weight will metabolize calories at the rate of 1,200 to 1,500 per day just lying in bed. More calories are burned in proportion to increased physical activity. Children's metabolism is perhaps even more activity sensitive than that of adults. Obesity almost always results not from genes, not from being big-boned, not from glandular problems, but strictly from consuming more calories than you burn.

Some have suggested that genes do play a role in obesity, because overweight children tend to have overweight parents.

Fat in the Family

- Likelihood of being a fat preteen or teen with one fat parent: 50 percent
- Likelihood of being a fat preteen or teen with two fat parents: 70 percent
- Likelihood of staying fat if you emerge from teenage years fat: 75 percent

However, we have no way of knowing if both children and parents are simply trapped together in the same response pattern to the two great risks of our culture—eating too much, especially the wrong foods, and staying inactive. Genes do not directly cause or control obesity, although genetic factors may help permit the development of obesity. In any case, until that fantasy future when "gene therapy" is available to make us thinner, it is not helpful to pursue this line of inquiry. Remember: genes will *not* stop you from losing weight.

Very occasionally, metabolic diseases exist. For example, some children cannot metabolize a particular sugar without turning it into a poison that results in brain damage and multiple deformities. Others are obese and also have stunted growth. Pediatricians can detect such rare diseases with a thorough clinical exam.

If an exam doesn't identify any fixable causes, and there's no family history of rare syndromes, obese children shouldn't be put through extensive tests. Medical "fishing expeditions" will probably make them anxious and even more self-conscious about such crucial matters as their eating and exercise habits.

Think before you talk with the child or teen. A loving, nonjudgmental, sensible parent is the one most qualified to talk with a child or teen about obesity. The second best choice is a significant family member or some responsible person whom the obese child can really trust. Genuine communication may take many attempts, but it is well worth it. A trusting and supportive relationship has proved to be the most vital component of obesity intervention in our New Orleans Program.

Before speaking to them, we should know what obese children and teens are going through. In the New Orleans Program, every one of our teens admitted to receiving frequent verbal abuse and derision from their peers. All of them had suffered considerable pain and endured numerous insults and slights. The obese child is called names, ridiculed, and not chosen for sports teams. Children can seem eager to display cruelty, and their overweight schoolmates are easy targets. Amato often overheard such taunts:

The kids just can't get up to their cognitive abilities when they've been yelled at or when they feel bad about themselves, or when they get embarrassed. It's the semblance of stumbling or falling and all the kids are laughing at them. You think, they get up, they dust off and they're normal. No. They're not prepared to learn for a good twenty minutes to half an hour.

In other words, it's hard to learn when you're being mocked. How ironic that while we're busily addressing racism and sexism, we can still allow ourselves to make obesity a social stigma! Physical activity is embarrassing for an obese child. All the teens in the New Orleans Program had poor self-esteem and body image. These situations can cause depression (recognized or unrecognized), and depression can stimulate more bad eating and more weight gain. This is a true self-feeding cycle. We know that depression can lead to teen suicides, and we have recently learned that antidepressants may themselves cause self-destructive behaviors. If a child seems depressed, obesity may be a contributing cause. Treating obesity does not require antidepressants. Treating obesity takes love and support, so that the child can learn to eat and exercise well.

What other troubles might an obese child have? Studies have demonstrated that higher fat consumption reduces learning ability. Cold drinks, with caffeine and additives, can bring behavior and mood changes. An obese child could also have other health issues: elevated blood sugar, high blood pressure, joint problems, or asthma.

Talk with the child or teen. When we've considered just how vulnerable an obese child or teen may be, we have some idea what *not* to say at the outset. These young people expect criticism, and they already feel inferior. Fat teens know they're fat and are reminded of this discomforting fact every day. They don't need moral lectures, constant prodding, or "motivation." They're conditioned to hear any reference to their weight as a humiliation. The teen has been lured to obesity by the American culture of food, which preys on our children's insecurities. Don't blame the child. A child has a sixth sense for detecting a parent's anger or disappointment.

Obese children and teens need someone to understand—someone who can acknowledge the problem along with them, and stick with them as a supportive partner. They need someone on hand and steadily available, with frank and positive advice. *Not a single teen we spoke to was willing to try the New Orleans Program on their own. They agreed to do it only when one or both parents also participated.* Parents and significant family members can make the biggest difference. Dr. Melinda Sothern and others, in the book *Trim Kids,* describe teen obesity as a deeply complex problem that needs a complex solution. We wonder how much of that complexity inheres in winning the trust of an obese teen. Dr. Sothern offers a far more complex approach than ours, and her approach may be needed in some cases. Whatever approach is used, help should be offered in a positive and supportive way. A friendly outside professional can often suggest ways to promote a positive conversation between parents and obese children.

Difficulties in communicating are almost inevitable between teens and their parents. Talking about a teen's obesity just sets up one more hurdle. For me, it was hard at first to discuss a weight problem with my own teenage daughter, until we could acknowledge the problem together. Working with my daughter was one of the sparks that ignited this book. It may have been encouraging for her that I had visibly reshaped myself, losing forty pounds on my personal eighteen-month trial of the New Orleans Program. Children often like to hear of their parents' struggles, especially when the parents admit to times of doubt or failure or hardship. It is through those admitted hard times that the humble parent can become a respected role model. Besides, everyone likes company in their misery. In our family, fortunately, the results of intervention have been positive.

Of course, obese parents have an excellent chance to empathize and act with their children. Parents and children worked together in our New Orleans Program, and in general they enjoyed success together (Appendix A).

We discovered the complexity of communicating with vulnerable teens the hard way. Talking with obese teens was the most difficult part of clinically road-testing our New Orleans Program. My own inquiries were met with hostility or indifference. We needed a peer interviewer to take information from teens about their patterns of eating and exercise. It was hard to find volunteers for our new program. It took us more than sixty encounters, including those in a community of faith where we held a successful adult participation group, in order to find five family units willing to give the New Orleans Program a try. Everyone in our program was there with at least one family member.

Once an obese child or teen is able to listen, many things are possible. Changing your habits can feel good and even be fun. The principles we followed in the New Orleans Program for working with obese teens are these:

- Teach the joy, enjoyment, and value of good food.
- Teach the joy of physical motion and exercise suited to age.
- Teach increased body awareness to assist in good eating choices and stopping when full.
- Expose the child to a variety of healthful foods.
- Be a parental role model, as much as possible.

Chef Bobo (Robert Surles) has himself been a role model in the New Orleans Program. In his own work with schoolchildren in New York City, he has demonstrated many times over that adult leadership can get children to say yes to fresh, whole foods and no to fries and ketchup. In a short time, friendly adults, especially parents, can win the day and convert unhealthy eaters to healthful choosers.

The informed-common-sense eating rules in the New Orleans Program are simplicity itself. The physical exercises in the New Orleans Program are comfortable specifically for children and teens who are obese and have little athletic ability. The spiritual exercises are easy and relaxing. In the appendixes, which contain the procedures and clinical results of the New Orleans Program, we include the specific rules and exercises we used.

Simple, clear, common-sense advice can change teens' habits drastically. We were surprised in our preprogram interview to see the near-uniform eating patterns of our five obese teens, as well as similar family attitudes towards food.

- All snacked constantly.
- All ate continuously while watching TV or the computer screen.
- All ate mainly fast-type food, such as hot dogs and hamburgers made at home.
- All described being served large quantities of food at home.
- All ate without attention to feeling full, and many were surprised to hear that there was such a feeling as "full."
- Most were encouraged to eat everything on their plate and as much as they could.
- All lived with at least one obese parent and, if siblings were there, obese siblings.
- All felt there was "no shame to their game" of eating constantly since "everybody else at home does it."
- All exercised little, if any.

SOME SAMPLE RESULTS

Everyone on our teen New Orleans Program lost weight—teens and family adults, a total of thirteen (Appendix A). The amounts of weight loss varied over our six-month observation period. Those with early metabolic syndrome lowered their blood pressure and blood sugar. All these good results came with no drugs whatsoever. What is more, everyone's attitude became more positive, especially for those who lost the most weight. As physical appearance improved, so did school attendance. Without so much TV, homework and other activities filled the newly available time. Some teens got higher grades, although several had earned good grades at the outset.

It wasn't all roses. For each teen, sticking to the program was hard at first, although it became easy by the end of the fourth month. The adults had a more difficult time at first, as they signed on not only to follow the program but also to limit TV and encourage exercise for their teens. Afterwards, three of the five teens have been able to continue their significant improvements for over a year. One person has kept a stable weight but has not lost more weight. One person began to gain weight again but returned to the program when asked and has since lost weight.

Our small but successful clinical experience tells us that next to preventing child and teen obesity, intervening with the participatory support of parents and family is the best choice. At the public-school level, would it be possible for dietitians, teachers, and administrators to replicate the success of the New Orleans Program with mass intervention programs for obese teens? We are doubtful. To the extent that an institution can lend a truly supportive and friendly ear, we suppose such widespread intervention might be possible. But direct intervention by a willing family member would be better.

So what can the schools do? What can we all do? We can provide healthier food at school and at home. We can make more time for quality exercise. We can be role models. The New Orleans Program will show you the way.

After all, prevention is the best cure.

CHAPTER 2

Mardi Gras: Laissez les Bons Temps Rouler!

If you don't enjoy Mardi Gras at least once, you must be dead.
—Mary Katherine Lonatro,
captain, Mystic Krewe of Shangri-La

As legend has it, French explorer Pierre Le Moyne, Sieur d'Iberville, landed at the mouth of the Mississippi River on Mardi Gras Day in 1699. He gave that muddy spit of land a European name: Pointe de Mardi Gras.

New Orleans' annual Mardi Gras celebration is a gift from the city to the world. Mardi Gras, or "Fat Tuesday," is all about the pleasures of good food, revelry, friendship, and tradition. It is not about the unchecked year-round excess that has consumed American eating habits.

TASTE OVER EXCESS: CHEF BOBO

To savor the spirit of Fat Tuesday, you don't have to be fat—or make yourself fat. In chapter 1 we praised Chef Bobo, a.k.a. Robert Surles, for introducing natural, healthy food to children at the Calhoun School in New York City. Chef Bobo returns to his native New Orleans each year for Mardi Gras, where he cooks for the krewe celebrities and royalty. His story shows a Mardi Gras experience that features the taste of great food and the joy of companionship, rather than simply stuffing the stomach.

I'll always go down for the frenzy of Mardi Gras time. It's a time for reconnecting with the best people in the world while at the same time eating the amazing food that trained my own personal palate to know the difference between really great food and good food. In New Orleans, the food has to be great. Anything less is unacceptable.

It is understood that I will be away every year [from the Calhoun School] for about ten days to go down to New Orleans to celebrate the best party in the world with my dear friends Sonny Borey, Derek Franklin, and all of the Krewe of Orpheus. It comes just at a time in the year when I'm feeling a little over-whelmed and realize that what I need is a good dose of Mardi Gras.

Once while I was working as a chef instructor at the French Culinary Institute in New York, that time of year came around, and, as agreed when I was hired, everyone knew I was planning to go down to New Orleans. But for this particular trip, two other chef instructors wanted to go with me to see what this was all about. One had been born and raised in New Jersey and the other in the Basque region of France. Whatever expectations they had were far exceed-ed by the biggest and best party this country knows. They had to try the gumbo and the jambalaya, they had to eat raw oysters and po' boys, and they were charmed by red beans and rice. Of course, they drank too many Hurricanes!

During the weekend, between partying and feasting, the three of us got togeth-er in Sonny's kitchen and cooked up a storm in preparation for the Krewe of Orpheus's Mardi Gras Day open house. We roasted beef and vegetables, we boiled shrimps and made remoulade sauce. There was guacamole, baked ham, and, of course, bread pudding.

But for my friends, the really big day came on Lundi Gras [the Monday before Fat Tuesday]. Every day during their visit to New Orleans they had seen one parade after another and had collected quite a treasure chest of beads and cups. Now it was their turn. When we reported to the New Orleans Convention Center for the Krewe of Orpheus parade, they were like kids in a toy store. I took them for a walk through the floats, and they marveled at the beauty and the incredible detail of the floats that make the Orpheus parade the premier parade of Mardi Gras. Their excitement began to grow. I took them to the dressing room to put on their costumes, and then we went to eat. The music being played really got them revved up, and they couldn't wait to get on their float and get started. That was the last I saw of them until their float came into the Convention Center.

I met them at their float, and when they got off they were bubbling over with stories and reactions and joy. There is no way you can describe the experience of a first Mardi Gras ride. You have to do it to understand it. But my friend Henri, the friend from France, said it best: "That experience could be addictive!"

I know. I'm addicted.

Addicted? To the Mardi Gras experience, yes. To constant excess in food, no. The typical American palate would stick exclusively to the po' boys and Hurricanes (in mass quantities). Yet most of the dishes mentioned by Chef Bobo are easily compatible with the New Orleans Program, such as gumbo, raw oysters, boiled shrimp with remoulade, roast beef and vegetables, and baked ham. Recipes follow for Chef Bobo's guacamole, as well as our program's Shrimp and Chicken Jambalaya, and Light Red Beans and Rice. And for a special Mardi Gras treat, we include Chef Bobo's Bread Pudding—not a low-calorie dish, but wonderful for an occasional feast.

We've include many recipes in this chapter and this book, and almost all of them fit into our New Orleans Program. We're demonstrating that well-chosen foods can be delicious enough for a joyous occasion like Mardi Gras and *still* be good for your health.

CHEF BOBO'S SIMPLE AND DELICIOUS GUACAMOLE

To me, guacamole is one of the most delicious party foods you can make. It seems everyone loves it. The key is to keep it simple and to make it fresh. If you want it really hot, add chopped habanero peppers instead of jalapeños. I'm happy with a bowl of freshly made guacamole and some thinly sliced raw vegetables, like carrots, celery, parsnips, and daikon radish, to scoop it up with.—Chef Bobo

4 ripe avocados, peeled and pitted (save pits)
¼ cup minced red onion
¼ cup fresh cilantro leaves, chopped very fine
2 fresh jalapeño peppers, seeded and chopped fine
Juice of 1 lime
Tabasco sauce to taste
Salt and black pepper to taste

Using a fork or potato masher, mash avocados, leaving them chunky. Stir in onion, cilantro, and jalapeños. Add juice and Tabasco. Mix well. Taste to see that there is a good balance of flavors. Then add salt and pepper. It should taste so good that you want to eat it all yourself. If the guacamole has to sit for a few hours, push some of the pits down into it—they will help keep the guacamole from oxidizing and turning brown. Cover with plastic wrap or put in an airtight container and store in the refrigerator. Serve with tortilla chips or fresh, thinly sliced vegetables.

SHRIMP AND CHICKEN JAMBALAYA

Jambalaya is a Louisiana rice dish of Native American origin. Our health-tuned version packs all the flavor of and much less fat than the classic preparation. When everything is prepped ahead, the cooking goes quickly.

If you choose to use brown rice, check the doneness, as it might require a slightly longer stirring time. I prefer my jambalaya dry; however, many good New Orleans cooks and eaters like a wetter style. You can choose by checking the liquid level as you fluff the rice: if you like it drier, cook it a little longer. This great centerpiece for a meal keeps well in the refrigerator and is terrific as part of a buffet. At home, I will often add some crushed red pepper flakes or a small, minced, not-too-hot serrano pepper to increase the heat.

3 tbsp. extra-virgin olive oil
1 large yellow onion, chopped
1 medium green bell pepper, chopped
3 celery stalks, stringed and chopped (tops too!)
1 large tomato, chopped
3 boneless, skinless chicken thighs or 1 large or 2 small boneless,
  skinless chicken breasts, sliced thin
3 tbsp. chopped parsley
2 garlic cloves, pressed
3 bay leaves
½ tsp. cayenne pepper
½ tsp. thyme
1 tsp. white or ½ tsp. black pepper
4 cups chicken stock (low-sodium, low-fat)
8 oz. tomato sauce (reduced sodium, no sugar added)
2 cups raw rice
2 lb. medium shrimp, peeled and deveined

In a large saucepan or covered skillet, heat oil. Add onion and stir just until it begins to be translucent. Add all but last 2 ingredients. Bring to a boil, stirring. Then stir in rice, and bring back to a boil. Cover and reduce heat immediately to low. Simmer 30 minutes. Stir to fluff rice (liquid should be almost all absorbed; if not, cook a few more minutes). Stir in shrimp. Recover pan and cook 5-7 more minutes until shrimp are just done. Adjust seasonings to taste. Enjoy!

LIGHT RED BEANS AND RICE

Mardi Gras wouldn't be the same without red beans and rice, traditionally cooked on Mondays while the laundry is being done but wonderful any day of the week. Like jambalaya, it is easily made for larger numbers of guests and easy to serve (even from the back of a truck outside Tipitina's on Mardi Gras Day).

1 lb. red beans
1 large sweet onion, chopped
1 large green bell pepper, chopped
3 large celery stalks, stringed and chopped
1-3 large garlic cloves, pressed
4 bay leaves
$\frac{1}{2}$ tsp. basil (fresh, if you have it)
$\frac{1}{2}$ tsp. thyme
$\frac{1}{2}$ tsp. sea salt
$\frac{1}{2}$ tsp. black pepper
$\frac{1}{2}$ tsp. or less cayenne pepper
$\frac{1}{2}$ bunch parsley, chopped fine (Italian flat leaf preferred)
$\frac{1}{2}$ bunch green onion tops, sliced fine

Place beans in a large pot. Cover to twice the bean depth with water. Bring to a rapid boil. Reduce heat to medium low. Stir occasionally and watch for sticking. Cook about 1 hour. Add water as needed.

Add all but last 2 ingredients. Cook for another hour on low, stirring occasionally. Add last 2 ingredients, and cook 15-20 more minutes, stirring. Serve with enough hot, cooked rice (white or brown) to accommodate all.

CHEF BOBO'S BREAD PUDDING
Serves 8.

Perhaps the best known of New Orleans' traditional desserts is our famous bread pudding. Chef Bobo gives us his secret recipe.

3 eggs + 2 egg yolks
1 tsp. vanilla
Pinch nutmeg or to taste

Cinnamon to taste
⅓ cup melted butter
1¼ cups milk
1¼ cups half-and-half
1½ cups sugar
½ cup raisins soaked in dark rum until soft
6 cups bread cubes (day-old challah or brioche preferred)
Softened butter for pan
Extra sugar for pan
½ cup chopped pecans
2 bananas, sliced

Note: This pudding is cooked in the oven with 2 pans, 1 inside the other. The outside pan holds the water, or *bain marie*. The inside pan must be smaller, yet still deep enough to hold all the pudding. I use a deep 9-inch cheesecake pan (not a springform pan) for the pudding and place it in a regular 10- or 14-inch cake pan.

Combine the first 7 ingredients with the sugar. Add raisins. Pour mixture over bread in a deep container. Cover surface with plastic wrap. Put weight on top of surface to hold bread down in liquid. *Let bread soak overnight in refrigerator.* Most of the liquid should be soaked up by the bread.

Take a deep baking pan that will hold all the soaked bread. Coat pan with butter and then dust all over with sugar. Put pan in freezer and allow to harden.

After about 30 minutes, remove pan from freezer, apply another coat of butter, and dust again with sugar. This time, press pecans over inside surface of pan, with most of them on the bottom. Return to freezer for another 30 minutes.

Remove pan from freezer. Pour half your soaked bread into it. Layer bananas over this half. If you have extra pecans, you can sprinkle these in as well. Then pour remaining soaked bread on top of bananas and smooth top.

Put this pan inside the larger pan and place in a 425-degree oven. Before closing the oven door, pour about 1 inch water into the larger outer pan. This will produce steam to keep the pudding soft and moist.

Bake about 25 minutes. Then lower heat to 350 degrees and continue to bake about 45 minutes. Keep checking to make sure there is still water in the larger pan.

When the pudding is done, it will feel firm in the middle, and a knife inserted in the center will come out clean. If it is not done, continue to cook, checking again after about 15 minutes.

Remove pudding from oven right away and let set about 30 minutes. Then turn out the whole pudding onto a plate or platter large enough to hold it. The outside will be crisp and crusty from the caramelization of the sugar and pecans. The inside will be smooth and moist with the fragrance of spices and banana. This pudding is very rich and stands well on its own, but on the side you can serve your favorite rum or bourbon sauce or just a little unsweetened whipped cream and a sprig of mint.

FAMILY RECIPES: CHEF BESH

In South Louisiana or "Catholic Louisiana," every community has its own version of Fat Tuesday. In the areas surrounding New Orleans, Mardi Gras is celebrated with parades, cookouts, and balls, from the cheap to the chic. Every socioeconomic group takes part in the celebration in one form or another. What they have in common is a feast for all the senses to precede the forty days of atonement of Lent. We love big pots of jambalaya, red beans and rice, gumbo, potato salad, fried chicken, sausages, po' boys, and king cakes. Not to mention Bloody Marys, Sazeracs, Hurricanes, Pimm's Cups, Mimosas, and of course beer.

In the areas west of New Orleans there is a different Mardi Gras. On Bayou Lafourche, you'll find boat parades and lots of boudin. In towns like Mamou or Church Point, west of Lafayette, you'll find revelers on horseback, either drunk or almost drunk, going door to door scavenging for ingredients to put in a gumbo, including live chickens, ducks, or geese. Later in the day, the loot is collected to cook a traditional gumbo. The feast is accompanied by more drinking, dancing, and singing—always lots of food and alcohol.

For myself, I prefer fried chicken and seafood jambalaya. Every year, we have the same argument: which batter for the chicken is better? I prefer a buttermilk and flour crust, while others may like the inferior qualities of cornmeal fried chicken. The jambalaya is made every year in the courtyard of Uncle Kurt's French Quarter apartment, just across from Jackson Square. The same pot is used every year, a well-seasoned cast-iron pot that is said to be 150 years old. More arguments erupt over who has the best recipe, or whether or not to use tomatoes. Creole jambalaya contains tomatoes, while Cajun jambalaya is much darker and has almost no tomatoes. I have the best recipe in the family—however, my father-in-law wouldn't agree. My brother-in-law makes a great jambalaya but is always trying to upgrade it; thus, it's not very consistent!

A *très* spicy Bloody Mary is a preferred breakfast drink, dressed with a tangy pickled green bean or okra. There is also the champagne and orange juice camp, which tends to look down on anyone drinking hard liquor before noon. These drinks are consumed while the men chop the onions, celery, and bell peppers, cut chickens, and season the flour. Meanwhile, the children enjoy hot beignets and fresh-squeezed orange juice prior to chasing pigeons on their way to Zulu (the first and best parade of Fat Tuesday).

Lunch is normally eaten throughout the day along with a few hors d'oeuvres, such as boiled shrimp with remoulade sauce, salty oysters with cocktail sauce, links of boudin, and hog's-head cheese with crackers. This is what I call Mardi Gras food!

Later in the evening, we'll have fried chicken and potato salad before the last parade, which I've never waited up for. It's usually an early night for us. After a day of feasting, it is actually quite easy to fast for Ash Wednesday. One small meal is usually eaten, and for us it's vegetarian red beans and rice with a little of that fluffy New Orleans-style "French bread." For the next forty days and nights, it means for me abstaining from alcohol (with a small exception made for St. Patrick's Day) and fasting on Fridays, especially from meat, as well as personal penance in one shape or form.

I'd always thought that it would be more of a sacrifice to eat meat on Fridays rather than to abstain from it. Seafood is almost all we eat in New Orleans!

MARDI GRAS RECIPES

When I asked Chef John Besh about his family's favorite Mardi Gras foods, his first response was "fried chicken"—and many New Orleanians would concur. Fried chicken recipes are often kept secret even within families. Each of my three aunts and my mother had a different way of preparing fried chicken.

New Orleans entrepreneur Al Copeland developed his own way, the Popeye's way of commercially preparing chicken, now available all over the country. We don't recommend commercial fried chicken, not just because the production techniques are controversial, but because of the trans fats, high calories, and relatively low food value.

I have worked for years to perfect frying good-quality free-range chicken, to maximize flavor and minimize calories. When friends visit at Mardi Gras time, nothing disappears faster than a platter of fried chicken. My family prefers thighs and drumsticks, although my technique works well for white meat and wings, too.

The secret lies in the egg wash and the temperature of the canola oil. (We recommend not reusing the oil.) This particular egg wash, or semi-egg wash if you choose the water technique, virtually seals the chicken off from the oil, thus keeping calories low while allowing spices and seasonings to permeate the meat. With this method of preparation, boneless, skinless chicken thighs and breasts come out nicely. Or the crisp skin can be removed after frying to lower calories (and heighten a sense of virtue). In contrast to beef or other meats, the fat in chicken accumulates between the skin and the muscle.

The cooking time for boneless, skinless pieces is less than it is for drumsticks. The cooking time for wings is less than for drumsticks. Cooking times are only approximate but can be judged nicely as the cooking proceeds. Turn the chicken frequently. The maximum cooking time even for larger drumsticks should be 35 minutes.

NEW ORLEANS PROGRAM FRIED CHICKEN

You will need a 12-inch skillet, a plastic sack for flouring, and tongs. The universally available, inexpensive triangular tongs grasp chicken the best.

Canola oil
³⁄₄ cup skim milk or water
White of 1 large or 2 smaller eggs
1¹⁄₂ tsp. sea salt
¹⁄₂ tsp. Louisiana hot sauce
8-10 pieces chicken
1 cup flour

1½ tsp. black pepper
½-1 tsp. cayenne pepper
Blended seasonings (lower-salt type preferred)

Add enough oil to fill skillet about one-third. Heat on medium high.

Combine milk or water, egg white(s), ½ tsp. salt, and hot sauce, mixing briefly with a fork. Coat chicken with this egg wash.

Combine flour, remaining salt, peppers, and 2 tsp. blended seasonings in the plastic sack. One at a time, lift each chicken piece out of wash and shake in coating sack.

When oil is hot (but not smoking!), add pieces one by one. Oil should bubble actively but not spatter. Sprinkle tops with more blended seasonings. Turn after 5 minutes. Sprinkle tops again. Turn after 5 minutes. Turn 2 more times, 10 minutes or so apart. Golden brown is the goal. Approximate times:

Drumsticks—30-35 minutes
Boneless breasts—25 minutes
Boneless thighs—20 minutes
Wings—20 minutes
Tenders—15-20 minutes

This dish delights hot (about 10 minutes out of the pan), cool, or cold. Leftovers with fried skin removed make great salads or salad additions.

Chef John has invented a calorie-sensitive, taste-rich, faux fried chicken breast that makes a good appearance on Mardi Gras plates, at picnics, and as the centerpiece of quick family dinners.

NONFAT OVEN-FRIED CHICKEN

Serves 6.

6 boneless, skinless chicken breasts
Salt and black pepper to taste
6 tbsp. Dijon mustard

2 tbsp. chopped thyme
2 tbsp. chopped tarragon
4 cups panko breadcrumbs

Rub chicken with salt and pepper. Mix mustard and herbs. Brush onto chicken. Shake chicken in a bag with breadcrumbs to coat, or toss together in a large bowl. Place on a roasting rack in the oven at 350 degrees and bake about 30 minutes or until chicken is no longer pink.

Though Mardi Gras attracts millions of visitors from around the world, it is also very much a local holiday, celebrated by everyone in the city. Transplanted natives of New Orleans, like Chef Bobo, use the occasion for a reunion with friends and family. In the lower French Quarter, where I used to live, one group traditionally gathers on Lundi Gras to make grillades and grits, the quintessential Mardi Gras breakfast.

The fun begins when everyone gathers to "make groceries"—that is, to shop—and then afterwards to pound out the flank steak into thin grillades and prepare the tomatoes and onion. The prep is usually finished in time to catch the Orpheus parade or even the Bards of Bohemia, which parades in front of Orpheus.

My first taste of grillades came at a midnight supper marking Twelfth Night. The following recipe reflects some personal preferences—I favor a dark roux with grillades and perhaps more tomato than other cooks might use. Some Creole cooks prefer a medium-color roux. I have also had grillades with sliced okra.

Traditional preparation requires that the tomatoes be peeled. Although tomato skins do offer some extra fiber, the final texture of the grillades gravy is nicer if the tomatoes are skinned. Grillades make an excellent, relatively low calorie dish, wonderful for serving to large numbers.

LOWER FRENCH QUARTER GRILLADES

You will need a meat tenderizer—the hammer type, *not* chemicals—and a surface to pound out the grillades. This can be a very liberating part of the dish preparation. The leaner cuts of beef may be less tender at first, but they tenderize nicely in the preparation, and they are lower in calories.

3 lb. eye of round beef
3 tbsp. extra-virgin olive oil
1 tbsp. butter
Sea salt and black pepper or blended seasonings to taste
4 tbsp. all-purpose flour (Swansdown Cake Flour also works well)
3 cups beef stock, yours or good, low-fat commercial
1 medium red bell pepper, diced
1 medium green bell pepper, diced
1 large or 2 medium yellow or Vidalia onions, diced
4 large garlic cloves, pressed
4 tbsp. parsley, minced (Italian flat leaf preferred)
½ tsp. cayenne pepper
3 bay leaves
3 tomatoes, peeled and diced*

Slice beef about ⅛ inch thick. Pound slices until they are about half that thickness. Cut each slice in half. Refrigerate, if preparing ahead for a crowd, or cook now.

Cover bottom of a large covered skillet with oil and add butter. Do not let oil get to smoking point. Toss in grillades, and quickly season tops lightly with salt and pepper or blended seasonings. Brown quickly on one side, turn with tongs, and season top while other side is browning. Remove from pan and reserve. Keep pan juice and oil hot.

Add flour, whisk, and make a medium-dark to dark roux. (Tips on roux making follow.) Rapidly stir in half the stock, avoiding lumps. Add remaining stock, stir well, and add all other ingredients, layering on tomatoes and then grillades last.

Cover and simmer 1 hour. Adjust seasonings. Serve with grits, the traditional accompaniment (recipe below), or boiled or mashed potatoes.

*How to peel tomatoes: Here's how easy it is. Fill a large saucepan or stockpot two-thirds of the way with water, and bring it to a rapid boil. Drop the (thoroughly cleaned) tomatoes into the boiling water for 20-30 seconds. Then remove them and refresh them briefly under cold running water. Use a small knife to pull up the skin—the easiest place to start is around the stem end. The skin should peel quickly from the tomato, leaving a beautifully skinned whole fruit ready for further processing. I usually remove the seeds.

FIRST YOU MAKE A ROUX

A *roux brun* forms the foundation of local gravies. In New Orleans, a sauce is usually called a "gravy"—for instance, spaghetti with tomato sauce is often referred to as "spaghetti with red gravy." To make a roux, you will need a large skillet, since usually other ingredients are added after the roux is made, and either a wooden spoon or a whisk. The roux can be varied by later additions, but proper initial preparation doesn't vary. The key proportions are 2 tbsp. flour to 1 tbsp. oil. You may wish to use butter and oil for a somewhat different flavor.

The color of the roux is determined by how long you cook it. I find the cooking is best done over at least medium-high heat, yet not high enough to burn. The color changes very quickly—hence my two cardinal rules for making a roux:

1. Avoid any distractions. It takes only a few moments to make a roux, but its success is critical to the success of the dish.

2. Never allow the least bit of burning to occur. Even a small amount of burning when you are attempting to make a dark, dark roux impairs irrevocably the flavor of the gravy and the dish. If the roux is burned at all, discard it. Wash the skillet and any implements that touched the roux thoroughly.

Here are the directions for making roux for the average dish.

2 tbsp. canola oil
½ tbsp. butter (optional)
4 tbsp. good-quality all-purpose flour
2 cups water or stock (or 1 cup water and 1 cup milk)
Additional liquid if needed

Heat oil over medium-high heat. Add butter if desired. Add flour all at once and begin stirring immediately.

Watch closely as it bubbles. The color of the flour will change rapidly. If cooking is stopped early, you can make a very light tan roux; further cooking creates a medium-brown roux and finally the dark-brown roux used in grillades.

The moment the roux has achieved the right color, stir in at least 1-2 cups liquid rapidly, keeping roux free of lumps. Immediately reduce heat and stir a few moments to smooth and thicken. Begin to add the other ingredients one by one as appropriate to the recipe. Remember that some ingredients will give off juice as they cook, so do not thin roux too much.

GRITS: NOTES FROM CHEF BESH

Breakfast before a big day is important. I grew up in a house where breakfast meant eggs, bacon or sausage, and grits. We always had sliced tomatoes, biscuits, and great butter to slather the biscuits with. Then we had homemade jellies and jams; I can just smell it. We always had orange juice and always coffee. Nowadays, it's inconceivable to begin every day with sunny-side-up eggs and grits or hash browns. We can't eat like that anymore. But I'd love to borrow some of those flavors and to eat like that on occasion, to eat like that responsibly.

Grits are now coming back into vogue after a long absence. I think we Americans the country over are waking up to the fact that grits taste great, and have a place in our diets along with potatoes. For so long we've gotten rid of our potatoes and all these other carbs that are really quite good—if you eat them properly. Again, this is all about moderation.

Grits start with corn that has been preserved as hominy. This hominy is then dried and ground into grits. The grits I love are organically grown and milled, mostly in the Carolinas. I think Morgan Mills in Brevard, North Carolina, and Anson Mills in South Carolina make the best grits on the market today. I love them because they're stone ground in these old mills. They aren't so precise. Some grits come out finer than others. So you have this dust that really adds a creaminess to the grits versus one of the quick varieties where everything is uniform and you add butter and other stuff. These are organic stone-milled grits. They become creamy on their own with just water. It's really interesting. I love eating them and I recommend going out of your way to find stone-ground grits.

CHEESE GRITS

Serves 6.

Grits traditionally accompany local breakfasts. Leftover grits can be transformed into other dishes like fried grits cakes. Grits lend themselves very well to additional ingredients, such as the cheddar cheese in this recipe. White or sharp yellow cheddar cheese is New Orleans' traditional choice. My favorite for breakfast, or with dishes other than grillades, would be a pungent domestic blue cheese such as Maytag. If you use blue cheese instead of cheddar, crumble and stir it in just prior to serving.

Grits come in two colors, yellow or white, depending upon type of corn and processing. Several suppliers of old-fashioned, stone-ground, whole-grain grits can be found on the Internet. Many local grocery stores also carry good-quality grits. Since it doesn't take long to cook unprocessed grits, I do not recommend using the processed "instant" types except in special situations.

An old Creole technique to enhance the flavor of grits is to use $2\frac{1}{2}$ cups water and $2\frac{1}{2}$ cups milk in place of 5 cups water.

5 cups water
1 cup uncooked grits
4-6 oz. white or sharp yellow cheddar cheese
1 tsp. or less sea salt

Bring water to a rapid boil. Stir in grits and return to boil. Crumble or cube cheddar cheese and add. Cover and simmer on low to medium heat. Stir occasionally. Grits should be tender in about 15 minutes. Stir in salt to taste.

CREOLE BREAKFAST GRILLADES

Grillades without gravy, quick and easy to prepare, play an important role in the traditional New Orleans breakfast. They can be served as a main course and require much less preparation than grillades with gravy. This dish, low in calories and loaded with flavor, makes a healthful, protein-based breakfast that can reduce one's appetite for the rest of the day. It is also an appropriate breakfast for extended test taking—like the morning of the SATs—and other events that demand concentration, such as courtroom appearances and important business meetings.

1 lb. very lean round steak
Sea salt and black pepper to taste
Blended seasonings to taste
1 tbsp. extra-virgin olive oil
1 medium onion, sliced thin

1 large garlic clove, pressed
1 medium tomato, diced
2 tbsp. chopped parsley (Italian flat leaf preferred)

Slice beef thinly, less than ⅛ inch thick. Rub both sides with salt, pepper, and blended seasonings. Heat oil in skillet until hot. Brown onion and garlic quickly. Do not burn. Add tomato and parsley and stir 1 minute. Move vegetables aside and place grillades on bottom of skillet. Cover with vegetables, cover skillet, and cook on medium heat until grillades are just browned and tender.

CHEF JOHN'S FAMILY-STYLE LIGHTER SHRIMP AND GRITS
Serves 6.

This interesting recipe really comes from South Carolina, but I've adapted it with some of our local products. The ham stock can be made from smoked turkey necks instead, which also provides a wonderful rich broth so full of flavor. It would cut back on the fat, and there's very little salt added either. The number of shrimp you should use depends on if you plan to serve this as an appetizer or a main course.

18-36 jumbo shrimp
Creole spice to taste
Salt to taste
6 tbsp. small-diced mildly spicy red peppers
2 tbsp. minced shallot
2 tbsp. minced garlic
12 oz. Ham Stock (see below)
24 oz. Tomato Sauce (see below)
Chopped chives
Diced tomatoes
Grits (see below)
6 sprigs chervil
2 tbsp. chopped thyme

Season shrimp with Creole spice and salt; sauté and hold on side. Sauté peppers, shallot, and garlic. Add stock and sauce. Let reduce a little, then add back shrimp to cook through. Add chives and toma-toes.

For each serving, place 2 tbsp. grits in the middle of a large bowl and arrange 3-6 shrimp in middle of bowl so they stand up (tails facing in). Spoon sauce around to fill space. Garnish with chervil and thyme.

Ham Stock
1 lb. smoked ham hocks
1 celery stalk, halved
1 onion, halved
1 carrot, peeled and halved
1 head garlic, halved
1 tsp. chopped fresh thyme leaves

Simmer ingredients in water, covered, for 1 hour, skimming off fat frequently. Strain and reserve liquid.

Tomato Sauce
Extra-virgin olive oil
1 lb. overripe tomatoes, quartered
1 clove garlic, chopped
Pinch crushed red pepper flakes
1 tbsp. chopped basil
1 tbsp. chopped tarragon
2 pinches sugar
Salt and black pepper to taste

Heat oil in a pot and hard sear tomatoes. Add garlic, pepper flakes, basil, tarragon, and sugar. Once tomatoes come to a boil, let them cook 5 minutes. Run through a food mill or food processor. Add salt and pepper.

Grits
4 cups water
Salt to taste
1 cup white grits

Boil water and add salt. Add grits and turn down to a simmer. Simmer grits on low about 20 minutes, stirring frequently.

One wonderful American food that occupies its rightful place at Mardi Gras is barbecue. Growing up in North Carolina, I learned early what good barbecue is all about. I realize those are fighting words to folks from Memphis, Alabama, Texas, and certain parts of Louisiana. The following preparation renders a flavorful, tender, low-fat, low-sodium treat that can be enjoyed with coleslaw and a pea or bean dish for a delightful meal. It can also be placed on a whole-wheat bun for an out-of-this-world sandwich—being from North Carolina, I prefer mine dressed with coleslaw. Any cut of beef or pork will do, as the preparation will tenderize it.

HOME-ON-THE-RANGE-STYLE BARBECUE

2 lb. lean beef or pork
4 bay leaves
1 tbsp. oregano (or equivalent, such as rosemary or thyme)
⅛ tsp. cayenne pepper

Trim as much fat as possible from meat. In large, covered saucepot, boil all ingredients in water to cover until meat falls apart, approximately 2 hours, adding water as needed. Remove meat from liquid. When cool enough to handle, pull meat into shreds. Discard bay leaves. Reserve 1½ cups stock, fat removed. While meat cooks, prepare sauce.

Sauce
2 celery stalks, stringed and chopped fine
2 ripe tomatoes, chopped fine
¼ cup tomato sauce (reduced sodium, no sugar added)
1½ tbsp. Worcestershire sauce
2 tbsp. cider, cane, or red-wine vinegar
2 tbsp. fresh lemon or lime juice (or 4 tbsp. orange juice)
2-3 tbsp. Louisiana hot sauce
2 tbsp. brown sugar
1 tsp. paprika (*not* hot)
1 tsp. Creole or Dijon mustard
1½ cups meat stock

Cook all sauce ingredients, uncovered, on a slow boil about 30 minutes. Add meat to pot, mix, cover, and simmer 45 minutes. Taste for seasoning, and adjust with black pepper, cayenne, or sea salt if needed.

Here is my recipe for a mayo-free coleslaw to accompany the barbecue. Be sure to choose the greenest cabbage head possible.

COLESLAW VINAIGRETTE

$^1/_3$-$^1/_2$ **small, firm cabbage head**
2-3 tbsp. extra-virgin olive oil
$^1/_4$ **tsp. black pepper**
$^1/_4$ **tsp. sea salt**
Dash cayenne pepper
$^1/_4$ **tsp. dry or prepared mustard**
1-1$^1/_2$ tbsp. cider vinegar or rice vinegar

Slice cabbage very fine or shred; do not grate. Toss cabbage first with oil and dry ingredients. Then toss with prepared mustard, if using, and vinegar. Check seasonings and adjust. Can be refrigerated, covered, 1 hour. Not bad kept overnight, but no longer. If you like, toss in a small amount of oven-crisped walnuts or sliced almonds just before serving. Great with barbecue in a sandwich or even with sesame or rice crackers.

MARDI GRAS FUN AND FESTIVITIES: NEW ORLEANS LORE

Mardi Gras caps the frivolity of the carnival season, which begins on Twelfth Night, January 6. Since 1870, the celebrations have been kicked off by the exclusive Twelfth Night Revelers Club. The carnival season peaks in the two weeks prior to Fat Tuesday, a day that falls between February 3 and March 9 every year. Pope Gregory, whose calendar we still use, set Easter as the first Sunday after the first full moon following the spring equinox. The day after Mardi Gras, Ash Wednesday, is automatically forty days and six Sundays before Easter. At midnight on Mardi Gras, carnival moves dramatically and suddenly into the abstinence of Lent.

Parades begin rolling weeks before the big day. Fat Tuesday break-fasts hail the morning arrival of Zulu, the oldest African-American krewe, followed by Rex, the King of Carnival. The Vieux Carré and Uptown are filled with the sounds of parades and band music. Bourbon Street is packed wall to wall with people. It may take the internationally famous clarinetist Pete Fountain and his Half-Fast Walking Club an hour to negotiate one block, as they deliver kisses and flowers to the ladies. The air is filled with laughter, music, and the shouts of a million revelers: "Throw me something, mister!"

There are several Mardi Gras celebrations in the United States, but New Orleans puts on a spectacle unlike any other. Debates continue about the origins of the American Mardi Gras. The tradition of Mardi Gras parties and balls may have drifted to New Orleans from French settlers in Mobile, Alabama. The first organized Mardi Gras parade with two floats, costumed maskers, and *flambeaux* (torches) was in New Orleans on March 24, 1857. The Mistick Krewe of Comus, the god of revelry, ushered in the tradition of Mardi Gras as we know it today. The city had seen Mardi Gras events for the two previous decades, but they had become somewhat dangerous. Instead of the candies and flowers originally given to parade goers, revelers had begun throwing sacks of flour containing stones and other objects, in the pagan tradition.

In 1872, all New Orleans was aflame with excitement in anticipation of the visit of the Grand Duke Alexis Romanoff of Russia for Mardi Gras. The young Romanoff was the closest thing in those days to an international heartthrob and rock star. Several New Orleans business-men, eager to show that the city could hold its own with such titled guests, hastily organized the Rex parade. The Romanoff colors of pur-ple, green, and gold became ever after the official colors of Mardi Gras in New Orleans. The Grand Duke's favorite song, "If Ever I Cease to Love," from the musical comedy *Bluebeard,* remains the official song of Mardi Gras.

The Zulu Social Aid and Pleasure Club organized its first all African-American Zulu parade in 1909. Zulu maskers today, including some non-African-Americans, all wear blackface and throw the most prized token of all Mardi Gras—the Zulu coconut. Each coconut is decorat-ed by hand, a unique piece of carnival art.

Everyone looks forward to the appearance of the Mardi Gras Indians, such as the Wild Magnolias. Southern Louisiana Indians such as the Houma Indians protected runaway slaves. In gratitude, African-

American men in New Orleans each year spend countless hours sewing lavishly detailed costumes of feathers in bright colors, forming "Indian gangs" with chiefs, scouts, and spy boys, and, of course, creating music.

The character of Mardi Gras in New Orleans has been transformed since the 1970s by the emergence of the super krewes. The super krewes, pioneered by the Krewes of Endymion and Bacchus, parade over a thousand maskers on thirty floats, interspersed with numerous marching brass bands. These huge night parades utilize lights, fiber optics, advanced sound systems, lasers, and elaborate decoration to provide a fantastic spectacle.

Perhaps the most outstanding recent addition to Mardi Gras is the newest super krewe, the Krewe of Orpheus. Native son musician Harry Connick, Jr., and his drama teacher at Jesuit High, Sonny Borey, conceived and created Orpheus in 1993. Their intent was to give the city the gift of a carnival krewe celebrating New Orleans' diverse heritage. Sonny, the krewe captain, tells the story of the krewe's founding.

Harry was Bacchus for the twenty-fifth anniversary. He loved being in the parade, and yet, at the same time, he saw that there really were not a number of African-Americans in the organization. There were obviously no women either, and he said, well, you know what? Why don't we try to do something for the city that helps bring Mardi Gras back together again? Why don't you and I start a parade?

I said, Harry, what have you been drinking this early in the day? Do you have any conception of what it takes, people-wise, energy-wise, financially, *to start a new parade, and especially to start a* super *parade? He said, yeah, but we can do it. I said OK. Let's get together. So we did.*

And over the next couple of months we got together with his dad, and some people that I knew, and with Blaine Kern, Jr. and Sr. (New Orleans' Mardi Gras float-making family), and said what we needed to do.

It was a great first year, and it has really taken off since then. One of the good things—and I think probably one of the reasons Harry asked me to do this—is that a Mardi Gras parade is like doing a musical. It's like doing a show. It's nothing more than the theater on wheels. It's watching a different act of the show go by as each float or band goes by. Now, putting on a Mardi Gras parade is like doing two musicals at once, but that's beside the point. It's a fun-loving experience. It's a gift.

For many years, including the year Harry Connick, Jr., reigned as

Bacchus, I was privileged to ride in the Bacchus parade on a certain float with a charter-member lieutenant of the krewe. One of New Orleans' most famous chefs of the moment, Emeril Lagasse, joined our float, which already boasted one of New Orleans' best-known "hereditary" chefs, Alex Patout.

Alex, generous gentleman that he is, made our float the envy of the entire parade. After mounting the floats at the New Orleans Convention Center and getting pulled slowly all the way Uptown to the starting point at the foot of Napoleon Avenue, next to the legendary Tipitina's Bar, it can sometimes be tedious waiting for the parade to roll. But Alex, using contacts and a bit of Mardi Gras gris-gris, obtained permits from the authorities and was able to bring trucks carrying tables, chafing dishes, silverware, candelabra, and linens to the banquette (New Orleansese for "sidewalk") next to our float. The feasts he set up were truly sumptuous. Other maskers from the Bacchus parade could only pass by and look on with envy as we sipped fine wine and ate wonderful Louisiana food.

FAT-LADEN FOOD: SPECIAL OCCASIONS ONLY

The early spring breezes of Mardi Gras carry with them the aromas of carnival street food: Lucky Dogs, corn dogs, po' boys, funnel cakes, French fries, boiled crawfish, fried chicken, alligator on a stick, grilled andouille, beignets, and more. It's no surprise, then, that when friends from Manhattan heard we were writing a guide to health with New Orleans recipes, they chorused, "Impossible!" Not so. Read on.

The beauty of Mardi Gras is that, like most things in New Orleans, it is part of a seasonal cycle that comes and goes. By the time Ash Wednesday rolls around, most New Orleanians are relieved it's over and ready to embrace the moderation of Lent.

Mardi Gras can be misunderstood when "you're not from here," as New Orleanians say. Some call it pagan and excessive, but Mardi Gras occupies a special place in the religious calendar. The celebratory nature of the spectacle uplifts us. It embodies the joy of being alive and of human community. Rich and poor, young and old, black and white and tan alike join in the festivities. Mardi Gras prepares us for Lent, a season of discipline and quietly joyful preparation. Discipline reminds us that fat-laden food eaten occasionally can taste great and not do harm. Daily overconsumption, on the other hand, can be dangerous.

A few years ago it was uncommon to see an article about obesity, high blood pressure, or diabetes in a nonscientific publication. These days, the local newspapers feature weekly headlines about our obesity epidemic. Obesity alone poses its own dangers, but far more dangerous is the full-blown metabolic syndrome that obesity can bring.

OBESITY AND METABOLIC SYNDROME

Obesity Alone	*Metabolic Syndrome*
Genes may predispose	Genes may play two roles
Not caused by bad and/or good fat consumption alone, but by too many calories in, too few burned	Aggravated by bad fat consumption
Risk of high blood pressure	High blood pressure of complex origin
No definite direct effect on arterial plaque disease	Arterial plaque disease of complex origin
No definite direct effect on increased blood clotting	Increased blood clotting tendency of complex origin, with increased risk of stroke and heart attack

Here's how the metabolic syndrome works. When we become obese, fat accumulates not just under the skin but also in our body cavities, especially the abdomen. This internal or "visceral" fat can directly harm us. Fatty tissues are blockers, interfering with the healthy metabolism of lean muscle tissue. Obese tissues can also block the hormone insulin from helping our main cellular fuel, sugar, get into our tissues. This blockade leads to a rise in blood sugar, insulin resistance, and Type II diabetes. When we add obesity's further associated risks of high blood pressure, stroke, heart disease, and cancer, we see that obesity and its attendant metabolic syndrome can be life threatening, with or without hereditary risk factors.

DEFINING OBESITY: YOUR BMI

There are two main types of obesity. In one, most fat collects in the upper body and abdomen; in the other, fat deposits build up on the hips and thighs. The first type is more risky, for it suggests hidden visceral or "inside the belly" fat around upper-body organs and abdominal cavities. Liposuction can remove fat between skin and muscle, but it's useless against visceral fat.

It's easy to tell if you're threateningly obese. First, simply measure your waist. Are you a woman with a waist thirty-five inches or more or a man with a waist forty inches or more? Then you are obese. This quick method is valid because visceral fat (the fat inside your belly) enlarges your waist, and large waist measurements are associated with heart disease and other diseases—even though some men still believe a large belly means virility. Some place emphasis on the waist to hip ratio (hip circumference in inches, divided by waist in inches). Better ratios are 0.9 or smaller. This number may be informative, but waist alone passes both the easy and informative tests.

Second, calculate your Body Mass Index (BMI), which is known to correlate with the amount of tissue fat one has. Here is the simplified Newsome/Besh formula.

Newsome/Besh Simplified Body Mass Index (BMI) Calculation

Your weight in pounds x 9.9 divided by your height in inches
For example, Chef John's Body Mass Index:
185 pounds x 9.9 = 1,831.5 divided by 72 inches = 25

Body Mass Index:	18.5 or less	Underweight
	18.6-24.9	Wellness Weight
	25-30	Overweight
	30.1-39.9	Obese
	40 or over	Morbidly Obese

The New Orleans Program will improve your BMI and your waistline, but these improvements will come slowly. We recommend that you not step on the scale every day. Rather, use the fit of your clothes, your reflection in the mirror, and the feedback from those around you as more helpful indicators of progress. When I had my own wellness epiphany, my Body Mass Index was over 29. It is currently under 25. That's fine, but what really pleases me is when patients who have not seen me in a while walk into the examining room and say, "Dr. Newsome, you look great!"

SCIENCE AND COMMON SENSE: YOUR BMR

Recent research has uncovered a small number of people who have a genetically determined "efficient" or "slow" metabolism. For these rare individuals, the old saying "I gain weight when I just look at food" seems almost to be true. These few persons, whose red blood cells create more metabolic products from fewer blood-borne sources, can indeed gain weight with fewer calories. The rest of us, however, are just taking in too many calories or not being active enough. Our "metabolism genes" do not make us fat. Our mouths do. Medical causes of obesity don't explain why there are 160 million fat people in the fattest nation on the planet.

We do need calories. We eat to live. Living has a metabolic cost that must be paid with food. Just staying alive requires consuming a certain number of calories per day. The Basal Metabolic Rate (BMR) estimates the daily calories you need just to support all your bodily functions, even if you're inactive.

If you remain physically inactive, how many calories will your body use for breathing, heartbeat, and other vital functions? Scientists have measured calorie needs in persons at complete rest. Adults need between about 1,200 and 1,500 calories to keep the heart beating, lungs breathing, and brain functioning.

More muscle mass increases your metabolic rate. Since men generally have more muscle mass than women, their BMR is proportionally higher than women's. Anyone adding muscle mass can increase their BMR—one reason that regular exercise is so important.

The more you weigh, the higher your BMR is. So if you're staying overweight, you're taking in more calories than a thinner person, by definition. Knowing this may make it easier to reduce your calories.

When we exercise, we can eat more than our BMR number and not gain weight. As a rough estimate, occasional exercise once or twice a week will increase your caloric expenditure by about 10 percent. Exercising six days out of seven will increase it by about 30 percent.

Since children are smaller than adults, their resting caloric expenditure is much lower. A twelve-year-old of average height and weight may have a BMR of only 1,100 calories per day. All these calories can be supplied by one Big Mac with supersized fries and soft drink. Without a lot of exercise, this fast-food meal—added to two other meals the same day—will contribute to making this child fat.

WHY DIETS DON'T WORK

As Americans, we don't know enough about what to eat, or even how to eat, in order to stay healthy. In practice, most of us hope that a loosely defined notion of "balanced" eating will somehow result in a healthful weight and improved appearance. Unfortunately, this simply isn't so.

The deck is stacked against us, beginning with the logistics of our food supply. Our caloric consumption has risen partly because fast foods, snack foods, and commercial bakery products are ever present in our culture. What we eat as a nation has caused adult obesity to spread in recent years and turned childhood obesity into an epidemic. The types of food we consume are often as bad as the excess amount.

We lack knowledge about our food choices, and the medical establishment doesn't meet our needs. The average family doctor or internist spends less than fifteen minutes a year per patient on preventive counseling. So we simply eat what we see others eating, all around us, assuming that our readily available foods and our large restaurant portions are "normal" and couldn't do us that much harm.

This is how we become obese. Many of us are in the boat I found myself in: the cargo ship carrying a stealth extra load—five more pounds of flab a year. It just creeps on. We read headlines about the obesity epidemic and recognize ourselves.

We feel the need to *do something*.

So we become obsessed with diets. This national obsession is misguided.

As scientific studies prove over and over again, diets don't work. Our "diet books" have a heritage at least a century old. Nearly one hundred years ago, scientists were clogging the arteries of rabbits with a high-fat diet and observing the results. Vitamins and minerals were being discovered. Our modern understanding about food's benefits and harms originated from this basic research.

The New Orleans Program is not a diet. *Diets don't work. Diets produce unhappiness.* We offer adaptable, sound food choices and exercise and self-nurture advice that will help us throughout our lives. We hope this advice will lead you to better health and happiness, once you've incorporated our guidelines into your own lifestyle. We believe you'll then find it absolutely natural to maintain a healthy weight.

The secret of the *temporary* success of our popular diets is calorie restriction. Yet beyond that golden bit of advice lurk problems.

Diets trick us into unrealistic, unachievable goals. Failure becomes standard. *Diets produce unhappiness.* They can cause yo-yo weight swings, a proven unhealthy state. Many make it prohibitively difficult to follow detailed rules for preparing food, combining foods, timing meals, and adhering strictly to eating patterns. Most people can't realistically limit daily fat intake to 10 percent. Diets revolving around pills, elixirs, juices, and other potions can harm people with health problems. Popular so-called "plans for lifetime eating" can hurt us in the long run. Many diets don't include frequent moderate exercise, which can check obesity and reduce disease. Most ignore spiritual self-nurture, an important component of overall wellness.

We designed our book to succeed where other programs fail because it is a complete vision of wellness for mind, body, and spirit. Our program features the pleasure and bodily satisfaction of eating well. We encourage a real connection with food. We believe there is no need to worry about how large a piece of chicken breast makes a "correct" portion. With few exceptions, all fresh whole foods provide support for health. In this and other chapters, we offer simplified recipes to encourage cooking. Preparing and serving good food at home does not have to be costly, either in terms of money or time. Our program has produced positive, long-term results for everyone who has used it.

Chef Paul Prudhomme, the dean of Louisiana chefs and one of the most loved media personalities of the cooking world, has been a long-time friend. I was shocked, after not having seen Chef Paul for a few months, to discover how much weight he had lost. In the past, he had battled his weight down from over three hundred pounds to below three hundred, but yo-yoed back up. As he related to me in a casual conversation in 1998, he resolved to tackle his weight problem once and for all. Tackle it he did. He changed his food choices, moderated the amount that he ate at any one time, and increased his exercise. Today, Chef looks thirty years younger and reportedly feels that way too. "There is no magic. It's just hard work and sticking with it over a long period of time," says Chef.

Chef Paul's battle with excess shows how difficult the relationship with food can be, but also that discipline can win in the end. It is indeed possible to enjoy sumptuous, tasty food without becoming a statistic of the obesity epidemic. In Jefferson Parish, next door to New Orleans, Sheriff Harry Lee, once a *Time* magazine cover personality, recently resorted to bariatric surgery in order to control his weight. Sheriff Lee grew up in a Chinese-American family who ran one of the first Asian restaurants in the New Orleans area. However, we know that prevention is the key. By making proper food choices over the long term, we can maintain a healthy weight without resorting to surgery.

FAT INTAKE: A QUESTION OF CHOICE AND BALANCE

Does eating more fat correlate with obesity? The evidence-based answer is no. Studies have indicated that up to 40 percent of what you eat can be fat without materially affecting your body weight. Minimizing fat in an otherwise low-calorie diet will enhance weight loss, but this benefit disappears after about a year.

It all comes down to calorie balance—if you consume a lot more calories than you burn up, you'll be obese. In fact, since the 1980s, the number of fat calories in the average American's diet has dropped significantly, but obesity has risen dramatically. Just as eating more fat will not necessarily cause a person to be fat, merely decreasing the amount of fat in the diet will not cause a person to lose weight.

Once you have become healthier after losing weight and revving up your metabolism, you will be able to tolerate more fats, especially the monounsaturated fats such as those in olive oil and canola oil. Consuming more of these better fats (chapter 3) is far preferable to eating more carbohydrates, which only worsen insulin resistance and may push the metabolic syndrome forward. When you are healthy, consuming more unsaturated fats can actually decrease heart and blood-vessel disease as well as Type II diabetes.

The American obesity epidemic has been accompanied by an increased intake not of fatty foods but of carbohydrates. (This statistic does not address the composition of the fats taken in.) This fact is cause for concern when we remember that obese people are less able to tolerate a higher carbohydrate load. Interestingly, in cultures where people consume lots of carbohydrates but accompany them with good fats, there is no increased risk of Type II diabetes or heart disease.

How much fat and what type of fat should we eat? With appropriate weight loss and exercise and the correct choices of dietary fats, we may enjoy more fat in our diets than previously thought and still maintain our health. In moderation, certain types of fats are consistent with healthful eating. Others are not. For health purposes, all fats are not equal.

For those special Mardi Gras occasions when we "let the good times roll," it always helps to choose good fats over bad fats. Healthful fats are every bit as tasty! With a little knowledge, we can make better fat-laden foods for our celebrations and our once-in-a-while indulgences. We take on this project in the next chapter.

CHAPTER 3

Lent: Sinners to Saints

Do not claim to be wiser than you are.   —Rom. 12:2

Lent arrives dramatically at midnight on Fat Tuesday. New Orleans sees its quiet season begin as crowds are hustled off Bourbon Street and indoors. "Mardi Gras is over! Get off the streets!" Shouts echo from the old walls as mounted police officially end Fat Tuesday, and the Lenten time begins.

The word *Lent* comes from an Anglo-Saxon word for spring. The word invokes our patience as we wait for the days to lengthen and spring finally to arrive. For Christians, Lent is a period of quietly joyful preparation for Easter, as well as penitence and sacrifice to commemorate Jesus' fasting in the wilderness. For some, it is a time to give up meat or fats or rich food. Small towns in France have long had Fat Tuesday pancake races, where housewives flip pancakes on lard-greased hot griddles to symbolize getting all of the animal fat out of the house for Lent. The movement from Mardi Gras to Lent to Easter can be seen as a ritual of balance, from celebration to restraint to renewed celebration.

By contrast, a childhood rhyme suggests the entrenched extremes of our American approach to eating rich foods:

Jack Sprat could eat no fat,
His wife could eat no lean;
And so between them both, you see,
They licked the platter clean.

In my nursery-rhyme book, this ditty was illustrated with Jack Sprat's wife in superabundant proportion and Jack himself thin as a rail. This cartoonish contrast might remind us of today's diet books, where eat-no-fat and fear-not-fat are familiar mantras of the Pritikin and Atkins programs, for example. When contrasting plans are advanced with equal fervor, it's a good sign that we are claiming to be wiser than we are. Instead of binding ourselves to either extreme, we should step back and consider how best to choose which fats to consume. We can't pretend to have divine wisdom, but we do possess some good, reliable, and recent information.

FATS OF YORE: WHAT OUR ANCESTORS KNEW

Fat as a desired food has an ancient history. Several millennia ago, animal fat was scarce. Animals ranged freely and had little muscle fat or external fat, so animal fat was not widely available. People valued fat in the animals they hunted for meat. Psalmists repeatedly celebrated fat and bone marrow as taste treats among the highlights of a banquet. In the *Odyssey*, Homer makes it obvious that the best cuts of meat, reserved for honored guests, are those with rich fat. The Prodigal Son in the biblical parable, who returns home a broken man after squandering his inheritance on wine, women, and entertainment (he would have enjoyed New Orleans), knows he is welcome when his father directs the servants to "kill the fatted calf." In the England of Johnson and Boswell, fatty meat was prized, as were the longhaired dogs kept around the table to serve as napkins.

Even in the 1930s, America was "eating hearty" by consuming a lot of saturated animal fat. We know this from partial results of the "What America Eats" study, a WPA-sponsored project during the depression in which fieldworkers surveyed work-kitchen environments and agricultural camps. There would have been a full report published in 1942, had not Pearl Harbor intervened. Our ancestors' respect for fat was not ignorance but a kind of wisdom—especially since the fats they ate were probably much healthier than the fats in our food supply today.

FATS VITAL TO OUR BODIES

We know today that we can't live without fats. They are a rich source of energy because they are calorie dense, with nine calories per gram of fat compared to four calories per gram of protein or carbohydrate. In all our worry about overweight, we tend to forget that we need calories to keep our hearts beating, our stomachs churning, and our brains alert and thinking. Fat enhances taste, adding flavor and texture, as we realize if we've tried low-fat versions of normally delicious foods. Certain fats provide the building blocks for chemicals that regulate inflammation and blood pressure, enable blood to clot, influence immune reactions and sex hormones, and lower the risk of heart disease. They influence the synthesis of prostaglandins, which can mediate damaging bodily reactions by affecting muscles and nerves and by influencing secretions and metabolism. We need a certain amount of fat to grow, develop, and maintain wellness.

Fats can be derived from both animal and plant sources. Whether they are called solid fats or lipids or oils, fats have varying numbers of fatty acid units linked together. Fatty acids, the building blocks of fats, exist in plants and animals, and in our own bodies, in association with a host molecule that acts like a coat rack outside a classroom in winter. Three fatty acid molecules can be "hung" on the "coat rack" of this host molecule, glycerol.

Not all fatty acid molecules are alike, though. Some have all their possible sites, or surfaces, decorated with hydrogen atoms: these fatty acids are said to be "saturated," or filled, with hydrogen. Saturated fatty acids are usually solid at room temperature. Others are monounsaturated (missing one possible hydrogen atom) or polyunsaturated (missing two or more hydrogen atoms). These unsaturated fatty acids are liquid at room temperature. Most glycerol host molecules will have different amounts of saturated or unsaturated fatty acids on their "coat rack." Therefore, most foods containing fat have varying amounts of different fatty acids.

Mono- and polyunsaturated fats, nature's own, rank high among good fats. These molecules, especially the monounsaturated one, promote better cholesterol balance. Perhaps more importantly, they can be anti-inflammatory. We now know that the anti-inflammatory properties of healthier, natural foods reduce the risk of formation and eventual bursting of plaques in our arteries and contribute to healthier tissues throughout our bodies.

When we digest fats, the fatty acids in our food are broken down in the small intestine by enzymes from the pancreas. They are emulsified by bile acids from the liver via the gall bladder. Finally, they are absorbed as fatty acids into our bodies, where they find new host glycerol molecules or "coat racks" and become triglyceride molecules. These triglycerides flow in our bloodstreams and participate in many beneficial reactions.

GOOD AND BAD FATTY ACIDS IN THE BODY

Some fatty acids are good for us. Others are bad. We'll summarize, then explain.

Omega-3 fatty acids: Essential. Good.
Omega-6 fatty acids: Essential. Good if in right proportion to Omega-3s.
Omega-9 fatty acids: Nonessential. Good in moderation.
Saturated fatty acids: Not good. Should be limited.
Trans-saturated fatty acids: Bad. Unnatural. Should be eliminated from our food.

Omega-3 fatty acids have strong protective roles in lowering the risk of heart disease. Nearly a hundred years ago, a study of the Inuit natives in Greenland found that they ate almost exclusively meat and saturated fat, yet they had no heart disease. These findings were confirmed fairly recently. Why no heart disease? Because the Inuit diet of mammal meat and blubber contains large amounts of Omega-3 fatty acids. However, when some of the Inuit relocated and switched to a typical Northern European diet, heart disease began to appear among them. Omega-3 fatty acids seem to protect us against bad fats. Recently, the presence of Omega-3s on adjacent transport molecules was found to offer some protection even from trans-saturated fatty acids, which are potentially lethal to the human heart.

Omega-6 fatty acids, together with Omega-3s, are essential for vital bodily functions. Our consumption of Omega-6s has accelerated in the last half century. Today, we have so many Omega-6s in our processed seed oils and polyunsaturated vegetable oils, our salad dressings and our marinades, that we now consume Omega-6s and Omega-3s in a ratio of about fifteen to one. This very high ratio may promote disease, including heart disease, according to some studies. More studies need to be done. We may conclude that a better ratio, one closer to the diet on which we evolved as human beings, would be two to one. Changes in our food supply have thrown our consumption of fats out of balance, and we can make food choices to regain our balance.

Omega-9 fatty acids are generally agreed to be beneficial. One of them, oleic acid, is the abundant lipid in olive oil.

Olive Oil

Foodie Myth: Olive oil is good oil and good for you.

The truth: Not all olive oils are created equal and some can be bad for you.

Experts tell us that the olive's tree position on the hillside and exposure to sunlight is much more important to producing good olives than is the soil or country of origin. Good olive oil starts with olives at any degree of ripeness. It's the *processing* that matters.

- Perhaps the finest, most delicate, most healthful, and most expensive form of olive oil is the "boutique"-produced *fleur d'olive*. This oil is obtained from crushed fresh olives that are allowed to drip the oil slowly. The yield is dramatically less than for any other process. The oil is completely free of any processing alteration and is light, delicate, and delightful in nose and taste.
- In countries where olive-oil production is regulated, such as Spain and Italy, extra-virgin olive oil is produced by "cold pressing." This is the first pressing of the crushed olives and is done without creating excessive heat. We recommend using this type of olive oil.
- Virgin olive oil is derived from the second pressing. Its production requires more force and carries the likelihood of being heated during the pressing, with subsequent degradation of the oil's integrity. We do not recommend using this type of olive oil.
- There is no such thing as "light" olive oil. All olive oil has 150 calories completely derived from fat per serving. After the olive pits and flesh have been processed for higher-grade oils, the mash is shipped to large processing plants. High-pressure commercial methods render a clear, virtually tasteless and less than healthful oil from this remainder. Despite its undesirable properties, it is valuable on the international market, being worth more than five times per barrel what crude oil brings. This oil may be used commercially and may be "enhanced" and appear on the grocery-store

shelves as "light" or "light-tasting" olive oil. We definitely recommend avoiding this product. It lacks the good fat balance
of better grades but still packs all the calories. "Light" olive
oil thus crosses the line into the bad-fat category.

Most better-quality olive oils produced according to the
guidelines above come with labels that, like wine, contain a
vintage date. Olive oil unopened can have a long shelf life,
but we recommend using the oil within two years of its pressing. Unused oil should be kept tightly closed and away from
light and heat.
Researchers have recently identified a natural chemical in
olive oil that fights inflammation in our bodies. This helps
us understand why extra-virgin olive oil provides the health
benefits it does. As with other plant products, there are likely other as yet unidentified components that promote tissue
health and longevity.

Essential fatty acids merit that designation because we must have
them to live, grow, and repair our tissues, and we must get them from
outside our bodies. We cannot manufacture them. Below are sources
for these acids.

Omega-3: Cold-water fish (mackerel, sardines, salmon, cod, trout);
tuna; nuts, especially walnuts, almonds, pecans; supplements. Green
leafy vegetables contain an essential fatty acid that is converted to the
protective Omega-3. Seaweed is another Omega-3 source, but few
other plant sources exist.

Omega-6: Canola oil, vegetable oils, butter (watch out for imbalance
with Omega-3s, a pitfall of the twenty-first-century American diet).

Omega-9: Extra-virgin olive oil; nuts, especially walnuts, almonds,
pecans, peanuts; fowl; pork; avocados.

In his research, Dr. Peter Verdigem has found confirmation that our
bodies need Omega-3 and Omega-6 fatty acids to function well.

*I was personally involved in a study that was done in adult dyslexics with a
fatty acid product [containing two Omega-3 fatty acids and one Omega-6 fatty
acid] that [the adults were] deficient in. . . . It's not going to dissolve the dyslexia*

like that. . . . But it's interesting to see how a number of symptoms which describe dyslexia and ADHD can be positively influenced by the supplementation of fatty acids. For example, reading speed, motor speed. In ADHD we have symptoms like attentiveness and compulsive behavior . . . positively influenced if you supplement those people with fatty acids. . . . People who had more fatty acid deficiency signs responded better to that treatment, to that supplementation, than people who had less fatty acid deficiency.

Butter

Foodie Myth: Butter is bad for you.

The truth: Chef Besh reminds us: *Butter is natural. Some butters are better.* Unsalted *butter usually made from higher quality cream has better cooking and nutritional qualities than salted butter. Salting can of course add sodium to what is a naturally sodium free product. It also can cover up lesser-quality flavors.*

The American Heart Association, among others, has demonized butter because it does contain 60 percent saturated fats. What's forgotten about butter?

- Butter has 40 percent monounsaturated and polyunsaturated fatty acids, "good" fats.
- Unsalted (sweet) butter is sodium free.
- A serving (1 tbsp.) of butter has a small amount of cholesterol (30 mg, about 10 percent of the recommended daily intake).
- Butter from grass- or pasture-fed cows has significant Omega-3 fatty acids, the very best fatty acids.
- A little butter goes a long way: less than one-third of a serving (tbsp.) added to extra-virgin olive oil will add a tremendous amount of flavor and negligible health risks (see our specific recommendation in recipes throughout this book).

Butter has no preservatives and can deteriorate. It should be used within a week or two of purchase. If you find butter on sale, you can preserve it by keeping it frozen.

Saturated fatty acids can be killers. They are found primarily in animal fats and dairy products, as well as in such tropical oils as coconut and palm. Eating a high level of saturated fat has been linked with cardiac disease.

Saturated fatty acids break down to form the building blocks of cholesterol. The more saturated fats you eat, the more cholesterol building blocks there will be in your body—especially if you also eat many refined carbohydrates. Dr. Ansel Keys concluded from his 1966 study, comparing heart-disease rates with saturated-fat consumption in seven different countries, that populations eating more saturated fats also died more frequently from cardiovascular disease. The Framingham [Massachusetts] Heart Study is generally considered to have proved that eating saturated fats produces cardiovascular disease in a "lock-step" fashion. We know that eating more saturated fats increases the elements of cholesterol, and we believe that increased cholesterol, in turn, leads to heart disease. Thus we have come to think that saturated fats increase the risk of heart disease.

However, recent studies have cast doubt upon this reasoning. For one thing, cholesterol may or may not be the real culprit in causing heart disease. Certainly cholesterol can be found in very bad company, as a component of atherosclerotic plaques on the interiors of artery walls. But this may simply be guilt by association. As far as I can determine, experts have not been able to "pin the rap" on cholesterol for initiating arterial plaque. The cause may lie elsewhere, according to contemporary research. For instance, cells that participate in the inflammation of the arterial wall, and cells that attempt to repair the subsequent damage to arterial wall tissue, may simply bring in cholesterol as "baggage." The cholesterol then gets trapped in the artery, as part of dangerous circulation-blocking plaque. Or it could be that LDL (low-density lipoprotein) cholesterol, the "bad" cholesterol, can easily form plaque deposits in arteries.

What is more, some of the major studies arguing for the saturated fat-cholesterol-heart disease link may be seriously flawed. The Keys study in 1966 used selective populations, a fatal scientific flaw. Keys may also have been subject to pressure from the cooking-oil industry. In the 1950s, Dr. Keys and other pioneer investigators like Dr. M. G. Enig reported that trans-saturated fats, which are easily made by heating polyunsaturated cooking oils as done in commercial fast-food establishments, are linked consistently to the rapid development of heart disease. The manufacturers of cooking oils were outraged. Later, the 1966 Keys study fell in line with the oil industry by ignoring these trans-fats and naming only saturated fats as the real culprit in heart disease. Curiously, the Framingham Heart Study reported one unusual and unexplainable result: those who ate the highest amounts of saturated fat and cholesterol had the lowest blood cholesterol. How could this happen? This inconsistency was highlighted by Dr. W. P. Castelli, one of the investigators of the study.

So we should not claim to be perfectly wise about the precise links between saturated fats, cholesterol, and heart disease. We do need more knowledge.

A NOTE ON CHOLESTEROL

We should also remember that we need cholesterol for our bodies to function. It is manufactured by our livers, sex glands, many other glands, and almost all our tissues for their own maintenance. It helps build cells that make up our tissues, our nerves and their insulation, and our sex hormones. Cholesterol is important not only to adults but especially to growing children. In large part, our genes determine, for each of us, the amount of cholesterol and the mix of cholesterol types our liver cells will make. We may or may not be able to influence our genetic programming.

Eating some cholesterol, within limits, is not so harmful as we once thought, because much of the cholesterol we eat does not pass into our bloodstreams. Natural digestive substances such as bile salt break down more than half of the cholesterol in our food. The remaining cholesterol is less than perfectly absorbed. For most people, eating less than 300 grams of cholesterol a day will have little or no effect on blood cholesterol. Consuming saturated fats is more likely to raise our blood cholesterol than eating a relatively small amount of cholesterol. This makes me personally very happy since such foods as shrimp, high in cholesterol but extremely low in saturated fat, are a much nicer component of my dinner plate now.

Yes, we should limit the amount of saturated fats we eat. But it's more important to minimize or eliminate from our diets the most dangerous and damaging fat of all: trans-saturated fatty acids. If we demonize saturated fats too much, we risk forgetting about another real enemy—trans-fats.

Trans-saturated fats are not found in nature. We manufacture them by hydrogenating otherwise innocent vegetable oils. We create them in our deep fryers by heating cooking oil to the smoking point or by reusing it many times.

In one dramatic demonstration, Australian investigators placed sensor gauges into the carotid arteries of healthy young volunteers and fed them meals of French fries. They measured the changes in the volunteers' blood flow after eating French fries cooked in oil used only once, then oil used five times. At this level, there was little change. But when the fries were cooked in oil used fifteen, twenty, or twenty-five times, arterial blood flow to the brain was as much as 20 percent restricted in these young volunteers after twenty to thirty minutes—a rapid and dramatic reduction. Even when cooking oil is unsaturated to begin with, we can contaminate that oil with unhealthy trans-fats simply by heating and reusing it.

- Trans-fats shift the cholesterol balance toward the "bad" (LDL) cholesterol.
- They chip away at the "good" (HDL) cholesterol.
- They contribute to arterial inflammation.

In 2004, the United States Department of Agriculture ordered that trans-fats be identified in labeling.

Fat and Cholesterol

Some fats are nonessential to life but can either be made by our bodies or eaten and affect health.

Omega-3s (alpha linoleic acid) include DHA (docosahexanoic acid) and EPA (eicosapentanoic acid).
- Reduce cholesterol (primarily "bad").
- Reduce triglycerides (the other potentially "bad" blood fatty substance).
- Reduce tendencies for blood to clot abnormally and be "sticky" (lower stroke and heart-attack risk).
- Reduce inflammation (a major factor in blood-vessel and tissue disease, aging).

- Increase "good" prostaglandins (powerful hormonelike molecule that can be "good" or "bad" or "good" in normal amounts or "bad" in abnormal amounts).

Omega-6s (arachidonic acid) include linoleic acid.
- Reduce cholesterol.
- Benefit blood pressure.
- Red meat is a common source.
- Can be made by our bodies.
- Needed for prostaglandin manufacture.
- Promote inflammation in excessive amounts.

Omega-7s (palmitoleic acid).
- Coconut is a common source.
- Elevate cholesterol, especially the "bad" LDL.
- May contribute to inflammation.

Omega-9s (oleic acid).
- Olive oil, nuts (e.g., pecans) are common sources.
- Promote healthy tissue renewal, in blood vessels, for example.
- Promote tissue repair.
- Do not adversely affect cholesterol.
- Reduce inflammation.

WHY HAVE WE PUT BAD FATS IN OUR FOOD SUPPLY?

It has been a mistake to stuff our food supply with trans-fats. In doing so, we have assumed our partial knowledge to be complete, and thus we have claimed to be wiser than we are. We have made trans-fats, but we can also stop making them if we will heed the warning signs.

In 1899, America saw the development of the Wesson oil process of partial hydrogenation, a huge commercial success because it greatly extended the shelf life of vegetable oils. This convenience has come at a price. As a side effect, partial hydrogenation converts otherwise healthful oils—even walnut oil or flaxseed oil—into trans-fats. Nutritional labeling that mentions "partially hydrogenated" oils is really saying "trans-saturated fatty acids." Many products, including most snack foods and fast foods, are loaded with trans-fats. They are good for business but very bad for our bodies. Snack companies like Frito-Lay began in 2004 to label certain snacks as containing "no trans-fats" because they are cooked in non-hydrogenated oils, but this labeling discounts the effects of the cooking process.

When we cook with good fats, we can turn them into bad. Polyunsaturated or non-hydrogenated oils such as soybean oil, cottonseed oil, olive oil, or canola oil can be at least partially converted to trans-fats when heated to the smoking point. The more you use and heat the oil, the more trans-fats you make. Oil that is not discarded after one cooking use will produce more trans-fats with each further heating. Since fast-food businesses need their profit margins, they are highly motivated to reuse their cooking oils. This is one good explanation for the danger of fast foods.

Unhappily, with good intentions and limited knowledge, we have sometimes even praised trans-fats. As late as the 1920s and early 1930s, heart attacks in our country were uncommon. Then some dramatic changes in our food supply began. The scarcity of butter in World War II drove us to use more butter substitutes, such as margarine and the processed oils. After the war, in the 1950s and 1960s, medical researchers linked heart-attack risk to elevated blood cholesterol. They did not yet know the difference between "good" (HDL) cholesterol and "bad" (LDL) cholesterol, and they did not give much attention to triglycerides. Thus dietary cholesterol became an easy target for scientists trying to be helpful. To save us from cholesterol, the American Heart Association began to recommend butter substitutes such as vegetable oils and especially margarine.

It is true that vegetable oils have little cholesterol, and margarine is indeed cholesterol free. *Yet, alas, both are full of trans-fats.* Our clever hydrogenation process, which seemed like a good idea when we invented it, has made both margarine and vegetable oils hazardous to our health. We obediently ate the recommended butter substitutes, along with the more calorie-dense fast foods and refined carbohydrates of the postwar economy. Before long, we found ourselves in an epidemic of heart attacks, strokes, and diabetes. Only recently has the American Heart Association stopped recommending margarine, and many still mistakenly believe that it is healthier than butter. The public still does not fully understand how dangerous trans-fats are.

The Truth Behind Trans-Fat Labeling

- Many snack foods trumpet "0 g trans-fats" (*g* means grams; 1 *g* is 1,000 milligrams [mg]), *but* the ingredients include "partially hydrogenated" oils, which have trans-fats.
- Nearly all grocery store baked goods have "partially hydrogenated" oils.
- Many margarines are still loaded with trans fats.
- No one knows precisely how many trans fats are safe.
- Reduce to a minimum or avoid completely if possible.

HOW HAVE WE REMOVED GOOD FATS FROM OUR FOOD SUPPLY?

Cows used to range on grasslands. They ate grasses and seeds. Their muscle was lean, and their food tissues built up good Omega-3 fatty acids, essential to human life. Milk and cheese from these cows also contained the healthful Omega-3s.

Then in the 1950s, we began the feed-lot production of beef, and it became widespread. This new feeding process increased the saturated fat in the beef muscle, once lean, that provides us with hamburgers, steaks, and chops. Feed-lot cows also have little or no Omega-3 fatty acids. Once again, we seem to have outsmarted ourselves by worsening our food supply.

Dr. Gerald Berenson, director of the Bogalusa Heart Study and the 2003 recipient of Cattle Breeder of the Year from the Cattlemaster Association, confirms this major change in our food supply.

The USDA grades beef higher that has higher fat. That also means more dollars, and often more hormones and other chemicals. [This is] not always really "better for you."

Grass-fed cows in other countries produce cheeses with more

Omega-3 fatty acids than do nongrazing cows in the United States. Perhaps this difference helps explain the puzzling fact that although the populations of some other countries consume more dairy products than the United States, they still have lower rates of heart disease.

WHERE CAN WE FIND BETTER FATS TO EAT?

As individuals and as a society, we can move away from trans-fats. We can limit our saturated fats. We can seek out Omega-3 fatty acids to consume and try to keep our Omega-6 fat intake down to twice the amount of our Omega-3s.

We recommend extra-virgin olive oil, canola oil, and butter. Butter! It has been demonized unnecessarily, and a little butter won't hurt us. We can also find healthier cheeses, with Omega-3 fatty acids, at some local farmers' markets. We are likely to find some cheeses there from artisanal cheese makers, many of whom start with dairy products from free-range, grass-fed cows.

Also available are some selected grass-fed beef products. Nolan Ryan, the baseball player, has worked with the Beefmaster breed, the same one used by Dr. Berenson, to produce a leaner yet tender product. As Dr. Berenson says:

It's all in the genes. There are genes for marbling; there are genes for tenderness; there are genes for every aspect of beef. It's a matter of selecting them. Right now we use the eye more than technology. But there is a lot of interest in breeding beef that will produce a superior product.

Some feel that the easiest way to get Omega-3s is via the supplement bottle. Recommended daily amounts of the essential fatty acids include:

- Omega-3s: 1,000 milligrams, tastier as a fish dish than capsule, but take the supplement if that's best for you. Fish oil is easier for men to digest, flaxseed oil easier for women.
- Omega-6s: 300 milligrams, easily obtained from canola oil.
- Omega-9s: 300 milligrams, from a handful of walnuts, avocado, pork, and other sources.

These sources seem somewhat limited, but they are easy to obtain.

The easiest approach is to eat fish several times a week, since all fish have Omega-3s.

Fish and Shellfish Ranked in Terms of Available Omega-3 Fatty Acids

- Chinook salmon
- Sockeye salmon
- Deepwater tuna
- Mackerel
- Herring
- Sardine
- Speckled trout
- Catfish
- Crab
- Crawfish
- Shrimp
- Cod

NOTE: This ranking refers to wild-caught, not farm-raised, fish—salmon in particular.

A recent physician's health study, which continues to follow more than 20,000 men, reveals the striking protective effect of eating fish. The group of male physicians who ate fish at least once a week lowered their risk of an acute heart attack by 50 percent, compared to those who did not eat fish. This is how important Omega-3 fatty acids can be to our health.

Here, we eat *pommes soufflé,* a unique fried potato shaped like a small, elongated balloon, lightly browned, crisp in texture, and delicate in flavor. Also, sticks of potato are partially cooked, flattened, frozen, and then popped in a hot skillet—a method that allows the *pomme frite* to retain comparatively little fat. Unless you insist on dipping these too deeply into the accompanying Béarnaise sauce, they exact a fairly low caloric cost and are, of course, absolutely delicious.

New Orleans restaurants, from the toniest white-linen establishments down to local po'-boy shops, have traditionally offered Lenten menus in recognition of the widespread local observance of this time of abstinence and fasting. Heavy meats are replaced by the locally abundant fish and shellfish, as well as by such vegetarian staples as beans and rice. Happily, Lent coincides with the crawfish season and the first availability of shrimp and crab.

CRAWFISH CAKES

This preparation makes flavorful, low-calorie, micronutrient-laden cakes that are colorful as well. Frozen crawfish tails are OK but you *must,* when they are thawed, *squeeze out as much liquid as possible* before chopping.

1 lb. crawfish tails, chopped
¼ cup destringed chopped celery
¼ cup seeded, demembraned, chopped green bell pepper
¼ cup seeded, demembraned, chopped red bell pepper
¼ cup minced sweet yellow onion
¼ cup thinly sliced green onion tops
1 small garlic clove, pressed
1 tsp. lemon juice
½ cup breadcrumbs
2 egg whites + 1 whole egg *or* 3 egg whites
1 tsp. Creole spice
¼ tsp. cayenne pepper
½-¾ tsp. sea salt
1 tsp. black pepper
1 tsp. Worcestershire sauce
¼ tsp. thyme
1 tsp. basil

Mix all ingredients in a medium mixing bowl. Mixture should be moist enough to form 2½-3-inch-diameter, ¾-inch-thick cakes that hold together. If too dry, add an egg white. If too moist, add some breadcrumbs. (I prefer them not too big—they cook faster and more evenly.)

In a large skillet, heat on medium high enough olive or good vegetable oil to come about a quarter of the way up the cakes. Place cakes into skillet. I use the "2-spatula technique": place each cake on 1 slotted spatula; lower into oil; slide off with other. This is good for turning too. Sauté until nicely golden brown, turn, and brown other side. Do not overcook: about 4 minutes per side should do it, but go by appearance. Drain on paper towels, and serve hot. You can reheat in microwave, on paper towels, on high for 30-45 seconds or so.

BELLE RIVER CRAWFISH SALAD

Serves 6.

2 tbsp. extra-virgin olive oil
1 shallot, diced small
1 lb. crawfish tails
1½ cups diced tomato
Vinaigrette (see below)
Leaves of 2 sprigs tarragon
½ tsp. salt
½ tsp. black pepper
½ lb. mixed greens

In a medium sauté pan over medium heat, heat oil until just lightly smoking. Add shallot and let cook 30 seconds (do not brown). Quickly add crawfish and tomato and let cook until hot. Add half the vinaigrette. Remove from heat and let come to room temperature.

Add tarragon leaves (reserve a few for garnish) and season with salt and pepper. Toss greens with remaining vinaigrette and place crawfish mixture on top. Garnish top of salad with remaining tarragon leaves. You can drizzle a touch of vinaigrette around the plate to garnish as well.

Vinaigrette
1 oz. rice-wine vinegar
2½ oz. extra-virgin olive oil
½ tsp. salt
½ tsp. black pepper

In a mixing bowl, whisk vinegar and oil. Season with salt and pepper.

DOWN-HOME CRAWFISH PIE

Serves 6-8.

4 tbsp. extra-virgin olive oil
3 tbsp. flour
1½ cups small-diced onions
¼ cup small-diced green bell pepper
¼ cup minced celery
1½ tsp. salt
¼ tsp. cayenne pepper
½ tsp. black pepper
1 bay leaf
¾ cup peeled, seeded, diced tomatoes
½ cup milk
1 lb. crawfish tails
Pie Crust (see below)
2 dashes Worcestershire sauce

Preheat oven to 375 degrees.

Add half the oil to a large skillet over medium-high heat. Add flour and stir until incorporated. Cook a few minutes.

Add onions, bell peppers, celery, salt, peppers, and bay leaf. Cook, stirring, until golden brown. Add tomatoes and milk and cook 15 minutes, stirring.

Add crawfish, remaining oil, and Worcestershire. Allow crawfish to simmer 2 minutes before removing skillet from heat and cooling. Pour cooled crawfish mixture into pie crust.

Bake 40 minutes or until crust is golden brown. Remove from oven, slice into 6-8 wedges, and enjoy.

Pie Crust
8 cups all-purpose flour
½ cup extra-virgin oil
2 tbsp. salt
Cold water

In a mixer, mix flour, oil, and salt. Slowly add water until dough is slightly damp and very firm. Roll out and place in a 9-inch pie pan. Trim off excess dough.

OYSTER-LEEK BAKE

The flavor of the leeks complements the oyster flavors, while the other "seasonings" (as we call chopped onion, etc., here) add extra but not overwhelming zest.

½ lb. whole-wheat fettuccine
3 medium leeks, well washed, sliced
3 medium garlic cloves, pressed
Extra-virgin olive oil
½ each red, yellow, green bell peppers, chopped moderately fine
1 bunch green onion tops, sliced
4 egg whites from large eggs
½ cup grated mozzarella or Swiss cheese
1 pt. fresh oysters, drained
1 small fresh hot serrano or other hot pepper, chopped fine
Sea salt
White pepper
Cayenne pepper

Preheat oven to 400 degrees.

Boil fettuccine 1½ minutes if fresh, 3 minutes if dried. Let cool so as not to cook egg whites.

Sauté leeks and garlic in olive oil about 5 minutes.

Squeeze liquid out of bell peppers just before use. Reserve 3 or 4 strips of each pepper. In large bowl, combine fettuccine and leeks with peppers, green onions, egg whites, cheese, oysters, and hot pepper. Add spices to taste.

Press into 10-inch, deep, nonstick dish that has been sprayed with nonstick cooking spray. Decorate top with pepper strips. Bake 35 minutes or until bubbling through.

"BREADED" SALMON WITH SHRIMP, FENNEL, AND ORANGES
Serves 6.

6 slices bread
6 6-oz. filets salmon
3 tbsp. chopped fresh tarragon

2 tbsp. butter, softened
2 qt. water
1 cup orange juice
½ cup fennel seeds
¼ cup salt
2 tsp. cayenne pepper
¾ lb. headless 16/20-count shrimp
2 qt. ice water
1 bulb fennel
3 oranges
1⅓ cups rice-wine vinegar
1 cup extra-virgin olive oil
1 tbsp. chopped chives
Black pepper to taste
3 lemons, sliced

Heat oven to 400 degrees. Using a rolling pin or pasta machine, roll bread until approximately ⅛ inch thick.

Season fish with some salt and a pinch of the tarragon. Spread half the butter on the bread. Stick 1 slice bread onto each fish filet by placing buttered side on fish. Turn filets over and trim bread so that edges are even are even with filets. Spread remaining butter on outside of bread. Reserve in cool place until ready to cook.

In medium saucepot, combine water, orange juice, fennel seeds, salt, and all but a pinch of the cayenne. Bring to a boil over high heat. Add shrimp and cook until just done. Remove shrimp and cool in ice water, then peel and remove vein from back of each one. Set shrimp aside.

Trim stalk and root from fennel bulb. Split in half from top to bottom and cut out root core. Slice fennel as thinly as possible with a knife, mandolin, slicer, or food processor. Place fennel in medium mixing bowl.

Cut tops and bottoms from oranges just enough to expose bright orange flesh. Cut away peel so that flesh remains with none of the bitter white pith. Holding oranges over bowl with fennel, cut out each orange section, allowing to drop into bowl. Add vinegar, oil, chives, and shrimp. Mix well and season to taste with salt and pepper and a pinch cayenne.

Roast fish filets, bread side up, on a buttered skillet in oven approximately 10 minutes or until a thin blade may be slipped through center without resistance and bread is lightly browned. Plate by surrounding with shrimp mixture and lemon slices.

QUICK-GRILLED SALMON, NEW ORLEANS PROGRAM STYLE
Serves 4.

Important! Do not try this with skinless fish unless you want a fiery mess on the grill. Wild-caught salmon is best, as is a filet of uniform thickness. Also, we do not recommend using either garlic salt or garlic powder. Good ground garlic can provide a quick substitute for fresh chopped or pressed garlic cloves.

1 lb. salmon filet, skin on
1 tsp. low-sodium soy sauce
1 tsp. hot sauce (not Tabasco)
Salt-free Creole spice, sea salt, black pepper, and ground garlic to
**   taste**

Preheat grill to medium (about 300 degrees). Wash and pat filet dry with paper towel. Rub soy and hot sauce on flesh side. Sprinkle on other seasonings.

Grill skin side down 20 minutes (or less, depending on grill temperature). Douse any grill flare-ups (which may happen in last 5 minutes of cooking, depending on oiliness of salmon). Salmon is ready to serve. Leftovers make tasty salad toppings, omelet additions, etc. Keeps well up to 2 days when refrigerated.

PERFECT POTATO CHIPS

1 potato
2 oz. extra-virgin olive oil
Salt

On a slicer or mandolin, slice potato very thin lengthwise and squeeze out water. Lay parchment paper on a baking sheet. Cover paper with some oil and lay potato slices one by one so they do not touch or overlap. Lightly brush potatoes with oil. Sprinkle with salt.

Place another sheet of parchment paper on top, and then another baking sheet. Place in oven at 225 degrees and rotate pan every 20 minutes for 2 hours or until potatoes are crispy.

MACQUE CHOUX WITH CRAB AND LEMONFISH
Serves 6.

2 oz. + 2 tbsp. extra-virgin olive oil
1 yellow onion, diced small
2 large red gypsy or bell peppers, diced small
4 large ripe tomatoes, seeded and coarsely chopped
3 cloves garlic, minced
1 celery stalk, diced small
6 large ears local sweet corn
Salt and fresh-ground black pepper to taste
Cayenne pepper to taste
2 cups crab claw meat, picked for shells
2 tbsp. chopped chives
2¼ lb. lemonfish (cobia) filets
2 lemons
1 cup flour
1 fresh summer truffle
3 tbsp. chive-infused extra-virgin olive oil
¼ cup fresh chervil

In a large sauté pan, heat 2 tbsp. oil and add onions. Cook, stirring constantly, until translucent but not brown. Add peppers, tomatoes, garlic, and celery and cook an additional 3-5 minutes or until peppers and celery have become tender.

Shuck corn and cut kernels from ears. Add corn to pan. Season with salt, black pepper, and cayenne.

Add crab and chives. Remove from heat and reserve in warm place.

Cut fish into 6 6-oz. steaks. Season with salt and black pepper. Sprinkle with lemon juice. Dust with flour.

In a large skillet, heat 2 oz. oil over medium-high heat. Place fish in skillet. Cook on both sides until golden brown. Remove. Allow fish to rest on a bed of absorbent paper for a moment.

Cut truffle in small rounds by slicing horizontally. Quickly sauté in a hot sauté pan with chive oil. Season with salt and black pepper. Reserve.

For each serving, place bed of corn macque choux in center of plate. Place fish on top. Spoon on some truffle. Garnish with chervil.

QUICK FRESH CORN MACQUE CHOUX
Serves 4.

The trick with this dish is the initial lower-heat sauté of the corn to bring out its sweetness and keep it tender, with a quick, slightly higher-heat finish after adding the other ingredients.

Extra-virgin olive oil
¹/₂-1 tbsp. unsalted butter
4 large ears fresh sweet corn, shucked and silked
Pinch cayenne pepper
¹/₂ tsp. salt-free Creole spice or blended seasonings
Sea salt and black pepper to taste
¹/₃ red bell pepper, minced
¹/₃ green bell pepper, minced
¹/₄ cup thin-sliced green onion tops

Add enough oil to thinly coat bottom of 9-inch skillet. Add butter. Slice kernels from corn and pour into skillet.

Over low to medium heat, melt butter and stir corn. Cook about 8-10 minutes, stirring until corn is sweet and tender. Add seasonings. Stir.

Add other ingredients, raise heat to medium high, and cook, stirring, 4-5 minutes. Check for doneness, and sauté a few more minutes if needed. Adjust seasonings. Can be prepared ahead and reheated when served. Do not overcook.

SHRIMP STIR-FRY
Serves 4. Easily reduced or increased.

Extra-virgin olive oil
1-2 tbsp. butter (no substitutes, or omit)
¹/₂ cup chopped yellow onion

1¾ lb. large shrimp, fresh or fast frozen
Sea salt to taste
White or black pepper to taste
Cayenne pepper to taste
¼ cup chopped red bell pepper
¼ cup chopped green bell pepper
3 tbsp. destringed chopped celery
3 tbsp. chopped parsley (Italian flat leaf preferred)
1 clove garlic, pressed

Cover bottom of a large skillet with oil. Add butter and heat on medium high. When hot, add onion and stir until beginning to turn clear.

Peel and devein shrimp, leaving tails on. Pat dry. Add to skillet. Season tops, turn with tongs in 2 minutes or so, and season other side. Add remaining ingredients and stir until shrimp are cooked but *not* overdone (about 3-5 minutes). Serve immediately alone or over cooked brown rice, whole-wheat pasta, or other starch of your choice.

STEWED STRAWBERRIES AND ANGEL-FOOD SHORTCAKE
Serves 6.

Unexpected Lenten-season delights include fresh, aromatic, flavorful strawberries from across Lake Pontchartrain. Chef John uses these to create a light, enjoyable dessert, a perfect Lenten grace note for special meals.

1 dozen egg whites
1 lb. sugar
6 oz. cake flour

Whisk egg whites with half the sugar until right before they reach ribbon stage. Add remaining sugar. Gently mix in flour.

Fill cupcake molds ¾ full or 1 cake pan. Bake at 325 degrees 25 minutes or until a wooden skewer inserted in center comes out dry.

Stewed Strawberries
2 pt. strawberries
¼ cup sugar

Quarter berries and cook down with sugar 10 minutes. If too thin, remove berries from juice and cook berries until desired consistency. Serve while still hot over individual cupcakes or large slices of cake.

GOOD AND BAD FATS: NOTES FROM CHEF BESH

By trade I am not a nutritionist. I am a chef who has been raised in and around New Orleans. I have a strong Catholic background, in which Lent is associated with some kind of sacrifice, like giving up the pleasure of eating certain things. The funny thing is that as a child, I'd look forward to Lent because you had to eat fish on Friday. My parents might fast all day on Friday and have a small seafood something at night. As a child, I remember this was the best. You were growing up in a place with wonderful seafood, and generally Lent meant crawfish on Friday nights.

I don't think that there's a civic organization or Catholic parish or school around South Louisiana that doesn't offer some sort of a seafood dinner on Friday nights during Lent. That brings to me memories of crawfish or oyster stews, crawfish pies, seafood jambalaya, seafood gumbo, and all of these wonderful things that I love to eat during Lent. In this chapter I wanted to showcase our local specialties like a crawfish salad and crawfish pie to relate to our good fat/bad fat ideas. I wanted to show people how easy it is to create the perfect potato chip, and to distinguish good oils from bad oils.

I've traveled extensively through Europe, and I fell in love with the way the Spanish eat. The amount of good fat that they consume, and the way that they limit the amount of bad fat—it's amazing. I like to choose my fats wisely. I love olive oil, extra-virgin olive oil in particular. My first time to Madrid, we were eating in a small bar having tapas and I asked if they would tell me what oil they were using to fry their foods. They said, "Well, certainly, Chef. We only use extra-virgin olive oil to fry foods." I thought that was amazing. You'd never think of that in America. We don't have their abundance of incredible olive oils, which are expensive here. Of course, some other oils like canola oil are invaluable. Then there's butter. Butter isn't talked about as much in nutritional circles as I think it should be. Butter isn't just pure fat. It has milk solids, water, and a number of different things. If you use it properly and within limits, butter has a lot of flavor, as does extra-virgin olive oil. That's why I prefer using those. Some people may think I'm crazy for even suggesting that we use butter, but in a lifestyle of moderation, it really shouldn't be a concern. Butter should be a tool, used and not misused.

I prefer unsalted butter. It's a higher grade of butter where salt is not added because it doesn't need to be. Along that same line, extra-virgin olive oil is the best of the best. After the olives are picked and milled, the first pressing of these olives yields the extra-virgin olive oil. Extra-virgin gives the most health benefit. But flavor is the overwhelming reason to go with that extra-virgin olive oil and a good unsalted butter.

I've put together a collection of recipes with a common-sense approach to using fat. Your body needs fat. We've all heard about the good fats that exist in certain species of fish like salmon. A fresh piece of salmon sautéed in extra-virgin olive oil is so good for you. A salmon steak, with the skin left on, cooked with a touch of butter gives this beautiful nutty flavor from the butter and the crispy skin. There are few things better in life. Not all fats are bad.

Lent here is like a new New Year's Day. It's a time to redefine how we're eating and drinking. In my life, it's a time to regain my balance after Mardi Gras—to say, hey, you know what, let me ease up on this. And there are parts of our lives besides just the physical. With mental and spiritual well-being, you're in tune with the way that you're supposed to live. Just as we need certain foods spiritually, Lent offers us a chance to spiritually or emotionally nourish ourselves through self-sacrifice. We might want to drink a little more water, try not to eat a certain type of cookie, refrain from big juicy steaks, or try to modify the portion size of our foods. There are many ways to help ourselves physically, spiritually, and mentally, to pull all the pieces of our being together. Lent is the perfect time for this.

On Fridays during Lent, when I return home from work, Jennifer will have a fish dinner waiting in the refrigerator, from one of the local churches in Slidell. It might be speckled trout, a fish fry, catfish with coleslaw, or spaghetti with oysters bordelaise. These are oysters poached in a white-wine sauce and tossed with pasta—phenomenal! The right way to fry fish is to slightly pan fry it in canola oil over very high heat, with a small amount of extra-virgin olive oil also. First toss the fish in some panko breadcrumbs. These Japanese breadcrumbs give the fish a flaky appearance. There are ways to fry things so that they will absorb as little oil as possible and also offer a taste of something real.

I like to use fennel during Lent because fennel, or anise, is one of the flavors that dominate our St. Joseph's altars around the city during March each year. You often find fennel cookies (aniseed cookies) at these altars. Almost any vegetable you can imagine can create nice, light slaws and salads. Carrots or celery are good choices. What we're really talking about is flavor. The more flavor you get for the caloric and fat dollar, the better.

As Chef Besh teaches us to create light salads and fry fish that absorbs only a little oil, he's illustrating the Lenten principle of balance—celebration, restraint, renewed celebration—as seen in Mardi Gras, Lent, and Easter.

CHAPTER 4

Crescent City Classic:
The Big Easy's Spring Ritual

We must all be foolish at times. It is one of the conditions of freedom.
—Walt Whitman

It's Saturday morning in the early 1990s, in the French Quarter. The lace-balconied, 200-year-old walls reverberate to the crack of the starting gun for the Crescent City Classic footrace. As we leave the French Quarter, we run through downtown (what New Orleanians refer to as "the CBD," Central Business District), across the Warehouse District (revitalized with apartments, condos, nightclubs, restaurants, and the D-Day Museum), and into the Lower Garden District. Modest nineteenth-century houses, for factory and river workers, give way to Italian-revival mansions, raised Creole cottages, and fancy iron fences. We are in the Upper Garden District.

At this point, I frequently visited my friend Joan's townhouse for a spicy Louisiana Bloody Mary in a go cup. It's amazing how a little fuel can help the rest of the race go better. This year, at Joan's, as with many houses along the route, people are gathered to party and watch the runners. As we pass through the Upper Garden District, we see the oldest continuously operating, not-for-profit hospital in the country, Touro Infirmary. In Uptown New Orleans, we cross the Emperor Napoleon's Avenue and go by the old St. Elizabeth's Convent—which Anne Rice, the author, once owned for the purpose of housing her doll collection. We run beside the varied architecture of Uptown and finally into Audubon Park. New Orleans, in mid-April, may sometimes be a little too warm for a comfortable run. Still, the morning always has a light mist, made golden by the sun.

The newer Mid-City course has increased the diversity of the scenery runners pass. And still there are parties, parties, parties! Spectators cluster on banquettes or front porches. After the final leg, runners have not only the customary T-shirt award but more partying! And they find lots of homemade food, including red beans and rice, of course!

World-class runners usually win the Classic. The rest of us have a great time whether we run, jog, walk, roll, or invent our own combo to get us across the finish line. How do we all make it? We burn carbohydrates, a ready source of energy. Yes, we're talking about the lowly and recently maligned "carbs." We could not make it without them.

CARBS ARE OUR SUNSHINE

Our bodies are solar powered. When we eat carbohydrates, for instance, we are consuming the energy of the sun that has been stored in plants. When plants absorb solar energy, or photons, they convert that energy through photosynthesis to sugars, starches, fibers, and the oils stored in seeds. Then these plants are eaten by animals, and the original solar energy is further concentrated into nutrients.

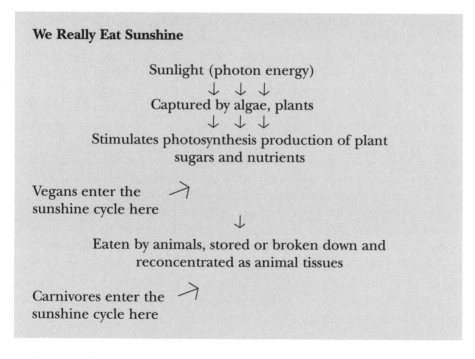

We Really Eat Sunshine

Sunlight (photon energy)
↓ ↓ ↓
Captured by algae, plants
↓ ↓ ↓
Stimulates photosynthesis production of plant
sugars and nutrients

Vegans enter the   ↗
sunshine cycle here

↓

Eaten by animals, stored or broken down and
reconcentrated as animal tissues

Carnivores enter the   ↗
sunshine cycle here

Carbohydrates range from simple to complex. The simplest carbohydrates, like glucose or fructose, have *one* sugar each. But lactose, in milk, is a simple carbohydrate with *two* sugars: galactose and glucose.

Table sugar is another two-sugar carbohydrate: glucose and fructose. Complex carbohydrates, with *three or more* sugars, are created when vegetables store their extra glucose as starches, like those found in potatoes or beans. Very complex carbohydrates are found in whole grains. Finally there is fiber, a complex carbohydrate that the body cannot digest, otherwise known as "roughage." The more complex the carbohydrate, the more time your body takes to digest it.

PASTA WITH FIVE-MINUTE TOMATO SAUCE
Serves 6.

Carb loading can be combined with quick homemade goodness, as Chef Besh shows us in this tasty pasta main course or side dish.

2 tbsp. extra-virgin olive oil
4 lb. overripe tomatoes, quartered
5 cloves garlic, coarsely chopped
1 tsp. crushed red pepper flakes
½ cup basil, chopped
2 tbsp. chopped tarragon
1 tbsp. sugar
½ lb. lean ground turkey
1 tsp. salt
1 tsp. black pepper

In a pot, heat oil and hard-sear tomatoes. Add garlic, red pepper flakes, basil, tarragon, and sugar. Bring to a boil. Add turkey, stir well, and cook 5 minutes or until meat is done. Run through food mill. Add salt and pepper.

Fresh Pasta
1 lb. all-purpose flour
1 tbsp. kosher salt
5 eggs
1 tbsp. extra-virgin olive oil

Combine ingredients into a smooth dough. Cut off golf-ball-sized chunk of dough. Working with a pasta machine on a floured board or countertop, form the dough into a 2-foot-by-2-foot square.

Pass dough through largest setting of machine 10-12 times. Roll out through smaller and smaller settings until it can get no thinner. Either cut through linguini attachment or by hand into pieces about 8 inches long. Hang pasta on a hanger to dry, or immediately blanch in boiling, lightly salted water.

Reheat sauce and serve over bowl of cooked pasta.

WHOLE-GRAIN PASTA WITH GARDEN-FRESH SAUCE
Serves 4.

Whole-grain pasta offers a different texture and taste. We find it particularly complemented by fresh vegetable flavors, such as bell peppers andgreen onions.

1 lb. whole-grain penne pasta
Extra-virgin olive oil
3-4 celery stalks, destringed and chopped
2 medium garlic cloves, pressed
1 medium sweet yellow onion, chopped
1 medium green bell pepper, chopped
1 medium red bell pepper, chopped
3-4 large tomatoes
$\frac{1}{2}$ tsp. sea salt
$\frac{1}{4}$ tsp. black pepper
$\frac{1}{4}$ tsp. cayenne pepper
$\frac{1}{2}$ tsp. oregano
$\frac{1}{2}$ tsp. basil
$\frac{1}{2}$ bunch green onion tops, sliced

Bring water to boil, and add pasta. Stir once, and return to boil.

Heat 3 tbsp. oil in skillet over medium heat. Add celery, garlic, and onion; stir until onion just starts to turn clear. Add peppers and stir. Cook about 5 minutes.

Peel, seed, and chop tomatoes. Add to skillet with seasonings and herbs and stir. Add green onions. Cook a few minutes until hot through.

Check pasta for doneness (prefer just slightly more cooked than *al dente*). Drain thoroughly in a colander. Toss immediately in colander with 1 tsp. or so oil to prevent sticking. Pour into bowl. Add sauce and toss; serve immediately. If you dare, grated Parmesan or other cheese enhances the experience.

WHOLE-GRAIN PASTA SALAD WITH ARTICHOKE VINAIGRETTE AND GRILLED CHICKEN
Serves 6.

This pasta salad can become vegetarian by omitting the chicken.

2 cups boiled, cooled whole-grain pasta (fusilli or macaroni preferred)
1 tsp. chopped fresh thyme
1 tbsp. lemon juice
2 oz. extra-virgin olive oil
½ cup chopped niçoise olives
½ cup diced celery
1 tsp. minced shallot
¾ tsp. kosher salt
¼ tsp. fresh-ground black pepper
3 boneless, skinless chicken breasts, grilled and sliced

Mix ingredients except chicken. Let marinate in refrigerator overnight.

Artichoke Vinaigrette
1 cup diced boiled artichoke hearts and bottoms
1 tbsp. minced shallots
1 tsp. chopped fresh thyme
¼ cup champagne vinegar
1 cup extra-virgin olive oil
Large pinch salt

Whisk ingredients together. Bring pasta salad to room temperature. For each serving, spoon vinaigrette around and over nice portion of pasta salad and ½ hot chicken breast.

LOW-FAT VEGETABLE RISOTTO

With the Crescent City Classic's focus on carbs, here is a really good vegetable risotto. It can be made with just about any type of vegetable any time of the year. This dish uses short-grain rice, usually an Italian rice known as arborio. It is cooked by adding hot stock to it, and you stir it to create a creaminess. That way you don't need lots of fat. However, a touch of really good Parmesan cheese does give the rice a little bit of a shine, providing maximum flavor with the maximum nutritional benefit of the mushrooms, tomato, and asparagus, which is in season during the Crescent City Classic. I can't think of anything I'd rather eat than a morel mushroom and wild asparagus risotto or green asparagus and spinach risotto. The combinations are absolutely endless when you think of a vegetable risotto, Chef reminds us.

1 cup small-diced porcini mushrooms
1 artichoke heart and bottom, sliced
1 tsp. minced shallot
1 tsp. minced garlic
Pinch chopped thyme
1 tbsp. diced tomato
Pinch chopped tarragon

Sauté ingredients in order listed, togther in same skillet. Keep warm.

Risotto
½ onion, minced
½ cup arborio rice
1 tbsp. extra-virgin olive oil
½ qt. hot white-meat chicken stock

Sauté onion until translucent. Add rice and enough oil to coat. Lightly toast rice. Add 1 cup stock and bring to a boil, stirring. Add more stock 1 cup at a time, stirring, to keep boil at a maximum so rice doesn't get too mushy. While stirring, allow most of stock to be absorbed by rice before adding more stock. When rice is a creamy texture, stir in vegetables.

Garnish
1 tbsp. sweet peas
1 tbsp. diced micro turnip
1 tbsp. edamame
1 tbsp. sliced wild asparagus

While rice is cooking, blanch ingredients. Shock in ice water. Garnish finished dish.

SEASONED COUSCOUS

Couscous is an excellent carb-loading dish that can serve as a tasty accompaniment to a number of protein main dishes. It comes in many sizes and colors, from the pure-white pearl to the rougher-looking whole wheat, which we employ in the following recipe.

2 cups water
1 small garlic clove, pressed
1 cup uncooked whole-wheat couscous
1½ tsp. extra-virgin olive oil
1½ tbsp. chopped parsley (Italian flat leaf preferred)
Dash sea salt
¼ tsp. white pepper
Dash cayenne pepper (optional)
Dash cardamom
Dash mace or allspice (optional)

Boil water with garlic and add immediately to couscous. Stir. Cover 15 minutes. Fluff and stir in oil, followed by other ingredients. Serve warm or at room temperature.

You can enjoy couscous by itself or with, for example, chopped tomato and/or green onions. You can turn it into a main dish by adding sautéed lean ground beef or pork, coriander, and cinnamon.

Our bodies metabolize carbohydrates—digest them and turn them into energy. We expend calories to make this transformation.

Digestion begins in our mouths. An enzyme in our saliva, amylase, starts breaking down carbohydrates into glucose. This simple sugar enters the bloodstream through the throat and esophagus. More complex carbohydrates, which are less susceptible to saliva, pass into the stomach and then into the small intestine. Eventually, at some point in this path, all carbohydrates (except fiber) are broken down into glucose, which enters through the digestive-tract lining into the bloodstream. "Blood sugar" is another term for glucose in the bloodstream.

Now glucose is in our blood. It's not quite ready to be used for energy. First, it has to enter our cells. How does it get there? Insulin provides the key. The glucose in our blood stimulates our pancreas (in the upper left abdomen) to release the hormone insulin into our bloodstream. The insulin then attaches to special "receptors" on our cell membranes. These receptors are like keyholes, and the insulin opens them—like a key opens a lock—to let glucose enter our cells. These "lock-and-key" mechanisms vary from person to person and even from one part of our body to another, but they all serve a common purpose: they let the glucose in. Now our cells and tissues can burn glucose for energy. The trip from sunlight to body energy is complete.

Our brains and nervous tissues burn the largest amounts of glucose whether we are resting, standing, or walking. Our muscles burn glucose, and they burn more with vigorous exercise. Eye tissues need a ready and plentiful supply of glucose to support the miracle of vision. Our livers and muscles can turn our excess glucose into a starch (glycogen) just as vegetables can make starches, and for the same reason—starches are stored energy. In times of heavy exercise or stress, our glycogen can be mobilized into glucose again. During my residency and fellowship in Boston, I would see people in restaurants eating huge bowls of pasta for several days before the Boston Marathon. These were prospective runners, of course. They were loading carbohydrates to store up glycogen in their bodies, to provide more glucose fuel for the race.

Because we need energy to live, we need carbohydrates. They are our source of glucose. This simple sugar supports our life functions. It may sound shocking to say there's nothing inherently wrong with sugar, but it's true as far as our energy needs are concerned.

So far, it's all good.

Then what can be bad about carbohydrates? How can a food element necessary for life create so many problems?

SHADOWED BY BAD CARBOHYDRATES

Too much of a good thing, too fast, can hurt us. Insulin is good. It's the lynchpin of our metabolism. It's necessary to admit glucose into our cells. But too much insulin, too fast, can hurt us. Here is the general picture. The simpler the carbohydrate, the faster it is absorbed into the bloodstream. The more simple carbohydrates we eat, the more insulin will be summoned into the bloodstream, and the faster it will get there. Many of us today eat mainly simple carbohydrates, and by doing so we're overstimulating our insulin production. In the long run, this is not good. We don't want large amounts of insulin flooding into our bloodstreams, nor do we want continuous insulin "spikes." This kind of carbohydrate consumption can turn a good thing into a bad thing.

Insulin

Too much insulin, too fast, can do the following:

- *Wear out cell-membrane receptors on cell surfaces, until those basic lock-and-key mechanisms don't work so well anymore.* This insulin resistance prevents cells from taking in all the glucose that they need for energy, and bloodstream glucose (blood sugar) will rise. All diabetics may have some degree of insulin resistance, a syndrome that is very difficult to treat.
- *Alter critical proteins and enzymes.* For example, blood sugars can attach to hemoglobin, the protein that carries oxygen in our red blood cells. Hemoglobin with tacked-on sugar is called glycosylated hemoglobin, and it is consistent with the increased scary stickiness that contributes to clogged vessels and premature aging of choked-up tissues.
- *Promote fat storage and likely derange normal metabolic pathways in tissues.* For instance, too much insulin can interfere with eye-lens tissue and promote cataract formation, alter the eye's drainage channel and cause glaucoma, and damage blood vessels and lay the groundwork for potentially blinding retinal disease.
- *Cause widespread problems in the heart and vascular system.*

- *Alter severely the functioning membranes and tissues in the kidneys.*
- *Inhibit the Holy Grail of weight loss—fat mobilization.* Too much insulin can raise triglycerides, metabolic fats that directly contribute to weight gain. Of course, calories *do* count, and at the most basic level all excess calories will make us fat. But too much insulin will make us even fatter.

Insulin affects not only sugar entry into cells but also general metabolism. Although some people may be genetically predisposed to insulin resistance, two causes we can control are obesity and lack of exercise. Insulin resistance develops alongside obesity. If you develop insulin resistance, your ability to tolerate a high-carbohydrate, low-fat diet decreases, and you're more vulnerable to elevated sugar levels, Type II diabetes, and a variety of chronic health problems.

In America we used to think that too many saturated fats were making us obese and sick—and granted, saturated fats are not good for us. Yet government statistics show that our fat consumption has in fact declined since the 1990s. It's our *carbohydrate* consumption that has increased, and most of those are simple carbohydrates.

If too much insulin is dangerous to our health, then we should naturally be wary of the foods that create too much insulin within us— namely, simple and "refined" carbohydrates. These take the fast-and-easy track into our bloodstream, either as glucose or as particles quickly made into glucose. Yet these are exactly the carbohydrates that most Americans eat—simple carbohydrates are all around us, attractively packaged. The average American eats relatively little else in the carbohydrate category.

Why? Because over time, our food supply has changed. We've posed new threats to our metabolism by working very hard to make our carbohydrates simpler and more delicious. Our road to simple carbohydrates has been paved with good intentions. But too often, we've left behind the healthier carbohydrates, the complex and unrefined carbohydrates.

OUR HISTORY: TURNING GOOD CARBOHYDRATES BAD

As long as 25,000 years ago, early bakers used whole grains: complex carbohydrates. When Egyptian royalty wanted an upper-crust bread, 6,000 years ago, it became popular to mill grains along the banks of the Nile. These grains were not wheat but millet-like grains, and their processed flour provided bread of a lighter texture and color, with carbohydrates less than whole due to partial processing. Later, the Egyptians added chemicals to bread dough to make it rise while baking, unlike the unleavened bread used by captive Jews. Just over 2,000 years ago, Rome boasted the first commercial food establishments: bakeries. Roman bakers practiced imported techniques they had learned from soldiers, and they made predominantly whole grain cakes, especially for the poor. Yet all classes ate bread, and it was prominent in the food supply. In 1771, London citizens learned that certain bakers were adding elements to expand their bread and their profits. Protests were widespread.

In Europe and America, little changed until the late 1700s, when flour-producing roller mills spread through the United States. Many people were concerned, including the Reverend Sylvester Graham, about the deleterious effects of this "refined flour," but their objections did little to stem the tide. The Reverend Mr. Graham's name lives on attached to the graham cracker. He likely would condemn some of the ingredients in the twenty-first-century version.

After the flour-processing roller mills, commercial bakeries appeared quickly. When the nineteenth century began, virtually all bread was baked at home, yet by the late 1800s, more than 25 percent of the bread eaten in the United States came from commercial ovens. It was then that Dr. Atwater, with the United States Department of Agriculture, unwittingly became an advocate for simple carbohydrates. He was looking for what he called the "fuel potential" or "efficiency" of various foods, so he naturally preferred foods that led to faster glucose absorption—these would have been the simpler carbohydrates. Bad idea. Nevertheless, Dr. Atwater recommended white refined flour as an "efficient" source of calories. He also thought potatoes should be baked instead of boiled—yet as we realize today, baking potatoes breaks down their starches further, making their carbohydrates simpler. Not only that, Dr. Atwater thought we should consume condensed milk with sugar for "efficient" energy. His recommendations can be seen as the granddaddy of the USDA Food Guide Pyramid. By the time the 2005 dietary recommendations were formulated, most of Dr. Atwater's specific recommendations had disappeared. Oh, well. Live and learn.

Home bread production decreased further in the twentieth century. Families started moving away from the farm in the first thirty years, and this trend accelerated during and after World War II. Commercial bakeries became dominant, and today all but a very small percentage of bread in the United States is commercially produced. Further, almost all of this commercial bread comes from highly refined and processed white flour that has been "enriched." Most of us today are familiar with this irony of bread history. The refining process strips wheat (a good food in its whole state) of its germ, its fiber, and most of its essential oils and vitamins. "Enrichment," initiated to create a robust population for the World War II effort, is a minimally useful attempt to resupply bread with some of the nutrients depleted by processing and "refining" wheat. Today our white bread, however "enriched" its label, is made of simple carbohydrates. Our other bakery products—cookies, crackers, hamburger buns—are almost without exception made from refined and processed white flour.

Let's examine a sample of today's bread. A serving of Bunny Bread® (copyrighted by American Bakers Cooperative, Inc., and distributed in the New Orleans area by Flowers Foods Bakeries Group, LLC) contains unbleached enriched wheat flour, malted barley flour, niacin, reduced iron, thiamine mononitrate (Vitamin B1), riboflavin (Vitamin B2), folic acid (Vitamin B6), water, high-fructose corn syrup, and yeast, plus a "2% or less" list of ingredients that includes wheat gluten, vegetable oil, soybean oil or canola oil, salt, and dough conditioners including sodium stearoyl lactylate, calcium, stearoyl alpha lactylate, monoglycerides, calcium peroxide, datem, soy flour, calcium sulfate, calcium propionate ("to retard spoilage"), monocalcium phosphate, yeast food, and ammonium sulfate. It's unclear exactly which of these helps Bunny Bread to make good on its claim to "stay fresh longer."

In our food supply today, simple carbohydrates lurk not only in our breads and cakes. Other foods that we call "sugar traps" are also laden with simple carbohydrates. Even though the American Heart Association has allowed the term "heart healthy" to be used by orange juice manufacturers, orange juice is usually a processed food. Unless it has really been "fresh squeezed" in your own home or a special restaurant, the orange juice you drink has been processed out of the orange, heat treated (pasteurized) to prolong shelf life, and placed into a bottle or carton. It may say "fresh, not from concentrate," but it is processed.

One of my children, studying nutrition modules at the Louise S. McGehee School, asked for help with a list of "processed foods" and was shocked when I named orange juice. We don't think of orange juice, or other fruit juices, as processed foods. We've been lulled into a false sense of nutritional security. Manufacturers have taken advantage of our public illusion that any and all fruit juice is healthful, and they often add high-fructose corn sweetener to the processed fruit juice.

The "Healthy Juice" Trap

- Based on 8 oz., calories can range from about 100 to 170.
- "Fresh" shelf juices, whether traditional brands or "organic" brands like Odwalla, are *all* pasteurized. Heat treatment reduces natural nutrients.
- Odwalla adds "evaporated cane juice"; others add high-fructose corn sweetener
- All calories come from sugar. Limit consumption.
- Just replacing sodas with juice in school vending machines won't help. Some juices have more sugar calories than do sodas. You still must moderate consumption.

Too much fruit juice can mean too many simple carbohydrates. We should minimize fruit juices and choose those with low sugar content. Our local citrus specialty, the satsuma, is available from October through early January. It has somewhat lower sugar content and easily squeezed pulp. It makes a nice addition to the pan water for roasting fowl or when preparing salad dressing.

Sodas, or what we New Orleanians call "cold drinks," are another simple-carbohydrate trap. The obese teenagers we interviewed for the New Orleans Program drank sugary sodas throughout the day. In the South, not only children but some adults drink a soda at breakfast, or wash down their meals with over-sugared iced tea. The "cold drink" snack habit adds over 100 calories of simple carbohydrates, rapidly absorbed as glucose that triggers insulin. When we take in these calories while we're working at a desk or watching TV, we're preparing our bodies to take on fat. If we're used to cold drinks and limit them to one per day (or less!), this reduction in itself can help us shed another pound or two per month. Cold drinks, by the way, can also unbalance calcium metabolism. Phosphates, present in many cold drinks and especially in colas, can reduce calcium absorption. If you're a child or an older person who is trying to build stronger bones, you want more calcium buildup, not less.

One humane exception is "flat" Coke. Many of us who grew up in the South were given a little of this when we were sick, feverish, and dehydrated. We called it "flat" because our parents let the carbonation escape before allowing us to drink it. When we were too sick to keep anything down, we took in valuable electrolytes, liquid, and energy-providing sugar from flat Coke. We used it only for the short run, though. Dehydration in an infant or small child who can't tolerate fluids can become a medical emergency and should be treated as such.

CHOOSING CARBOHYDRATES TODAY

We don't have to be victims of our food culture. We may be surrounded by simple carbohydrates, but we won't starve without them. Many of us are virtually addicted to simple carbs. Yet when we break that addiction, when we learn healthier eating and exercise patterns that shift our metabolism, then we'll be able to work some simple carbs back into our meals.

How are simple carbs addictive? Eating too many will cause an unhealthful hunger driven by insulin fluctuations. Even when we don't need more food, we feel hungry. We're trapped in the mood swings of simple-carb consumption: sugar highs and sugar lows or "crashes." Insulin ups and downs also trigger our fat cells to send out their "hungry" signals. Metabolically, we're out of balance.

Participants in the New Orleans Program were asked to set aside many of their simple-carb foods for the six-month initial phase of the program. Omitting these simple carbs was one feature we designed to create a metabolic shift and put their bodies into a proper balance. Another essential feature was exercise. Along with fat loss, our exercise program (including resistance exercises) promotes a higher ratio of lean muscle mass in the body. Lean muscle mass burns glucose in the bloodstream much faster than do other tissues, and it even keeps burning carbs when you are asleep. This benefit of exercise is like discovering your own oil well or gold mine.

Anyone can choose to follow the New Orleans Program, of course. For the general reader caught in the swings of carb consumption, we recommend following the no-nos in Appendix B for at least two to three weeks, while exercising, to create the metabolic shift that will make you more comfortable eating fewer refined carbohydrates.

While we are avoiding simple carbs, what about sweeteners? Many popular sugar substitutes are found in foods labeled "low calorie" or "low carb," and some of these chemicals have been around for decades. They're hard to avoid, even though many of them, historically, have cautions associated with their pre-FDA approvals. In general, we have a troublesome number of food additives in our food supply. One way to work around this problem may be to reconsider plain old table sugar—sucrose—for our tea or coffee. Yes, sucrose is a simple carb, and it is refined from cane or beets, but used in moderation it may be better than one more dose of sweetener. One teaspoon of table sugar, at 16 calories, is very unlikely to cause an insulin spike.

A November 2005 study of effects of the artificial sweetener aspartame created some new shock waves. Research in the peer-reviewed *Journal of Environmental Health Perspectives* clearly showed that rats eating 20 mg per kg of body weight developed multiple types of cancer, including leukemia, lymphoma, and tumors in multiple organs. Currently the U.S. sets acceptable daily human intake at 50 mg/kg; Europe sets it at 40 mg/kg. The controlled scientific study involved hundreds of rats that were fed the aspartame with regular chow and allowed to live out their natural lives (averaging just over three years). This finding contradicts studies by aspartame producers, who got FDA approval in 1974 and supply the sweetener to manufacturers of over six thousand products.

How Sweet It Is!

Sugar: Natural
Other sweeteners: Not natural (includes Splenda or sucralose, which is artificially modified sugar)

Sugar: Only 16 calories per teaspoon
Other sweeteners: No calories, but unknown effects on your body

- Most people blame sugar wrongly. Cola has high-fructose corn sweetener, *not* sugar, for its 39 grams of sweet carbs. "Sugar-free" foods can pack calories and trans fats.
- Sugar can kill bacteria.
- The American Diabetic Association agrees that a moderate amount of sugar with balanced eating, as in the New Orleans Program, is all right.

Don't forget fiber. Fibers are carbohydrates that we can't digest, so they don't raise our insulin level at all. In fact, they're a bright spot in the insulin picture. They slow the passage of simple carbs from stomach to intestine and therefore "smooth out" possible insulin spikes. Fibers are usually larger molecules, like cellulose—which New Orleans termites can digest, but we can't. Fiber-rich foods include beans, onions, celery, cabbage, and green leafy vegetables. Mushrooms contain raffinose, an indigestible carb. Fibers also can act as "sponges" to remove cholesterol and other undesirable elements. Whole-grain oatmeal, through its fiber, can lower cholesterol.

Why do we pass more gas when we eat fiber? Because our intestinal bacteria *can* digest fiber, even though we can't. For most people, the increased gas is not uncomfortable. People with diverticulosis or irritable bowel syndrome, though, may have a more noticeable reaction to increased fiber.

Choose complex carbohydrates, and don't overcook them. Complex carbohydrates, those with a lower glycemic index, are found in starchy vegetables, beans, and whole grains.

A Note on the Glycemic Index

The term "glycemic index" is a complicated way of stating a simple observation about carbohydrates. Some food advice writers, Dr. Arthur Agatston, for example, tend to lump whole and processed or simple carbs together. We simplify this observation here:

Simple carbohydrates = high glycemic index = bad. Eat comparatively less.

Complex carbohydrates = low glycemic index = good. Eat comparatively more.

In order to choose healthy food, we don't need to become mired in a scientific classification of every carbohydrate source. Many systems and even academic careers have been built around describing our bodies' reactions to certain carbohydrates. For our New Orleans Program, we found that our above equation was usually sufficient.

The more complex the carb, the lower the glycemic index, which varies from food to food. Lower glycemic indexes are, of course, better. *The more complex the carbohydrate, the longer it takes your body to digest it.* Slow digestion of carbohydrates is the best. Even the absorption of the simplest carbs into the blood can be slowed by eating them with protein or fat. This fact adds fuel to our recommendation of varied foods at each meal. We really don't need to fear carrots, for example, unless we cook them to mush and eat heaps of them.

Another word of caution: overcooking whole carbs can break down their starch structures until they become simple carbs. We may be tempted to bake or overboil our carbohydrate foods because it makes them taste sweet. Scientific studies tell us that even babies prefer the sweet taste over all others, and most of us will admit to a sweet tooth. A raw "sweet potato" is not sweet, yet. When we bake the potato and reduce it to its very simple constituent sugars, then *they* taste sweet. A better method is to gently boil vegetables and pasta until they are barely tender—*al dente.* Remember that a century ago Dr. Atwater advised baking instead of boiling potatoes? Disobey him. Boil them lightly.

We also don't recommend the marathoner-style carb loading for the general reader. Instead, we recommend proteins and exercise to prepare for strenuous short-term performance like final exams, SATs, the courtroom, and family reunions (see chapter 1).

Balance meals to modify sugar absorption. By minimizing simple carbs, our goal is to minimize how much glucose (sugar) our bloodstream absorbs, and how fast. We're glad to observe that a meal that contains a balance of good fats, proteins, and complex carbs can modify or prolong sugar absorption. Proteins themselves modify sugar absorption, and they are less dense than fat: 4 calories instead of 9 calories per gram. (The pancreas also produces a fat mobilizer, called glucagon, after we eat protein-containing foods.)

Fat can prolong the time it takes the stomach to empty into the small intestine, so that sugar, wherever it is absorbed, will enter the bloodstream at a more gradual pace. Acidity contributed by fruits, the vinegar in salad dressing, and some vegetables may also slow down sugar absorption. Adequate stomach acid also plays a role. There are even nutraceuticals and pharmaceuticals today that claim to lower sugar absorption (for more details, visit our Web site).

As long as we've broken the addiction to simple carbs, as long as we're exercising, and as long as we're eating meals that balance proteins, complex carbs, and good fats, we can take in a few simple or refined carbs with our meal. And our resulting glycemic index for such a meal will be in a healthy zone. Certainly brown rice and wild rice are healthy whole grains, but white rice, a Southern favorite and a simpler carbohydrate, need not be demonized—as it has been in the Atkins, South Beach, and Sugar Busters! diets. Prepared correctly and eaten moderately with a balanced meal, white rice is not harmful.

Nearly every "diet" guru maligns white rice. You can certainly use brown rice with any of our recipes. We New Orleanians, however, prefer long-grain white rice with many dishes. Here is how to get perfect rice every time.

NEVER-FAIL RICE

Please note—this recipe is 100 percent guaranteed only if you use a Louisiana rice: white, brown, or "popcorn." One cup cooked rice serves 4.

2 cups water
1 tbsp. good vegetable oil
2-3 good pinches sea salt
1 cup rice

Place water, oil, and salt into heavy pot that has a cover. Bring to rapid boil, uncovered. Add rice, stir once, and cover. Watch for 1-2 minutes until it returns to a boil. *Immediately* reduce heat to low. Do not touch pot for 30 minutes. Then, uncover, fluff the perfect rice, recover, and turn off heat. Rice is ready to serve in a few minutes, or will keep hot in pot for 20-30 minutes. If you need to reheat, microwave, covered, on high power 30-45 seconds, but try to use rice before it needs reheating.

Another Southern favorite that can be enjoyed while still revving up the metabolism and contributing to a balanced meal is the tomato sandwich. Take 2 thin slices white bread (yes, white bread), a moderate amount of canola-oil mayo, and 3-4 thin slices fresh Creole tomato. Assemble with light sprinklings of salt and black pepper. Eat immediately. This "decadent" sandwich has less than 200 calories and is a relatively sound choice. The acidity of the tomato (an excellent food) and the fat of the canola-oil mayo both slow down the absorption of the simple carbs in the white bread, lowering the glycemic index of the whole. In the same context, we can approve another classic Southern delight, the cucumber sandwich.

Enjoy!

CHAPTER 5

Earth's Bounty and Rebirth:
Easter Feast

It is Easter morning, 1990. I pass through the doors of the Creole Cottage at historic Arnaud's Restaurant on Rue Bienville in the French Quarter. My friend Susan has invited me to join the Friends of Germaine Wells Traditional French Quarter Easter Parade.

Sunlight and chandeliers illumine a scene like a movie set for a Southern belles' party. Ladies in wide hats festooned in lace, flowers, feathers, and bunnies (and yes, sometimes beads) are in lively conversations with each other and with gentlemen in vanilla or white linen. Ma chère, these are real chapeaux!

After a light cocktail breakfast, the ladies mount horse-drawn carriages to parade through the French Quarter, while the gentlemen prepare to walk. Some of us drive white convertibles with two or three lovely ladies on the deck. The route snakes through the quarter. What a large crowd has gathered so early! The paraders toss fresh or faux flowers to the adults, stuffed bunnies to the children. The destination? Jackson Square, in front of St. Louis Cathedral. We all second-line into the square, ladies and gents, for champagne before noon mass. During the service, one of the longtime Easter paraders, who holds a reserved pew in front, kneels at the prie-dieu of the side chapel, places flowers, and says a prayer for the soul of Germaine Cazenave Wells.

After Mass we return to Arnaud's for Easter feasting. Our typical choices include seafood gumbo, shrimp bisque, shrimp Arnaud, Creole panéed veal, sautéed or broiled speckled trout straight from the Gulf, roast beef, many vegetables, and crème brûlée. Children, a prominent part of our Easter parade for decades, can choose fried chicken Arnaud's style. My two daughters have grown up dressing for this parade, and they've enjoyed throwing stuffed bunnies to other children along the route. Councilwoman Jackie Clarkson, with her daughter Patricia—now a famous stage and film star—recently rode as the grand marshal.

Chef Besh gives us his update on a classic Easter dish.

VEAL PANE OVER HEIRLOOM TOMATOES

Serves 4.

4 2-oz. veal cutlets
1 cup panko breadcrumbs
Creole spice
¾ cup low-fat milk
1 large egg
1 cup all-purpose flour

Pound veal thin. Mix breadcrumbs and Creole spice. Make an egg wash by whisking milk and egg together. Dredge veal in flour, egg wash, then breadcrumbs. Roast in oven 10 minutes at 375 degrees. Keep warm.

Heirloom Tomatoes
4 thick slices various heirloom tomatoes
8 ¼-inch slices smaller tasty heirloom tomatoes
Sea salt and fresh-cracked black pepper to taste
1 tbsp. 30-year-old sherry vinegar
1 tbsp. red-wine vinegar
3 tbsp. canola oil
3 tbsp. walnut oil
25-year-old balsamic vinegar
1 cup mustard or turnip greens

Season tomato slices with salt and pepper. Whisk together sherry and red-wine vinegars and canola and walnut oils. Place tomatoes on a plate and drizzle with some sherry-walnut vinaigrette and balsamic vinegar. Top tomatoes with veal and with greens that have been tossed in the vinaigrette.

Germaine Wells started this parade in the 1940s, after seeing the Easter Parade on New York's Fifth Avenue. With her awareness of New Orleans finery and her own taste for fancy hats and dresses, she felt that a New-Orleans-style Easter parade could only spice up an already spicy place. Her father had founded Arnaud's in 1918.

Archie Casbarian, a true host and leader of the New Orleans

hospitality industry, relates why Germaine Wells chose him to purchase the family business. Mrs. Wells said, "You know why you got it? Well, because you're the same age as my dad was when he started the restaurant. You're foreign born; he was foreign born. Your initials are the same. You smoke cigars; he smoked cigars. You both wear nice clothes and most importantly you both like cognac."

Casbarian corroborates reports that Mrs. Wells, into her eighties, regularly sought male companionship using her restaurant bar as a source. She also stayed active in many Mardi Gras krewes. Casbarian describes the 1983 opening of the Mardi Gras Museum at the restaurant:

We documented which Mardi Gras balls she was queen of, and what the theme of that was, and then we got the curator of a local museum here and we took all the dresses and all the costumes and where help was needed, help was done. We got all the mannequins. We identified and actually put up cards on which events these were, which Mardi Gras balls, which Mardi Gras krewes. So as you entered the museum then there was essentially a link from Mardi Gras ball to Mardi Gras ball that this lady was queen of. According to her, she was queen of more Mardi Gras balls than anybody in New Orleans. So the day came that we wanted to promote the opening of the museum. She said she had a duplicate of one of the gowns that was on display. I said fine. I went to pick her up and here she was in this gold lamé dress that she wore when she was in her thirties and now she was in her eighties and there was a part of her that was overflowing. . . . Nevertheless, my staff and I were able to maneuver her down the steps and then the cocktail party was held in the Count's Room, which is one of the private dining rooms on the second floor and requires access through a number of stairwells. This lady was so tightly packed in this dress that she was basically lifted until we got to the entrance to the Count's Room, where the cocktail party was in full swing. She had the scepter in her hand and she said to me, "Sonny (she never knew my name; I was always Sonny), have you ever escorted a queen?" And I said, "No, ma'am, I never have." She said, "Well, you know what we're going to do now? We're going to walk. I'm going to hold on to your arm and we're going to walk slowly and we're going to circle the ballroom. When I squeeze your arm, we're going to stop and I'll wave my scepter at the group." So we walked in, a sight to behold—she was in this gold lamé thing; she had a tiara, a scepter, and little gold slippers. Everybody thought it was the biggest riot.

After Germaine Wells passed away in her nineties, Arnaud's, a cluster of twelve historic buildings, the largest block of French Quarter buildings used as a business, experienced what Casbarian describes as "haunting" by Mrs. Wells. He went so far as to ask his priest, Rev. Hil Riddle, to perform an exorcism. He reports, "It worked. Things stopped moving and breaking."

Today there are other Easter parades in the French Quarter, and newly on St. Charles Avenue. The internationally known Bourbon Street entertainer, Chris Owens, leads a nontraditional Easter parade. Easter is always fairly close to Passover, and the New Orleans Jewish community has put its own stamp on a Passover tradition thousands of years old. Coauthor of Creole Jewish cookbooks Mildred Covert and the Honorable Miriam Waltzer agree that "a little purple, green, and gold" never hurt any traditional meal.

In the Creole tradition, the quiet time of Lent has passed. The Easter feast has arrived. And in our feasts, throughout history, we have always eaten protein.

OUR BODIES ARE MADE OF PROTEIN

Our bodies are continually renewing themselves. Little by little, old cells die and new cells must replace them. To feed this process and keep ourselves alive, we must take in protein foods that have the eight essential amino acids. Through digestion, we break down protein food into constituent amino acids, which travel to our liver and into our bloodstreams. From there, we rebuild and maintain vital parts of our bodies, such as muscles, nerves, hormones, enzymes, blood, skin, hair, and cell membranes. Structures like these carry out most of our life functions. It is a protein-to-protein cycle: we eat proteins, break them down, build them up, and thus reconstitute our protein-based bodies. We are made from these eight amino-acid blocks, which are called "essential" since we cannot synthesize them, and the other twelve "nonessential" ones, which we do create in our own tissues.

We need to eat the right kinds of proteins to supply ourselves with all the essential amino acids. Animals and animal products provide our most-often consumed sources of protein. Our top sources in the United States today are beef, pork, chicken, turkey, milk, cheese, and eggs. Fish and shellfish, especially shrimp, take second place as sources, and plant proteins come in third.

Meats, eggs, dairy, and fish each provide complete proteins, with all the essential amino acids. Plant-derived foods are incomplete in essential amino acids, however, so vegans and vegetarians must plan their meals strategically for protein intake. Long ago, George Washington Carver said, "I would rather have a handful of peanuts than a steak." He was almost right. In the 1970s, we learned how to combine grains, beans, nuts, seeds, and vegetables sources to make "complete" proteins for our bodies. Frances Moore Lappé, who wrote *Diet for a Small Planet,* might have suggested that Dr. Carver eat some sunflower seeds or whole grains along with his peanuts, or drink a glass of milk. Through informing themselves and varying their protein sources, vegans and vegetarians can indeed obtain all of the life-necessary amino acids.

Even though some claim a totally vegan or vegetarian diet brings long life, it remains controversial. It takes vigilance to consistently include all necessary amino acids in a vegetarian meal plan, and amino-acid deficiencies are dangerous. Such deficiencies can severely derange a normal protein metabolism, with tragic results like diminished brain function, accelerated aging, and poor structural body integrity. Scientists have not yet determined exactly how much protein we should eat to stay healthy. Not all food constituents are known. For reasons we cannot fully discern, it is clinically true that in certain situations, adding animal proteins can boost immune and healing responses, or help a pregnant woman bring her baby to term. So vegetarians should be very careful with their protein intake.

The "diet gurus" recommend a wide range of daily protein intake to keep healthy, from 20 percent to the whopping 70 percent of daily calories from protein that Dr. Atkins advises. When we look for basic scientific observations, we find that in areas where people suffer less from heart disease and diabetes, and live longer, protein makes up about 30 percent of a typical day's calories. This percentage seems to us reasonable. Yet certain situations can call for more daily protein, or less.

So when should you eat more protein? Our guiding principle here is that protein is needed to build up or repair tissues, whether they are muscle tissues, nerve tissues, or others. That's why growing children need more protein. Women in the third trimester of pregnancy also need more protein, as do people recovering from surgery. Those in stressful situations can benefit from higher protein. Active individuals need more protein than sedentary individuals. Regular heavy exercisers need more protein. Athletes and bodybuilders have their own protein intake regimen. Whey now occupies some of the spotlight among body-builders and buffer-uppers as a source for additional protein. Little Miss Muffet must have broad-jumped away from that intrusive arachnid.

Protein has another metabolic advantage. Eating protein stimulates our pancreas to make glucagon, which stabilizes our blood glucose (blood sugar) and also inhibits that sugar from turning into fat. If we exercise and also eat enough protein, we'll maintain or even (with resistance training) increase our muscle mass. Lean muscle burns the largest amount of glucose. We've used this knowledge to design our eating and exercise guidelines for the New Orleans Program.

We have noticed, though, that different individuals can react differently to consuming protein. Some will feel as if they have low energy without a certain amount of protein; others may feel sluggish after eating protein. Each of us must make a personal decision about when to eat protein and how much to eat, within overall guidelines. It's important to eat a balance of protein, carbs, and fats.

We believe that too much protein *can* hurt you. Proteins, like carbohydrates, are 4 calories per gram. If you eat too much of anything—even protein—it can be stored as fat. But there can be even worse results. Excess amino acids in your bloodstream can metabolize into ammonia. Anyone who has used household ammonia is familiar with this noxious substance. In our bodies, too much of it can damage the liver and kidneys. For those with weakened livers, struggling to make ammonia into urea for the kidneys to excrete, this ammonia from excess amino acids will be toxic. This excess ammonia can also damage our kidneys when it filters through them. Many people have undiagnosed borderline kidney problems. For them, the extra ammonia will add insult to injury, kicking the fighter when he's down.

All those with liver or kidney problems should lower their protein intake. Yet even for a healthy person, just as repeated assaults of high blood sugar can weaken the insulin receptors on our cells, so repeated assaults of amino-acid breakdown products can weaken our kidneys. Even in the short term, too much protein could bring on an ammonia load that would cause serious bodily dysfunction. Ammonia directly poisons brain cells and may interfere with the functions of many tissues. All in all, the high-protein consumption touted by Atkins and others may be hazardous to your health.

OUR FOOD SUPPLY: BAD "BAGGAGE"
HARMS GOOD PROTEINS

We are omnivores. Our jaw and tooth structures equip us to eat meat as well as vegetation. Tens of thousands of years ago, human beings began to eat more meat when they learned to hunt more efficiently. The result? Our brains got larger, our musculature improved, and we grew taller. Being omnivorous has historically done good things for human beings.

Protein intake has played a vital part in human history. *Homo erectus omnivorous* ate a high proportion of meat and bone marrow, balancing this with roots, nuts, fruits, berries, green vegetable sprouts, and whole-grain cakes. Fish entered our diet when we devised fish hooks, around thirty-five thousand years ago. Of all our protein sources, animal protein has historically been our favorite. In our feasts, we have prized animal protein: roasted pigs, ducks, geese, turkey, sides of beef, venison.

Let me hasten to add that all this meat was free range, until very late in our history. As recently as my childhood, we were eating free-range meat. I grew up in a family that hunted. At age eight I was given my first hunting rifle, a .22-gauge "short," and a few years later a 410-gauge shotgun. As a very good shot, I fit right into our family's hunting tradition. We shared the excitement and camaraderie of hunting, which culminated in preparing and eating our game. We also bought our beef from farmers who raised cattle naturally, feeding them on a variety of plants.

Those days have passed. Now almost all of the animal protein foods in our grocery stores are loaded with such potentially toxic "baggage" as antibiotics, hormones, and traces of heavy metals. We find it ironic that in the 1970s, while our popular diet books were busy demonizing sucrose and canonizing protein, our commercial food supply of animal proteins was steadily absorbing more potential toxins. In our New Orleans Program, we have chosen protein sources with the least harmful "baggage."

Commercial farmers routinely feed their animals antibiotics. As a result, the beef, pork, chicken, and turkey in our grocery stores routinely contain antibiotics. Why is that dangerous? The lesser risk is that certain people are allergic to selected antibiotics. The greater risk is that some bacteria will multiply rapidly enough to generate antibiotic-resistant offspring within a matter of hours or days. The more antibiotics we consume in our meat, the more likely we are to harbor antibiotic-resistant strains of bacteria in our bodies. The threat of antibiotic-resistant bacteria in the human population is an ongoing concern to the medical community. And then we have the hormones that farmers feed to cows and chickens, to increase the production of beef and milk, chicken and eggs. Should we be consuming all these hormones? In one case, a man who ate large amounts of chicken that had been fed with estrogen, a female hormone, actually began to develop breasts. We might think that government agencies would not approve of feeding hormones and antibiotics to the animals that supply our protein. And yet they have given their approval. We don't approve.

Then there is our secondary-level protein, fish. It's hard to keep up with the latest warnings about mercury or other heavy metals in our fish supply, especially when environmental toxins can vary so dramatically from one area to another.

Toxins

Environmental pollutants and toxins end up in certain otherwise delicious elements of our food chain (e.g., mercury in tuna, swordfish, salmon). We recommend consulting frequently updated Web sites to stay current:

- environmentalnutrition.com
- theneworleansprogram.com
- cspinet.org

Several years ago, I founded a charitable eye-care project in Port-au-Prince, Haiti. One doctor and three nurses, who had come from the Midwest to work in the eye clinics there, developed a fondness for grouper—a fish that was prepared in a restaurant just outside the city and right on the beach. They thought it was delicious. They ate grouper in that restaurant three nights in a row. The next morning, they all awoke with headaches, vomiting, vertigo, and vision disturbance. They were diagnosed with acute heavy-metal poisoning from copper or lead. The grouper, it turned out, were feeding not far from the restaurant, at the ocean bottom contaminated with runoff from a bauxite (aluminum ore) refining plant. The grouper flesh had absorbed enough toxic metals to poison these three people after only three meals.

SHOPPING (HUNTING) FOR GOOD PROTEIN TODAY

Fish and shellfish are both excellent protein sources. It turns out that my grandmother and mother were right when they told me, "Eat your fish. It's brain food." This was handed-down wisdom, but today we've confirmed that fresh fish, carefully chosen, is easily digestible and complete protein, which provides us with good Omega-3 fatty acids.

We recommend buying fish from local markets rather than chain grocery stores. With local markets, we can more likely find out whether the fish are harvested from clean waters. On this question, there's no substitute for informing ourselves and "asking around"— and these efforts are worth it for the sake of our health.

None of us is alone in searching for uncontaminated sources of fresh fish. In fact, our search itself creates pressure on suppliers—pressure for change. That's a good thing. Dean Pigeon, executive caterer to the New Orleans Saints football team, worries about his fish supply just like the rest of us. When we interviewed him for this book, he revealed some of his fish-hunting strategies:

We'll try and find fresh fish. We have a few places if we need flounder, I'll call so and so and get flounder. [One caterer] has a fish program. If you call today before 11, you can get fresh beautiful trout if that's what is available, or red snapper. It's a good program they have. You just have to call in before 11 today and tomorrow you'll have the freshest fish they have. I don't know if they go to the docks, but I know fresh. I've had not-fresh fish before and you just know. Fish is the scariest thing. I would never buy fish from the grocery store because you don't know. I think [one particular grocery] is pretty decent but you just don't know how long it sat on the dock. From the dock it went to the supplier, and then the supplier might have had it for four days and then they send it to [the grocery]. To me your average grocery store, you're starting at seven days. That's my opinion. I knew somebody that worked at a fish house and what they used to do. They get the fish and after seven days if it wasn't moving they'd take it and take baking soda and lemon and dip it into that and it took the odor out. That's one of the tricks of the trade. To me, [it's good to] buy IQF [individually quick frozen] farm-raised catfish. They clean and freeze it immediately. It's as fresh as can be. They have everything—grouper, red snapper— and it's all IQF-layered and you know that stuff didn't sit around for three-four days before it even started to move.

Sometimes our inquiries will yield comforting, certain knowledge. In our area, I've found out which oyster purveyors definitely harvest their tasty bivalves from clean waters. Knowing that, I feel reasonably safe eating them raw. As I'm preparing them for cooking, I'll pop some of the plumper ones into my mouth with a bit of Louisiana hot sauce. But as for oysters or other shellfish from unknown sources? I don't eat them raw.

Fortunately, there are ways to cook oysters that retain their delicate fresh flavor. Here is one.

OYSTER STEW

Serves 6.

3 cups fumet (see below)
2 tbsp. minced shallot
2 tbsp. minced leek
6 tbsp. diced tomato
1 fresh artichoke heart, blanched and sliced thin
6 oz. oyster liquor
Juice from 1 lemon
10 dashes Tabasco
1 tbsp. fresh thyme
1 tbsp. minced chive
Salt and black pepper to taste
30 oysters

Combine fumet, shallot, leek, tomato, artichoke, oyster liquor, lemon juice, Tabasco, thyme, and chive in medium pot and stir. Add salt and pepper. Heat to just before boiling. Add oysters, heat just until edges curl, and serve immediately.

Fumet
1 onion, coarsely chopped
⅓ celery stalk, coarsely chopped
1 bulb fennel, coarsely chopped
3 cloves garlic, halved
Extra-virgin olive oil
Salt to taste
1 pt. vermouth
1 sprig thyme
1 sprig tarragon
1 bay leaf
1 pt. fish stock
1 cup heavy cream

Sweat onion, celery, fennel, and garlic in small amount oil until onion is transparent and add salt. Add vermouth. Reduce until alcohol is evaporated. Add thyme, tarragon, bay leaf, and stock. Reduce by ¼ over low heat. Add cream, heat to just before boiling, and remove from heat. Strain. Keep chilled until final assembly of stew.

In Southern Louisiana, we're blessed with crawfish (a.k.a. mudbugs) that propagate in our bayous. The crawfish season lasts from about early February to early May, depending on rainfall, temperature, and other factors. Flash-frozen, processed crawfish tails are available year round. As with many shellfish, crawfish are "purged" in cool, fresh water for up to twenty-four hours before boiling. Properly spiced, they're a delicious, high-protein, low-calorie, high-micronutrient food. We can say the same for crabs, scallops, shrimp, mussels, and even the non-New Orleanian clam.

CHILLED BUTTERMILK AND
CUCUMBER SOUP WITH SEAFOOD
Serves 6.

½ cup jumbo lump crabmeat, picked for shells
½ cup cucumber flesh

Lemon juice to taste
Salt to taste

Mix crab and cucumber together. Lightly season with lemon juice and salt.

Olive-Oil-Poached Lobster
1 lobster tail
Extra-virgin olive oil to cover
Thyme to taste
Salt to taste

Combine ingredients in a small pot or skillet. Poach lobster over low to medium heat until firm, about 15 minutes. Remove lobster from shell in one piece and cut meat crosswise into medium slices.

Boiled Shrimp
1 lb. medium shrimp, peeled and deveined
1 gal. water
½ cup salt
¼ cup sugar
½ cup salt-free Creole spice
¼ cup lemon juice
4 bay leaves
1 tbsp. coriander
1 tbsp. black peppercorns
1 sprig thyme
1 onion, halved
1 head garlic, halved

Combine ingredients in a large pot. Boil until shrimp are tender and just cooked through. Remove shrimp and shock in bowl of ice water.

Soup
Juice of 4 cucumbers
3 cucumbers, peeled, seeded, and pureed
½ cup buttermilk
1 tsp. garlic powder

1 tsp. onion powder
1 tsp. celery salt
1 dash Tabasco
1 tbsp. lemon juice
Salt to taste

Combine all soup ingredients and chill.

Garnish
Chive blossom
Chopped chives

To assemble, use 6 large bowls. In each bowl, place crab in bottom, top with lobster slice(s), then shrimp. Pour about 6 oz. soup around each seafood tower and garnish.

CRAB CAKES

Serves 4.

Most Baltimorians would never admit it, but the majority of crabs served there come from Louisiana. If you don't believe us, just follow many members of the Baltimore political establishment and members of the Orioles baseball team to Bud's Crab House in East Baltimore and ask one of the servers for the truth. Here are crab cakes with a Creole flair. Crab claw meat will do, but only if it is not all in fine shreds.

½ **pt. fresh lump crabmeat**
¼ **cup destringed, minced celery**
¼ **cup demembraned, minced green bell pepper**
¼ **cup demembraned, minced red bell pepper**
¼ **cup thinly sliced green onion tops**
½ **cup breadcrumbs**
2 **egg whites**
½ **tsp. Worcestershire sauce**
1 **tsp. blended seasonings**
½ **tsp. sea salt**

½ tsp. black pepper
¼ tsp. cayenne pepper
Pinch basil and/or thyme

Check the crab for cartilage and remove. Combine crab, vegetables, and breadcrumbs in a medium mixing bowl. Add remaining ingredients and mix well.

Form into 4 2-inch cakes. (If too dry, add egg white or a whole egg if you dare. If too moist, add small amount breadcrumbs until good.)

In large skillet, heat olive or good vegetable oil over medium-high heat. Place cakes (see "2-spatula technique" in Crawfish Cake recipe) in oil. Sauté until nicely browned on one side, turn, and sauté until nicely browned on other side (medium dark). Do not overcook, about 4 minutes each side. Drain on paper towels. Enjoy!

SCALLOPS GRANNY

Serves 2.

½ cup fat-free, well-seasoned chicken stock or vegetable stock
⅛ tsp. thyme leaves
1 large Granny Smith or other tart apple
Lemon juice
8 large scallops, fresh or quick frozen, thawed
Sea salt and black pepper to taste
Paprika (not hot) to taste
Extra-virgin olive oil
1 tbsp. sliced green onion tops

Place stock and thyme in a skillet. Bring to a gentle boil.

Peel about 12 strips peel from apple. Peel rest of apple and mince apple. Sprinkle strips and apple with small amount lemon juice to keep from turning brown.

Add strips and apple to stock, and stir to soften. Remove strips.

Pat scallops dry and season on both sides. Heat oil and add scallops. Sprinkle with green onions. Sauté scallops, turning until nicely browned and done through. Plate by placing apple stew *around* scallops and strips on top. Serve immediately.

SEA SCALLOPS WITH SQUASH SAUCE

Serves 2.

Extra-virgin olive oil
10 pearl onions, peeled and halved
1 tbsp. flour
¹/₂ cup medium-dry to dry white wine
Sea salt and white pepper to taste
¹/₂ cup cubed butternut or pumpkin squash
8 large scallops, fresh or quick frozen, thawed
Blended seasonings to taste

Heat a small amount of olive oil in a pan. Add onions and caramelize to a medium degree. Remove.

Add about 1 tsp. more olive oil and heat. Add flour. Let bubble while stirring, 2 minutes (it should cook but not darken).

Add half the wine while stirring rapidly, making a roux as you deglaze pan. Add remaining wine, stir, and cook 2-3 minutes. It should be a lovely, medium-light brown.

Add salt and pepper. Taste for seasoning. Return onions to pan.

Cook and drain squash cubes well. Add to pan, stir to warm, and taste for seasoning.

Pat scallops dry and season on both sides with salt, pepper, and blended seasonings. In another skillet, heat oil and sauté scallops until nicely browned and done through. Plate with sauce and serve immediately.

BESH'S CIOPPINO

Serves 6.

The following mélange shows its European and Creole roots in the exciting combination of herbs and seafood, reminiscent of a more sophisticated court-bouillon.

1 oz. extra-virgin olive oil
¹/₂ cup minced onion
2 bunches scallions, diced

1 green pepper, diced
4 oz. fennel, diced
4 cloves garlic, minced
4 lb. tomatoes, chopped (or 2 28-oz. cans diced tomatoes)
6 oz. dry white wine
1 bay leaf
½ tsp. salt
½ tsp. black peppercorns, crushed
12 clams
12 shrimp, peeled and deveined
2 lb. grouper or any white flaky fish
2 tbsp. fresh basil, chopped
2 sprigs thyme

Heat oil in a soup pot. Add onions, scallions, peppers, and fennel, Sauté until onions are translucent.

Add garlic and sauté until aroma is released. Add tomatoes, wine, and bay leaf. Cover pot and simmer about 45 minutes. Add small amount water, if necessary.

Add salt and pepper. Remove and discard bay leaf. Add whole clams. Simmer about 10 minutes.

Add shrimp and fish; simmer until fish is just cooked through. Add basil and thyme; adjust seasonings to taste. Ladle cioppino into heated bowls.

SHRIMP CASBARIAN

Serves 4.

This classic Creole shrimp dish—usually served over good lettuces and Creole tomato slices—opens a meal with gusto and, with enough to sauce, the sinuses too. Arnaud's remoulade sauce, a true family recipe, is available on grocery-store shelves.

1 lb. 24-count shrimp
½ tsp. sea salt
¼ tsp. cayenne pepper
1 tsp. blended seasonings
1 small head Boston or red-leaf lettuce
1 large or 2 medium ripe tomatoes, sliced

Remoulade sauce to taste
Lemon or lime wedges

Bring enough water to cover shrimp to a boil. Add shrimp and seasonings. Stir and boil about 5 minutes, until shrimp are just nicely cooked through. Do not overcook. Drain; cool under some running water until comfortable to handle. Peel and devein.

Wash lettuce leaves and pat dry. Remove stems and heavy ribs. Place layer of lettuce on 4 plates. Arrange shrimp on lettuce. Top each plate with tomato slice and large dollop sauce (not *too* much, to keep calories lower). Garnish plates with lemon or lime.

MEATS AND OTHER PROTEINS

Some ranchers and farmers don't use antibiotics or hormones for their food animals, and they raise them in a free-range habitat. We hope this practice is a trend. For example, according to a recent article, the fast-casual Restaurant Chipotle, in Manhattan, uses free-range pork: "Fresh tortillas are heated on a griddle, then piled with fillings like rice flecked with fresh cilantro, naturally raised Niman Ranch pork and organic beans" (Amander Hesser, "The Way We Eat: Tex Macs," *New York Times,* Feb. 27, 2005). Perhaps ironically, McDonald's is a majority investor in Chipotle's. Is free-range protein in our future?

Perhaps. Yet most of us still have to hunt down stores that sell meat from free-range chickens, turkeys, cows, and pigs. Many health-food stores and some environmentally conscious chains like Trader Joe's (in twenty states) do offer free-range animal protein (visit our Web site for additional information). These are worth seeking out. By inquiring in our local stores, we can minimize our risk of bad protein baggage. Wild game, like venison and duck, is a good source of low-fat protein. American buffalo (now home again on a limited amount of the range) provide meat with very low fat protein, as do ostrich.

If we can't find free-range animal protein, however, we should nevertheless eat protein—from varied sources and in moderate amounts. Chickens and turkeys, because of their briefer life spans, are exposed to hormones and antibiotics for a shorter time. Beef and pork, well selected and correctly trimmed in the New Orleans Creole tradition, are still excellent sources of protein. Creole housewives have always bought the best cuts of beef and pork they could afford and had them completely trimmed of fat.

FRENCH QUARTER SKILLET CHICKEN

Extra-virgin olive oil or good vegetable oil
2 medium frying chickens, halved and patted dry
3 cloves garlic, crushed
3 tbsp. butter (optional)
1 bunch fresh asparagus, trimmed to small tender spears
8 oz. very fresh button mushrooms
1-2 oz. small shiitake mushrooms, stemmed and caps halved
Sea salt to taste
White pepper to taste
Cayenne pepper to taste
Paprika (not hot) to taste
½ tsp. oregano (fresh if available)
1 tsp. basil (fresh if available)
½ cup chicken stock
2-3 oz. snow peas or young sugar snap peas, destringed
1 bunch green onion tops, sliced

Place oil in frying pan and heat over high heat. When hot, add chicken and garlic. Turn frequently to brown nicely on all sides. If garlic looks as if it is burning, take out. Remove chicken from pan.

Reduce heat to medium. Add butter, asparagus, and mushrooms. Stir frequently and cook 5-6 minutes.

Return chicken to pan and stir. Sprinkle seasonings over chicken and cook, turning, about 5-6 minutes. Add stock, peas, and green onions. Cook, stirring, until chicken is fork tender. Do not overcook vegetables. Adjust salt and pepper to taste.

PROTEIN: NOTES FROM CHEF BESH

Easter brings the breaking of the Lenten fast, along with the craving for and abundance of meats. In a culinary sense, Easter is that time that we break away from the dull foods of winter and enjoy life, vibrancy, spring, and foods perfumed by fresh herbs and sweet peas and crunchy fava beans and maybe a new artichoke and things of that nature. I look at spring as an exciting time to put the winter behind us. In my house on Easter I love nothing more than to whole roast a lamb or a baby goat, or enjoy some grilled racks of American lamb, maybe with some grilled pork chops served with fava-bean and artichoke salad, or fresh baby greens tossed with a heady dried-cherry vinaigrette. Sometimes I add baby beets and a few pieces of bleu cheese and pecans. It's a time of excitement in food and excitement about life that I really enjoy.

I'm very careful about where our beef comes from, where the lamb comes from and how is it raised. I like to look for American lamb. At all of our restaurants we use only American lamb. These days we focus on the small farmers and the artisan producers of lamb—and beef and poultry—because it does matter what an animal eats. A smaller producer is more apt to focus on the individual animal and its diet. We look for animals that have not been confined to small cages but have been allowed to range more freely, with less stress. With pork production, there's an effort to allow the animals to live in a much more natural environment. (I hate to use the term "free-range" because the animals aren't actually free-ranging.)

I have a steakhouse where we focus mainly on hormone-free and antibiotic-free meats. It's important to really highlight the smaller artisan producers that raise their animals for the flavor and not just for the buck. Often this extra step, and the extra time, is more expensive and is passed on to the consumer. But it's money well spent, I think.

It's good to buy a chicken that really tastes like a chicken. These animals aren't raised to be taken to the slaughter in record time. As a chef and a father, I need to know that I'm feeding people what is good for them. This is especially true with chicken. With some kids being raised on chicken nuggets, it's really scary to think how polluted our chicken population is. Cage after cage after cage of these chickens eat nothing but little pellets full of hormones and everything else. By contrast, my friends Jim and Gladys Koor in Folsom, Louisiana raise chickens in a wide-open pen, eating everything from corn that's tossed to them to cabbage to crickets. When you have an egg from one of these chickens, it tastes like an egg. It has a bright yellow yolk, almost orange, that looks and tastes beautiful. The chicken itself is yellow. The skin is yellow. The bones are very strong. These are healthy birds that we're eating, not sickly birds pumped up on every sort of chemical known to mankind. We'd like to control what we are putting in our bodies and not leave it up to fate.

Thanks in a large part to our growing Muslim and Latin American populations, we also have a number of locally raised goats. We have more of a demand now for cabrito, the meat of a young goat.

VEGETABLE PROTEIN

Some people choose to avoid animal-derived proteins entirely. High-school girls, in particular, often become vegetarians for a while. My older daughter has been on a vegetarian regimen for several years—she eats fin fish as well, but not shellfish, since she has a mild allergy. To help vegetarians obtain all the amino acids they need for good health, plant genetic engineers and hybridization specialists are working to improve the amino-acid content of popular vegetables, beans, and roots. Information about amino-acid "coverage" is easy to find. If, for example, we eat corn, deficient in the essential amino acid lysine, we should eat it together with certain beans, peas, or root vegetables. Canadian dietitians published an article in a recent issue of the *Journal of the American Medical Association,* concluding that "well planned" vegan and vegetarian eating can sustain infants, children, adolescents, and pregnant women. Whether older individuals do as well remains unclear. The key to success, especially in pregnancy, is in the choice of building-block amino-acid sources.

Planting season begins here in the Delta much earlier than in other parts of the country. When we see fresh beans and peas at our farmers' market, it's a sure sign that our spring harvest has begun. It's best not to overcook beans, as often happens in the Southern country-style "mushy" tradition. Contemporary Creole cuisine offers firmly textured cassoulets, with a bountiful variety of beans.

Chef Besh utilizes fresh free-range chicken in the recipe below to enhance the flavor of a simple but delicious and novel vegetable complement.

GRILLED CHICKEN WITH CELERY-LEAF SALAD
Serves 6.

2 cups yellow celery leaves
2 tbsp. Pepper-Jelly Vinaigrette

Lightly toss ingredients together.

Pepper-Jelly Vinaigrette
2 red bell peppers, minced
1 cup pepper jelly
½ cup red-wine vinegar
1 tsp. sambal chili paste
¼ cup sugar
½ cup water

Heat all vinaigrette ingredients together until dissolved. Add salt and black pepper to taste, then cool.

Celery-Root Puree
¾ lb. celery root, cut in large dice
¼ lb. potato, cut in large dice
1 onion, thinly sliced
2 cloves garlic, halved
Salt to taste
¼ cup 2 percent milk, hot

Combine vegetables in large pot and fill with water to cover by 2 inches. Salt water appropriately and simmer about 45 minutes or until vegetables are fully cooked but not waterlogged. Drain well and, while still very hot, puree in food processor with hot milk. Season with salt. It should be almost as stiff as mashed potatoes.

Grilled Chicken
¼ cup sea or kosher salt
½ gal. water
6 boneless, skinless chicken breasts
Salt and black pepper to taste

Dissolve the salt in the water. Brine chicken in this mixture overnight at least 12 hours but no more than 24 hours. Remove from brine and pat dry with paper towels. Season with pepper and small amount salt. Grill about 10 minutes until no pink remains in center. To assemble, place chicken over salad, and dollop puree decoratively around plate.

Not All Salts Are Created Equal (in Taste or Nutritional Value)

The common salts are:

- Ordinary table salt (plain old sodium chloride)
- Iodized table salt (iodine was one of the first nutritional additives to be widely used; prevents enlargement of the thyroid—goiter—in areas with iodine-deficient water, soil)
- Sea salt, ordinary (may not provide iodine)
- Kosher salt (coarse sea salt, usually with iodine and other trace minerals, not to be confused with rock salt, which is used on highways in icy climates)
- Sea salt, Fleur de Sel (top crust of the first crystallization in the sea-water evaporation tray)
- Exotic salts, from Red Hawaiian to Pink Spanish, Celtic gray, and others

Everyone knows that too much salt intake is a potentially serious health risk. But we all need some sodium daily to stay healthy. You can reduce your use of salt by keeping it off the table and following our recipes and New Orleans Program recommendations. Sea and other less usual salts often, due to their trace micronutrient content, can impart a saltier taste with less quantity. (See "Resources" chapter for a source of information on specialty salts.)

Brining is an ancient food-preservation technique brought to Southern Louisiana from Europe. In making kim chee or sauerkraut, brining kills off the bad spoilage bacteria but keeps the good fermentation bacteria. It is also used as a food treatment—for example, to reduce the gaminess of wild duck. It results in tenderness and juiciness in fowl, helping you to avoid a dry turkey on holidays.

Brine usually contains a 10 percent solution of kosher or other coarse salt. A somewhat weaker brine is acceptable. For a strong brine, mix 1 gal. water and 1½ cups salt or 1 qt. water and 6 tbsp. salt. A 10 percent brine will float a small to medium egg.

THE SAINTS IN TRAINING: A PROTEIN FEAST

On a sunny Tuesday before Thanksgiving, Dean Pigeon's voice came over the phone: "You'd better be here by 11:30 or you'll miss it!" As executive caterer to the New Orleans Saints, Dean was chaperoning my visit for lunch with the team.

The Saints' top-of-the-line training facility lies beside Airline Highway, the old access road to Louis Armstrong International Airport. Their dining hall is a well-lighted room in black and white linoleum tile, with flexible chairs and a mix of table sizes. Dean had arranged the food pickup area in a *U* shape. There was a table d'hôte of prepared-to-order ravioli, stuffed with spinach or Italian sausage sautéed in extra-virgin olive oil and topped with marinara, pesto, or garlic-olive sauce. Parmesan cheese completed this dish. The salad bar offered high-quality lettuces and toppings like sunflower seeds, bean sprouts, tomatoes, bell peppers, tuna salad, white-meat chicken salad, and egg salad.

Hot main courses included lasagna, spaghetti with meatballs, and burgers—all made with ground turkey breast. Chicken breasts sautéed in a light gravy, several other pastas, and low-fat hot dogs filled the thirty-foot main table. There were a few choices of dessert.

I was impressed. This was not my preconceived notion of how football players eat. I was expecting huge fatty steaks and baked potatoes. Instead, there was an amazing variety of high-quality, lean protein. In our interview, Dean told me that in addition to fish, he prefers chicken and turkey over beef, for animal protein. For tacos, he'll use ground turkey. Beef at the evening meal is restricted to training camp. During the football season, if he uses beef, it will be a lunch dish with leaner beef—such as his homemade vegetable beef soup with filet mignon tips.

Dean also cooks without heavy creams and butters in his sauces. And he doesn't give the players fried chicken. Instead, he uses such good fats as extra-virgin olive oil, and he limits these.

I use olive oil and just limit it. We use a lot of [cooking] spray, just to wet the pan when we're doing eggs. We don't put butter in the pan to cook the eggs. . . . Over here, that's a full omelet bar with your [egg substitute] and the egg whites. That's [coach] Jim Haslett . . . he has an egg-white omelet without fail.

Of course, these players are not eating a low-carb menu. As Dean says, "They need their carbs." They have turkey sausage for breakfast, but they also are offered grits, oatmeal, and hash browns, as well as pork bacon: "They need their bacon." These players are not eating to lose weight. Yet most of them, in their practice gear, appeared trim. Many of them, I noticed, took one large helping and did not return for seconds. Here is Dean's observation of the lunch routine.

It's crazy, their schedule. [The coach] brings them out on the field at 1:00 so they eat at 12:00 and at 1:15 they have practice. They really watch what they eat. They rarely grab a lot of food. It's not a ton. Most of them get up with half of it on the plate because they know in an hour they're going to be running all over the place.

Everyone at lunch had apparently heard Dean's warnings to be prompt. The players descended before noon, and by 12:20 "it was all over" for attacking the food lines. Players took time to eat and chew their lunches before the 1:00 wrap-up. Coaches and front-office managers ate with the team. When I asked Dean what the coach eats for lunch, his answer evolved into a full picture of the Saints' eating habits—lean and high-quality protein, excellent variety, and choices free of excess fat.

He'll eat plain pasta. He likes spaghetti with the turkey, or shrimp; he loves jambalaya and that's about it. He loves the turkey burgers. I don't know if you've ever had one but it's all white meat. No dark meat, all white turkey meat on. . . . They're absolutely delicious. We put a little Lea and Perrins, garlic; I love them. . . . Your hamburgers, the turkey burgers, that's there every day. . . . [At the sauté station,] we started with some crab cakes. . . .

Dinner that night we had a carving station; we started off with tenderloin. We have one of those rotisserie smokers on wheels. One day we did a tenderloin on the smoker. You can cut it with a plastic knife; it just melts in your mouth. Then we have a pasta bar, so we have a carving station there. . . . It's an incredible amount of food. . . . We have garlic mashed potatoes, baked potatoes, whole sweet potatoes, asparagus with a tarragon cream but we basically do asparagus with a little lemon on it. There's no cream or butter on the asparagus, just a touch of oil.

During training camp, we have a huge table set up with the desserts, the cheesecakes, but with that we have the yogurt machines and we have the cookies that this lady makes that are all natural that they really like. . . . Fresh fish, lots of fresh fish, especially during training camp. We sauté it in light olive oil. We don't fry it, just lightly flour and sauté. That's how we do the fish. We had a lobster night. . . . You're in the middle of training camp, change of pace. . . . You have to do it. They get tired of looking at me and I get tired of looking at them so you bring in [a particular caterer] and we just stand back. . . . We still had to have our staples for people who don't like lobsters.

None of us could match a football player for food intake, nor should we. Calories do count! But Dean Pigeon's protein choices are exceptional. We'd do well to imitate him in that department.

Chef Besh gives us his take on what I know from experience is a tasty main dish. (Watch the portions!)

SPAGHETTI WITH TURKEY MEATBALLS
Serves 4.

For most home cooks today, some things are just more trouble than they are worth. Making homemade pasta falls into this category. Many brands of "fresh" pasta are available, which will do nicely.

1 lb. ground turkey
½ cup breadcrumbs, seasoned or plain
¼ cup minced sweet yellow onion
1 large egg or 2 egg whites
Sea salt to taste
White pepper to taste
Dash cayenne pepper
½ tsp. oregano
Extra-virgin olive oil

Combine all ingredients in bowl except oil. Form meatballs about 1 inch in diameter. Coat bottom of skillet with oil. Sauté balls over medium-high heat until nicely browned all over. Place on paper towel; reserve.

Sauce
¼ cup minced sweet yellow onion

¼ **cup minced green bell pepper**
¼ **cup minced red or yellow bell pepper**
¼ **cup minced celery**
1 **clove garlic, minced**
2 **tbsp. extra-virgin olive oil**
10 **oz. low-sodium tomato sauce***
½ **tsp. oregano**
½ **tsp. basil**
1 **tsp. Creole spice or blended seasonings**
Sea salt and black pepper to taste

Sauté onion, peppers, celery, and garlic in oil until onion is just clear (4-6 minutes). Add tomato sauce, stir, and simmer 3-4 minutes. Add oregano, basil, and Creole spice or blended seasonings. Stir well. Add salt and pepper by dashes, stirring, until to taste. Keep sauce on simmer. Add meatballs.

*You can make a different sauce by substituting 4 large ripe tomatoes, cored and seeded, cooked in their own juices until mushy. You will need to add a little more salt at the end, but with fresh tomatoes the taste is subtler and the sauce lower in sodium.

Spaghetti
1 **lb. fresh or dried spaghetti**
1 **tbsp. sea salt**
3 **tbsp. extra-virgin olive oil**
1 **tbsp. unsalted butter**

Boil spaghetti in water with salt and oil until al dente. This degree of cooking not only tastes best; it lowers the innate glycemic index of the pasta. Drain in colander and add butter to prevent sticking (you can use oil if you wish). Serve immediately, topped with meatball sauce.

QUICK TURKEY CHILI, NEW ORLEANS PROGRAM STYLE
Serves 6.

Chili, done correctly (every chili cook has his or her own personal definition of "correctly," namely their recipe), may be one of nature's nearly perfect foods. Our easy, savory mix uses ground turkey and is lower in fat and sodium than many preparations. You can make it with lean chili beef if you wish. But no, you cannot make a smaller amount. Chili does not work that way. Also, we recommend *never* using the garlic in oil that is commercially available.

Extra-virgin olive oil
2 sweet yellow onions, chopped
2½ lb. ground turkey
3 garlic cloves, minced, or 4 tsp. garlic powder
3 tbsp. mild chili powder
3-4 tbsp. hot chili powder
3 tsp. cumin
2 tsp. oregano
2 tsp. marjoram
1 tsp. paprika
1 tsp. salt-free Creole spice
1 tsp. sea salt or to taste
7-9 oz. commercial chili sauce
2 tbsp. masa harina (optional)

Coat bottom of skillet with oil. Sauté onions until clear (about 5-6 minutes). Add turkey, stir thoroughly, and sauté until nicely browned.

Add garlic, stir to cook 1-2 minutes, then add all other ingredients except sauce and masa. Cook 4-6 minutes, stirring. Stir in sauce, adjust seasonings, and simmer 45 minutes-1 hour.

Chili should be rather thick. A teaspoon should be able to stand in it at least briefly. If after 40 minutes of simmering the chili seems too thin, add masa, stir well 5 minutes, then adjust thickness with water added in small amounts, stirring.

CHAPTER 6

French Quarter Festival:
Rolling on the River

Like our renowned food and drink, the city of New Orleans has a layered history. In 1682, the Robert Cavelier, Sieur de La Salle and his companion explorers rounded a bend in the Mississippi River and saw a small area of high ground, used by local Native Americans as a trading spot. Nearly forty years later, Jean Baptiste Le Moyne, Sieur de Bienville, returned to this same area and claimed it for King Louis of France. This place would become the city of New Orleans.

New Orleans, encased in swamps and bayous, was six feet above sea level at its highest. French entrepreneurs used the day's most advanced civil engineering to drain and fill an area of six by thirteen city blocks. Levees held back the river. Fortifications protected the other three sides of the city. The city's main grid anchored on the central square, the Place d'Armes, which belonged to the occupying military forces. A Roman Catholic church of timbers and brick faced the square, completing the scene.

Over eight hundred of the city's structures, which were made of wood, burned in the Great Fire of 1788. Because the fire flared on Good Friday, the cathedral staff refused to use the church bells as an alarm. A few structures survived. The Old Ursuline Convent, the oldest recorded edifice in the Mississippi Valley, is a simple but beautiful French stucco building rebuilt in 1834. The building that would later become Lafitte's Blacksmith Shop is now a piano bar.

Both French and Spanish flags have flown over New Orleans. The Place d'Armes, renamed Jackson Square for Andrew Jackson after the 1815 Battle of New Orleans, survived the Great Fire and was first commercially developed by Don Andres Almonaster Rojas. His daughter, the Baroness Micaela de Pontalba, brought the first apartment buildings to the United States. She supervised the construction of these elegant apartments in the 1850s by climbing ladders in her crinolines, creating a sensation.

This original city of New Orleans is known as the French Quarter, and its history—with its repeated destruction by fire—can be seen in its architecture today. Dominating its streets are Creole cottages as well as Spanish and French colonial houses, whose deceptively plain stuccoed facades conceal the balconies and central courtyards behind them. Modest houses with gracefully tapered Ionic columns stand as examples of the Greek revival. Our streets have kept their original names. St. Louis Street honors Louis XIV, the French king when New Orleans was founded. The street names of Bourbon, Burgundy (we say, "bur-*gun*-dee"), Chartres (we say, "charters"), Conti (we say, "cont-eye"), Dumaine, and Toulouse honor the king's sons, sons-in-law, and other family ties. Streets with saints' names, like St. Ann, are designated to separate the streets named for sons and sons-in-law who were embroiled in feuding and "bad blood." Rue Barracks, on the downtown side of Jackson Square and the cathedral, marks the site of old military barracks.

As New Orleans spread along the crescent bend of the mighty Mississippi, with large plantations established on either side, the original city became known as the Vieux Carré, French for "Old Square." Its plan dates from 1722, yet not many years ago it was home to 12,000 residents. Today 4,000 people live there, but full-time residents are increasing these days after years of decline. Nearly three hundred years since it was founded, the French Quarter, or Vieux Carré, has survived nearly everything—fires, hurricanes, floods, yellow-fever epidemics, and wars. Preservationists in the 1960s, in a struggle now celebrated as the Second Battle of New Orleans, fought successfully to keep the French Quarter from being buried under an elevated expressway.

The French Quarter escaped the great flood in 1878. Due to its elevation, it also escaped the flood after Hurricane Katrina. Except for the "new" strip of high land the military created in the 1930s out of Lake Pontchartrain swampland, the map of dry New Orleans after the 2005 flooding looks surprisingly similar to 1878 maps of the city.

Diversity rules in the Vieux Carré. Artists love to work there. Haunted houses and legends abound. Gabriel Garcia Marquez dubbed it "the northernmost Caribbean island," for amidst the French and Spanish colonial architecture and the hidden courtyard gardens of bananas and jasmine, there is a sensibility that is distinctly "other." Joshua Clark, editor of *French Quarter Fiction: The Newest Stories of America's Oldest Bohemia,* says it is "arguably the oldest neighborhood in the United States that has kept a true sense of its history and original culture and is as well the oldest bohemian village." According to this rising literary star and true New Orleans bon vivant, "We still have stories to tell the world."

When I first moved to New Orleans and lived on Bourbon Street in the lower French Quarter, I got to know the people there as friends and neighbors in a tight-knit community. This community readily stretches out its hand to newcomers and provides a living environment where with a little walking one can buy groceries, make friends, eat at great restaurants, attend plays, and enjoy life in general. There is also enough room to escape Mardi Gras, the biggest free party on earth, if that's what you choose. Here everyone is free to choose.

French Quarter inhabitants are uncommonly long-lived. Residents thrive in its atmosphere, walking rather than driving to do their errands, and participating actively in neighborhood events. Recent studies have linked sedentary lifestyles and disease to suburban living. One big temptation of suburban life, to drive everywhere and get little exercise, is easily avoided in the French Quarter.

Each April, the French Quarter Festival attracts tourists and locals. It is a four-day food and music party over a long weekend, celebrating the birth of jazz and the area's famous restaurants. Six bandstands showcase local music along the river, on Royal and Bourbon streets, and in Jackson Square. Several dozen booths provide New Orleans-style refreshments, and most items are cooked on the spot. Delicacies include crawfish pies, crawfish ravioli, alligator sausage, shrimp étouffée, barbecued shrimp, flash-grilled catfish, and traditional French Quarter restaurant pot roast. Here Chef Besh offers several delicious dishes that reflect the spirit of this springtime Vieux Carré celebration.

BLACKENED CATFISH SALAD WITH LAVENDER HONEY VINAIGRETTE

Serves 6.

6 4-oz. catfish filets
½ cup canola oil
Salt and black pepper to taste
¼ cup Creole spice
2 heads frisee lettuce, cleaned and picked apart
Lavender Honey Vinaigrette (see below)

Heat a large iron skillet over high heat. Coat catfish with a little oil. Season with salt and cover with spice. Fish should be completely coated and spice should appear wet.

Add thin layer oil to skillet. Sear fish on each side until spice becomes black but not yet burned. Remove from skillet.

Lavender Honey Vinaigrette
¼ cup rice-wine vinegar
¼ cup Provençal lavender honey
½ cup canola oil
½ cup extra-virgin olive oil
1 shallot or green onion bulb, minced
½ tsp. minced lavender

Mix vinaigrette ingredients. Toss lettuce with enough vinaigrette to coat nicely but not overwet. Season with salt and pepper if necessary. Place piece of fish in center of each plate and cover with tumbleweed of lettuce. Finish each plate with drizzle of vinaigrette. Remaining vinaigrette will keep refrigerated for one week.

GRILLED REDFISH AND GRILLED CORN VINAIGRETTE
Serves 6.

The summer and the grill go together. For quick, easy, low-fat, flavorful cooking, a grill is the best piece of cooking equipment to own. Any bass or drum fish may be substituted for the redfish in this recipe.

Nonstick vegetable cooking spray
6 6-oz. redfish filets
Salt and black pepper to taste
2 cups Grilled Corn Vinaigrette

Heat grill and spray with nonstick spray. Season fish with salt and pepper. Lay fish diagonally on grill. Leave alone 2 minutes; this is important in order to get beautiful grill marks and not tear fish.

Turn fish 90 degrees and let cook 3-4 more minutes. Flip fish over, cooking to medium doneness (about 4 more minutes). Place spoonful of vinaigrette in center of each plate. Place fish on top. Spoon remaining vinaigrette around.

Grilled Corn Vinaigrette
1 cup kernels cut from grilled corn

¼ **cup rice-wine vinegar**
1 cup extra-virgin olive oil
1 tbsp. chopped chive
1 tsp. lemon juice

Whisk ingredients together in bowl.

JIM CORE'S HEIRLOOM TOMATO SALAD
Serves 6.

Jim Core, a farmer north of Lake Pontchartrain, has one of the largest collections of heirloom tomatoes in the country. He is a regular vendor at area farmers' markets.

6-8 different heirloom tomatoes from Jim Core
Salt and black pepper to taste
1 cup shredded basil
¼ **cup red-wine vinegar**
1 cup extra-virgin olive oil
Balsamic vinegar
1 cup shaved Parmesan cheese

Slice tomatoes about ½ inch thick. Lightly season. Sprinkle with basil.

Combine red-wine vinegar and oil and add tomatoes to marinate 1 hour or so refrigerated. To serve, arrange tomatoes nicely in large bowl or on 6 plates. Sprinkle with balsamic vinegar and Parmesan.

LOW-FAT RED BEANS AND RICE
Serves 6.

2 tbsp. extra-virgin olive oil
1 cup small-diced onion
½ **cup small-diced celery**
½ **cup diced red bell pepper**
½ **cup diced green bell pepper**
Salt and black pepper to taste
Creole spice to taste

2 cups red kidney beans
2 qt. smoked turkey-neck stock
2 cups raw Louisiana jasmine rice
4 cups water

Heat oil and sauté onion, then celery, then peppers, until they get nice and caramelized. Season with pinch salt, pepper, and spice. Add beans and sauté 5 minutes.

Add stock. Simmer 2 hours or until beans are nice and soft. Season with more salt and spice to taste.

In separate pot, cover rice with water. Add pinch salt. Bring to a boil, cover, and simmer on lowest heat 20 minutes. Let sit covered 10 more minutes before fluffing with fork. Serve rice with beans on top.

For creamier beans, remove 1 cup beans and puree in a food processor until smooth. Add back to pot.

GREAT VEGETABLES: SOIL OR GENETICS?

The French Quarter Festival, like all such festivals, is a free party open to the public. A delightful array of musical performers might include the Olympia Brass Band, Dwayne Doopsie and the Zydeco Hellraisers, Lucien Barbarin and His Traditional Jazz Band, Ronnie Magri's Shim Sham Review Band, The Hackberry Ramblers, Steve Riley and the Mamou Playboys, the Pfister Sisters, Ya Ya Sol, Jimmy LaRocca's Original Dixieland Jazz Band, and the Red Hot Blues Mamas. Laced among these entertainments are special events for children, and on Festival Sunday, over fifty restaurants host "The World's Largest Jazz Brunch."

In April, we celebrate not just the music, dancing, and freestyle enjoyment of the French Quarter. We celebrate the parade of fresh local produce.

As usual, Mother was right: "Eat your vegetables." Vegetables in New Orleans taste good enough even for children to eat. Our lettuces, for example, stay crisp in the refrigerator drawer. They are fresh, flavorful, organically grown, and nutritious. Since January and February weather here can be as warm as eighty degrees, lettuce can appear in early spring at the farmers' markets.

Headlines across the country decry soil depletion from intensive farming techniques. Our local lettuce farmers, like the producers of our Creole tomatoes, are convinced that the alluvial soil of

Plaquemines and surrounding parishes gives their lettuces exceptional taste. This may be another Foodie Myth, albeit an attractive and nostalgic one. In fact, with modern agricultural techniques, our vegetables are routinely given all the nutrients and soil tending they need. What is not being replaced in soil is micronutrients. This depletion is *not* a Foodie Myth. It supports the use of vitamin-mineral diet supplements.

Once a rootlet has internalized a phosphate molecule, for example, the plant cannot tell whether it came from native soil or fertilizer. What is more worrisome is the application of hormones and other chemicals to boost production. The absence of these chemicals is what distinguishes farmers' markets, community-based agriculture, and certified organic produce.

The differences seem to be in the genetic makeup of the particular vegetable. Not all lettuces are created equal. All have vitamins and minerals, and all have some fiber, yet some lettuces provide better taste and nutrition than others. Which lettuces should we choose? It's a matter of taste. The only lettuce I avoid is iceberg, a variety selected for its growth rate and shipping hardiness. It's all crunch, with little taste or nutritional value.

The following nutritional profile of lettuce is per 3½ oz. raw (100 g).

	Calories	Fat (g)	Carbs (g)	Protein (g)	Calcium (mg)	Vit. C (mg)	Vit. E (mg, alpha-tocopherol)	Beta Carotene (mg)
Boston	13	0	2	1.3	35	8	0.5	0.6
Iceberg	13	0	2	1	19	4	0.3	0.2
Loose-leaf	18	0.35	3.5	1.4	68	18	0.4	1
Romaine	16	0	2	2	68	24	0.4	2
Arugula (½ cup)	3	0.1	0.4	0.3	16	2	0	24
Chicory (½ cup chopped)	21	0.3	4.2	1.5	90	22	0	260
Watercress (½ cup chopped)	2	0	0.2	0.4	20	7	0.17	80
Mache	21	0	0	0	38	38	0	4

SALAD DRESSING: NOTES FROM CHEF BESH

Whatever your choice of lettuce, I have some advice about salad dressing. Unless you are certain that the salad dressings you wish to enjoy at a restaurant are homemade, use extra-virgin olive oil and vinegar usually available on the table along with a small amount of salt and pepper to taste. This is far preferable to most of the bulk-prepared salad dressings used in many food establishments. These bulk preparations may not taste too bad but they are largely chemical based and not part of eating fresh and nutritionally sound ingredients. Using one of these nutritionally negative dressings may be the only way that an otherwise terrific salad could fail to be part of the New Orleans Program.

We present here low-fat dressings to accompany some of the salads that you can have prior to eating other dishes without filling up. Or you can use salad after other courses to refresh your taste buds. My dressings blend different flavors to offset the acidity of some vinegars. We use good vinegars.

I say "good vinegars" because nowadays we have so much more available to us. We have wonderful balsamic vinegars from Italy. We have some great American wine vinegars produced from famous vineyards in California. We have cider vinegars that are really great. Vinegar can have an acidity of 10 percent to as low as 4 percent. The lower the acidity, the lower the amount of fat you need to add to make tasty salad dressings.

We offer a nonfat salad dressing that includes orange juice. This way, you get the same effect of full-fat vinaigrette but with half the calories and none of the fat.

SALAD OF ORGANIC GREENS, CANE-SYRUP VINAIGRETTE, AND SPICED NUTS

Serves 6.

1 oz. canola oil
2 tsp. Creole spice
1 tsp. sugar
1 tsp. brown sugar
1 tsp. salt
2 cups pecans
Organic greens
Cane-Syrup Vinaigrette

Heat oil and whisk in seasonings. Toss in nuts. Lay out on baking sheet and toast 10-15 minutes in oven at 350 degrees. Toss greens with vinaigrette. Sprinkle with nuts.

Cane-Syrup Vinaigrette
1 cup rice-wine vinegar
2½ cups canola oil
½ cup Steen's cane syrup
1 tbsp. sea salt

Whisk together. Toss greens with just enough vinaigrette to coat nicely. Remember the cardinal rule: Do not put so much dressing on salad that it drips off the greens. Just enough dressing allows the flavors of all ingredients to shine and keeps calories down. Remaining vinaigrette will keep refrigerated for one week.

SPICY SPINACH SALAD DRESSING

Serves 4.

3 tbsp. red-wine vinegar
1 tbsp. extra-virgin olive oil
5 tbsp. good vegetable oil (not canola)
1 tsp. fresh lemon juice
1 tsp. dark brown sugar
⅓ tsp. paprika (not hot)
⅛-¼ tsp. cayenne pepper
⅓ tsp. dry mustard
¾ tsp. garlic powder
⅓ tsp. sea salt
⅓ tsp. black pepper

Mix dressing ingredients together with fork in cup or bowl. Dress spinach just before serving. Do not use too much dressing! This dressing will keep 2-3 days refrigerated and is also good for coleslaw.

PARSLEY DRESSING

4 tbsp. good vegetable oil

2 tbsp. water
2 tbsp. cider vinegar
Leaves from 3-4 sprigs parsley (Italian flat leaf preferred)
Dash cayenne pepper
Dash white pepper
2 pinches blended seasonings

In a blender, combine ingredients on "mince" until smooth. Should be only moderately thick. Keeps overnight in refrigerator, but not longer.

CLASSIC OIL AND VINEGAR DRESSING
Serves 4.

3 tbsp. extra-virgin olive oil or good vegetable oil
1½ tbsp. cider or wine vinegar
2 pinches dry mustard
¼-½ tsp. sea salt
¼ tsp. white or black pepper

Whisk all ingredients together.

BALSAMIC VINEGAR AND OIL DRESSING
Serves 4.

3 tbsp. extra-virgin olive oil
1 tbsp. balsamic vinegar
¼ tsp. sea salt
¼ tsp. white pepper

Whisk all ingredients together.

NONFAT SALAD DRESSING
Yields 2 cups.

1 cup rice-wine vinegar
¼ cup orange juice

2 tbsp. soy sauce
2 tbsp. molasses
Pinch salt
$\frac{1}{2}$ tsp. smashed garlic
$\frac{1}{2}$ tsp. smashed ginger
$\frac{1}{2}$ tsp. smashed shallot

Whisk all ingredients together. Keeps up to 10 days in refrigerator.

GRILLED TOMATO VINAIGRETTE
Serves 6.

1 cup grilled, seeded, and peeled tomatoes
$\frac{1}{2}$ cup red-wine vinegar
$1\frac{1}{2}$ cups extra-virgin olive oil
2 tbsp. chopped shallot

Cut tomatoes in small dice. Whisk in vinegar. Add oil and shallot.

Fastest Salad in the World

So many fresh vegetables now come in convenient packages. Here are our shopping and preparation recommendations.

- Purchase *good-quality* salad greens, now available in salad-bowl-ready packages.
- In our experience, those in "tub" containers have better refrigerator life than those in plastic bags.
- Do not purchase if even one blackened leaf is visible.
- Even though most packaged greens need no washing, a little grit ruins a salad. We suggest a quick rinse anyway.

GENETIC MODIFICATION: RISKS AND BENEFITS

Today, genetic modification of vegetables and fruits is fairly easy. Scientists can chop up genetic material, or DNA, from a given plant by using chemicals or enzymes. Then they can select and remove certain desired genes—like the stay-red-longer gene in tomatoes—and insert those into the genes of the plant they are growing. Much of our high-fructose corn sweetener comes from corn modified genetically. Most Americans are not aware of how much genetically modified food we already have on our grocery shelves. And of course, farmers have practiced crossbreeding (genetic modification the old way) for tens of thousands of years—like Dr. Berenson, whom we met in chapter 3 trying to breed cows for protein with less harmful fat and greater tenderness.

Perhaps because it is so easy to do and so likely to become more widespread, genetic modification has its opponents. Among them are several environmentally conscious groups, such as the GAIA Foundation in London. The European Union Congress at first blocked the United States' initiative to export genetically modified crops. Then in early 2004, the EU was not persuaded when we argued that we'd certify these crops as harmless, by labeling them with the specific scientific technology used to produce them. Recently, under our lobbying efforts, the EU has somewhat relaxed its ban.

These opponents are not mere extremists, fearful of glow-in-the-dark "Frankenfood" tomatoes with lurking primate genes. They have genuine, justified concerns. Consider the following example. Recently our EPA approved a genetically modified corn plant that produces its own insecticide to kill rootworms. Since rootworms cost corn producers a billion dollars a year in pesticides and crop loss, this new corn plant should be good, right? Not entirely. Its self-produced insecticide is low intensity, giving generations of rootworms a greater chance to develop resistance to it. The long-term outlook is therefore risky, as with the low-level antibiotics in our meats that might give rise to resistant strains of bacteria. What is the solution, at least theoretically? We should grow ordinary corn plants next to genetically modified ones, alternating row by row. Regular rootworms will then breed with insecticide survivors and dilute the resistance gene. This could work. There have already been instances, in some areas, of genetically modified corn pollinating ordinary corn and passing on modified traits.

Proponents of genetic modification believe it to be a brand-new day for reducing agriculture costs and feeding the hungry. These proponents include Monsanto, a major producer of modified seeds, as well as the Bill and Melinda Gates Foundation, the Rockefeller Foundation, and experimental groups in Africa. They advocate high-salt, low-moisture-resistant crops in Africa, where famine is an everyday issue. Critics point out that simple genetic modification does nothing to address basic needs there, such as adequate roads, fertilizers, and machinery, which are essential to grow food and combat hunger.

Nevertheless, in certain settings, genetic modification seems both sensible and safe. Take for example East African highland bananas. They're propagated by cuttings, since bananas lack seeds. For that reason, it would be safe to modify them, because they can't spread on their own. Genetic modification for increased growth could benefit Uganda, where people rely on these bananas for their daily food and even for beer. Joseph Mukiibi, former director of Uganda's National Agricultural Research Organization, said recently that famine is unknown in Uganda "to a great extent because of bananas."

Perhaps someday genetic modification can even produce a lettuce with increased antioxidants and nutrients that surpasses our lettuce in New Orleans.

If scientists want to carry genetic modification to absurd lengths, we suggest they not worry about making low-carb wine or a mild habanero pepper (real examples, the latter created by Texas A&M Agricultural Experiment Station researchers). We suggest they work on making green peas taste like French fries.

"ORGANIC" FOODS AND PESTICIDES

Rachel Carson, author of the 1962 bestseller *Silent Spring*, must be smiling. Decades ago, she was the first to dramatize the environmental dangers of pesticides such as DDT. In late 2004, with noticeable growth in the "organic" food industry (see below), the USDA finally published strict guidelines to make the "organic" label signify low pesticide amounts. These USDA guidelines help prohibit not only pesticides but also hormones, antibiotics, irradiation, chemical fertilizer, organic sewer-sludge fertilizer, and genetically modified organisms in foods labeled "organic." (What *have* we been eating?) Consumers should be aware that there are different levels of "organic" (see label standards below).

Growth of the Organic Food Industry
(Source: Organic Trade Association)

- "Organic" product sales: $9.3 billion in 2001; $11 billion in 2002; $22 billion in 2005.
- "Organic" products have garnered shelf space in many conventional grocery stores, as well as "organic" stores and farmers' markets.
- Despite the increase, today "organics" have only about 3 percent of the market share.

USDA 2004 "Organic" Label Standards

Categories:
　　100 percent organic, completely produced *without:*
- Pesticides
- Antibiotics
- Hormones
- Chemical fertilizer
- Sewer-sludge (fecal) fertilizer
- Irradiation
- Genetic modification

and with:
- Sustainable farming practices
- Humane animal treatment
- Hand weeding or mulching

　　Organic: 95 percent or more "organic" ingredients
　　Made with organics: at least 70 percent "organic" but cannot be labeled simply "organic"
　　Some organic parts: "organic" parts can be identified, but product cannot use term "organic"

　　Note: The label "100% natural" does not mean "100% organic." Natural products may or may not have pesticides, antibiotics, or other harmful ingredients.

Organic goods still cost more. There is neither scientific data nor a common-sense guarantee that organic foods have better nutrition for improved health or longer life. Even junk food can be labeled "organic." Yet such nutritional "baggage" as pesticides and chemical fertilizer is certified to be lower in organic foods, and this assurance may be important for children.

J. I. Rodale originated the term "organic" and founded numerous publications, with *Prevention* magazine as the flagship. Wherever he is, he must also be pleased. In the early 1950s, Rodale was scorned by doctors, government agencies, and even Congress for claiming extravagant benefits from "organic" food. He may have overstated his case, but he opened the door for the growth of the organic food industry to its current and rising level. He exited this life dramatically by collapsing and dying on national television.

Pesticides are a subject of controversy. Are pesticide residues toxic to us, or not? The answer is still not known. Fortunately, our bodies can detoxify a certain amount of damaging material, so the definite toxicity of pesticides is hard to prove. Science cannot tell us how much pesticide is safe or unsafe. Such consumer groups as the Consumers Union and the Center for Science in the Public Interest have studied this question, and they've found that even "organic" foods have pesticide residues—from preexisting land contamination or nearby non-organic farms. A recent Consumers Union analysis of "organic" produce discovered pesticide residues in about 25 percent of the samples. At least this is lower than the pesticide residue found in 75 percent of ordinary fruits and vegetables at our grocery stores. Many specific items have scored high on this toxic index: peaches, apples, grapes, pears, spinach, squash, and green beans—especially green beans grown in the United States. The Consumers Union tells us that eleven of the twelve highest toxicity scores belong to foods grown in this country. Some apples had over thirty different toxic residues!

Tommy Thompson, former Secretary of Health and Human Services, said in late 2004 that our food supply was vulnerable to terrorist activities, since nearly half our food is imported. Yet so far, imported foods actually have fewer pesticide residues and health-threatening contaminants, a statistically lower risk even though pesticides may be used illegally in other countries.

Children, who are still developing brain and functional connections into their teenage years, should be protected from pesticides. In 1996,

Congress passed a Food Quality Protection Act to protect children from hazardous residues like DDT. For adults, pesticide residues can interfere with tissue repair. Of course, consuming pesticides does us no good, and common sense would suggest we reduce them whenever possible.

Canned fruits and vegetables have lower pesticides traces, although green beans and squash are still our outstanding offenders. Fruit juices have residues much lower than the fruits themselves. When you use canned food, we suggest draining the liquid thoroughly and then rinsing the contents three times in water. This lowers not only the salt but the pesticide content. When you bring home fresh fruits and vegetables, here is what to do.

Easy Steps to Reduce Pesticide and Other Toxic "Baggage"

- Wash fruits and vegetables in a diluted detergent (½ capful or 1 small squirt unscented dishwashing detergent per gallon water). Rinse thoroughly in cold water.
- Peel apples, pears, peaches, melons, other fruits, and vegetables, especially celery (you'll want to "destring" them anyway).
- Choose a wide variety of fresh vegetables and fruits, as the New Orleans Program recommends.
- Emphasize vegetables (including such "technical" fruits as tomatoes) over fruits in your fresh, uncooked eating.
- Remember that a "quick boil" sacrifices few nutrients, makes vegetables more digestible (you get more nutrient "goodies"), and further washes off some toxic load.

The New Orleans Program emphasizes eating fresh vegetables, and some fruit, every day. Those with diabetes should watch the sugar content of such fruits as watermelon and pineapple.

Although grapes score poorly for toxic residues, they are delightful for table use when washed. For many, they suggest the pleasant thought of wine.

WINE AND OTHER ALCOHOLS

Wine has played a part in human history since the dawn of agriculture, ten thousand years ago. In the New Testament, when the host of the wedding party at Cana ran out of wine, Jesus of Nazareth changed water into wine so as to continue the feast. Guests marveled that the host had saved the best wine for last, instead of the usual custom of serving the best wine first. Perhaps people have always been able to tell which were the better wines.

We in New Orleans rank among the very highest per-capita wine consumers in the country. We are happy to say that wine, beer, and even distilled spirits are not prohibited in the New Orleans Program. Moderation is the key. We should remind ourselves that alcohol has calories, and that the newly popular "zero carb" cocktails made with diet drinks are by no means zero calorie. In fact, ethanol, the ingredient that gives us the pleasant effects of an alcoholic beverage, has a few more calories than carbohydrates. Alcohol calories are metabolized somewhat like carbohydrates, but more like fat. Too much ethanol, like too many calories in any form, will be stored as fat in your body.

Of course, we fully endorse warnings about driving when intoxicated, which can lead to serious or fatal accidents involving innocent people. We also recognize the dangers of disease from drinking to excess, and the prohibitions that must be followed in certain religions. On the other hand, we realize that kosher wine is important to Jewish festivals, and that priests at mass pray over the fruit of the vine before consecrating the ritual wine. Choosing to drink alcohol at all is a personal decision. We repeat: *moderation* is the key. A conservative study has found that one small glass of wine for a woman, and two for a man, is a safe daily amount for consumption.

Although alcohol doesn't give us nutrition, wine seems to have some health benefits, or good "baggage." Consumed properly, wine relaxes us and even provides some vitamins and minerals. Red wines contain phenols and other compounds that can contribute to cleaner arteries. The French have a reduced risk of heart attacks and other vascular problems. Is it because they frequently drink red wine? That's our theory. Red wine has also been suggested to reduce heart disease and even to help prevent colds.

Researchers at the University of Buffalo studied hundreds of people with varying alcohol consumption and discovered that white wine improves lung function. They don't yet know why, but their findings are statistically significant. We think it's safe to assume that white wine, although it has a bit more sugar than red wine, can confer overall health benefits. Skeptics may say that wine drinkers simply lead healthier lifestyles, but this observation doesn't hold water (or wine). We believe that moderate wine consumption itself is beneficial.

Wine Tips

- Actually, there are few tips needed for drinking wine. Drink the wine *you* enjoy with the food *you* enjoy.
- Some Meursaults (white) can stand up to steak. Some pinot noirs (red) work with spicy grilled fish. Inexpensive Muscadets (white, 2000 vintage) are never "cheap" on enjoyment.
- Champagne and white wine should be colder than reds: 50 degrees for whites (two hours in the refrigerator); 64 degrees for reds (thirty minutes in the refrigerator).
- Forget the stuff about letting a bottle of red wine breathe. Let the reds open in the glass, and follow with your nose and tongue.
- When sampling a wine at a restaurant, don't slurp. Look and smell. If the wine has the least brownish tinge or smells or tastes oxidized (called "corked" in the trade), send it back. The restaurant gets it replaced by the distributor in most cases. You are not penalizing the restaurant. And bad wine, even if just a little "off," upsets the stomach and spoils the taste and enjoyment of even the best food.

A French researcher recently answered this earth-shaking question: why does champagne bubble? The answer: dust. Who knew? It seems that champagne opened in hermetically sealed and dust-free rooms and poured into dust-free glasses just sat there, as still as any wine. We're lucky to live in less immaculate air, where we can enjoy our bubbles. In New Orleans, champagne often marks the critical passages in life—not only birth and marriage but also deaths, at wakes—so a little dust may suit the occasion. If we shake and open a champagne bottle all at once, as we've all seen done in locker rooms after the Super Bowl (alas, not with the New Orleans Saints), we maximize the bubbles. But if we open a champagne cork too quickly at home, we can "bruise" the champagne by stirring the effervescence prematurely.

A recent article in the *British Medical Journal* reveals that Ian Fleming was right. When spymaster James Bond ordered his martini "shaken, not stirred," he was increasing its life-protective, antioxidant content a thousand fold. This more vigorous method doesn't seem to have been adopted yet by Hollywood or Broadway, or Manhattan's East Side toffs. Yet since we now know how good antioxidants are for you, our advice is to lose the wimpy silver stirrer and go for the shaker instead.

In a classic well-chilled, thin-stemmed martini glass, traditional gin gives an authoritative medicinal bite. Some of the vodkas from eastern Europe are smoother and more pleasant. Many are "doctored" for the American market by adding "sweeteners" such as ethylene glycol. This includes "top shelf" brands such as our household preference, Belvedere.

WINE AND FOOD

The New Orleans Program promotes enjoying food. Wine can help! People have made careers from pairing wine with food, but we can summarize the elements for you right here.

"Secrets" of Wine Pairing

- Remember the five cardinal taste sensations: sweet, sour, salty, spicy, and bitter.
- In your mouth, because of how your tongue sensors work, these taste sensations play off of and influence each other.
- For example, a "sour" salad dressing counterbalances a drier Chardonnay, making the wine taste sweeter.
- Eating flavorful but not sweet red meat balances the tannin in a robust red wine, and the tannin rebounds nicely, producing a happy pairing and a fuller wine sensation. Some whites, especially Meursaults, pair nicely with red meat.
- Some champagnes can, as the Europeans discovered in the late 1700s, pair nicely with all courses.

With our local spicy foods, the delicate sweetness of a modern German Riesling connects nicely. German wines, underappreciated in the United States, have recently become more sophisticated, with less soda-pop sweetness. Caution: Many German wines are converting to screw caps, so don't bring out the corkscrew unless you're going for standup comedy.

The following soup from Chef Besh is a wonderful way to begin a summer dinner party. Perhaps try it with a glass of champagne.

SOUP OF LOCAL MELON AND CHAMPAGNE
Serves 10.

The idea of such a chilled soup came from a recent cooking trip to Provence, where I was asked to make a guest-chef appearance in late May at the famed Relais & Chateau hotel, Chateau de Montcaud. We journeyed to the small village of Bagnols just across the Rhone River from Chateauneuf-du-Pape and Betunes-de-Venise. Our host, a Mr. Baur, who owns the hotel, requested that I create a menu that would reflect the food of New Orleans while using ingredients from the Provençal larder. How wonderful it was to shop the vast outdoor markets of Avignon, Bagnols, and Orange for ideas and products from which I was to prepare a special menu. I finished my week of cooking at the chateau by presenting a large jazz brunch under shady trees. The French prize the small melons from the area around Cavillon, which are often served halved and doused with the sweet dessert wine of Betunes-de-Venise, for which the town is famous. Among the many items featured at my brunch was a chilled soup of these Cavillon melons and muscatel de Betunes-de-Venise. Upon returning to the States, I was able to reproduce such natural classics with our local products.

2 overripe cantaloupe melons
2 overripe honeydew melons
1 tsp. sea salt
2 oz. sugar
Juice of 1 lemon
½ bottle champagne
Crème fraiche
Mint sprigs

Peel, seed, and cut melons into 1-inch dice. Puree melons while slowly adding salt, sugar, and lemon juice. Strain through fine sieve. Combine with champagne. Chill 1 hour. Serve cold with spoonful of crème fraiche and some mint.

The New Orleans Wine and Food Experience is an annual indoor/outdoor festival. Dickie Unangst, a founding member, says this event was started in 1991 by three local businessmen to boost the New Orleans economy during our hot summers. The concept is to pair diverse New Orleans cuisine with wines from around the country. This festival has grown over the years into a five-day gala that spotlights several venues. We have the Vintner Dinners at our most prestigious restaurants; the Royal Street Stroll through hospitable antique shops in the French Quarter; the Grand Tastings at the Convention Center, where a hundred restaurants and wineries serve their favorite pairings; and the traditional New Orleans Jazz Brunch. Here is an example of the joyful and healthful atmosphere at the Grand Tastings, from a 2005 radio broadcast connected with this book.

David A. Newsome: I'm here at the Saturday afternoon Grand Tasting with Southern Louisiana chef Alex Patout and as I'm talking with him, he's stirring a fragrant pot of a medium-dark roux for "crawfish stew." I wish everybody could be here with me and get this aroma. That looks beautiful, Alex. What we're talking about in this book is that in New Orleans not only is eating a delight, but if our food is eaten in moderation, and is well-prepared, fresh stuff, it won't make you fat, but it will make you healthy and maybe even pretty.

Alex Patout: The thing about it is, I'm a chef by profession. I weigh 160 pounds and I don't diet. . . . I do some walking because I like to walk. . . . The point simply is that what we're blessed with is an abundance of fresh seafood— all protein oriented—and we have some great sauces that we make with butter and flour a little bit, but the point simply is that it's not about the carbohydrates, it's more about the protein: the speckled trout, the red snapper, the crawfish, the oysters, the crabmeat. You go right down the line: wild duck, fresh roasted pig. This is what we grew up eating. What people don't realize is also how big Louisiana is on fresh vegetables—snap beans, butter beans, black-eyed peas—all home grown, all out of the garden.

Alex Patout knows all about the New Orleans attitude towards cooking. We use local seafood and vegetables right out of the garden for our Wine and Food Experience, our French Quarter Festival, and our Grand Tastings. The result? Our celebrations are as fresh and tasty as you will find anywhere in the world.

CHAPTER 7

Jazz Fest: The Greatest Picnic on Earth

An appeaser is one who feeds a crocodile, hoping it will eat him last.
—Sir Winston Churchill

Jazz Fest! This annual seven-day celebration of music, food, and culture is a true extravaganza as only New Orleans can present it. Begun in 1970 as the New Orleans Jazz and Heritage Festival, it has long been one of our city's best-loved events. Conceived by George Wein and overseen by local maven Quint Davis, Jazz Fest provides late-spring magic both for locals and a growing international audience.

For many non-New Orleanians, the pilgrimage to Jazz Fest takes on a religious quality. The Pet de Kat Krewe, a group of Floridians who style themselves as a "loosely disorganized professional" band of aficionados of Louisiana music, spend much of the year counting down to Jazz Fest. One member, sporting a customized Pet de kat Krewe T-shirt, compared the experience of Jazz Fest to an annual rebaptism in Louisiana culture. Many of us locals go in sizeable groups. It's not unusual to see five or six couples who stay together in the ambling crowds by homing to a standard bearer with a tall, befeathered, bejeweled, or beribboned cane pole.

If Mardi Gras is the harbinger of spring in the Big Easy, Jazz Fest heralds our long, hot summer. It occupies the entire area of the Fair Grounds, a nineteenth-century racetrack once depicted by the French painter Edgar Degas, whose mother was a New Orleanian. The festival stretches across two weekends. The opening Thursday traditionally gets its own baptism from the skies. In 1995, a brief, intense storm pounded the Fair Grounds and toppled some sound-equipment towers, delaying the opening by several hours. The photographs of the collapsing towers have become a part of local pictorial lore, much like the photos of New Jersey's Hindenburg disaster. The weather always clears, though. Thousands of festgoers drift over the Fair Grounds property from stage to stage to hear over five hundred musical offerings, ranging from Rockin' Dopsie, Jr., and Zydeco Twisters to the Wild Magnolia Mardi Gras Indians, from Fats Domino to the Funky Meters, from Gladys Knight to Crosby, Stills & Nash, from the Zion Harmonizers to LL Cool J, from Nicholas Payton to the Neville Brothers.

The food offerings are as crucial as the music to the Jazz Fest experience. Each year festival officials carefully select only the best of the best to be represented among the seventy-odd vendors. Competition is fierce for the coveted slots. For example, there might be only two gumbos available: a delectable seafood gumbo and an amazing game gumbo of pheasant, quail, and andouille sausage. Each in its own way expresses the absolute heights of gumbo cuisine. One can only imagine how many gumbos the New Orleans Jazz & Heritage Festival and Foundation has from which to choose!

Jazz Fest Temptations

I recommend here some Jazz Fest temptations. Follow the New Orleans Program, but life's too short *not* to *laissez les bons temps rouler* sometimes!

Crawfish Monica: Perhaps the quintessential Jazz Fest dish; a Creole preparation of crawfish tails in a nicely seasoned creamy sauce mixed with *al dente* spiral pasta.

Crawfish Strudel: German immigrants helped build and run New Orleans. These flaky, crusty gems with a tasty filling speak well for that heritage.

Fresh-Shucked Oysters: Are dem de "salty" ones? Always good quality, from good sources. I "let 'em slide" with either a small dash of Crystal or Louisiana hot sauce, never lemon or the horseradish sauce. They, and the vinegary Tabasco, can overwhelm the delicate oyster essence.

Soft-shell Crab Po' Boy: Louisiana soft-shell crabs delicately, almost greaselessly fried, filling a crispy only-in-New Orleans po' boy loaf. "Dressed" or "naked," cher?

Cochon de Lait: Southern Louisiana crisp roasted suckling pig, sliced thin, nestled in pistolettes with a little jus: delicate, delicious.

Oyster-Artichoke Soup: A Creole combination guaranteed to delight.

Crawfish Zucchini Spinach Bisque: Another Creole combo with an authentic local flavor. Even spinach and zucchini haters would enjoy!

Meaty White Beans, Seasoned Local Style: No better way to get your fiber plus great texture and flavor!

Jama-Jama: Fresh spinach, cooked in a skillet just right. Great alone or with other dishes.

Fried Green Tomatoes: Light enough to write a book about. If you don't feel more local after eating these, check your pulse.

Natchitoches (say "Nack-uh-dush") Meat Pies: Always served hot, a moderately spicy (I always add some Crystal hot sauce) filling in a crispy crust. My personal favorite "guilty Fest food pleasure."

Barbecued Turkey Wings with Coleslaw: Sauced just enough to enjoy without getting it all over you and everyone else. The slaw, not overdressed, adds a great counterpoint.

There are also dishes like fried chicken, shrimp and okra, Caribbean fruit salad, Key lime pie, and dozens more. The www.nojazzfest.com Web site carries complete listings.

When I lived in the French Quarter and attended St. Anna's Church nearby, I was one of a group of parishioners who competed for a food-vendor slot at Jazz Fest. Some of us unearthed information showing that the pirate Jean Lafitte, a great ally of locals during the War of

1812, had once kept mistresses on grounds next to St. Anna's. Lafitte's main base of operations once occupied nearly a block in the lower Quarter. So our group wrote a history and applied to the foundation. We were excited to be chosen for the food auditions!

We created Spicy Roast Pork Jean Lafitte Style with Barataria Sauce on a multigrain bun. The Barataria Sauce, appropriately piquant, was named for the marshes where Lafitte and his pirate band lurked to surprise their prey along the Mississippi. On the appointed day, each team member appeared at the French Quarter church where the food auditions were being held—well, all but one member. That person failed to order the crispy round rolls that provided nuttiness and texture without being overly sweet. In emergency mode, we ran to the J. Alois Bender Bakery in the Faubourg Marigny and bought small white-bread French pistolettes. Our creation was good, but it didn't measure up. We got a "try again next year."

SPICY ROAST PORK JEAN LAFITTE STYLE
WITH BARATARIA SAUCE

Serves 4 to 6.

For the Barataria Sauce, sugar-cured, applewood, or corncob-smoked bacon is preferred, but any kind is OK. Microwaving it on paper towels until crisp renders most of the fat.

1 lb. boneless pork loin, nicely trimmed
2-3 satsumas or blood oranges (preferred by pirates, of course)
1 tsp. hot sauce
1 tbsp. garlic powder or 2 small garlic cloves
Sea salt and black pepper to taste
1 tbsp. oregano
Barataria Sauce

Preheat oven to 500 degrees. Wash loin in warm water; pat dry. Place into foil-lined roasting pan.

Squeeze satsuma or orange juice over loin. There should be enough juice to form a ring of liquid around loin. Pour hot sauce on loin and spread with fingers over surface, mixing with adherent citrus juice.

Sprinkle on garlic powder or press out fresh garlic and spread out on loin. Sprinkle on salt, pepper, and oregano. Cook 20 minutes.

Reduce heat to 200 degrees, and cook 1 more hour. Do not over-cook. Serve with Barataria Sauce. Refrigerated leftover roast makes great sandwiches (on multigrain buns) or additions to soups or salads.

Barataria Sauce
4 strips uncooked bacon
¹/₂ cup extra-virgin olive oil
1-2 tbsp. red-wine, cider, or rice vinegar
1 tsp. salt-free Creole spice
¹/₂ tsp. dry mustard
Salt and white pepper to taste

Place bacon between paper towels on a microwave-safe plate. Microwave bacon until crisp (about 5¹/₂ minutes on high, depending on microwave). Cool and crumble.

Combine ingredients in glass measuring cup. Warm in microwave just prior to serving with roast. A prepared sauce, such as Arnaud's Remoulade Sauce, also complements this roast.

Of course, we New Orleanians are thrilled by the diverse musical talents appearing every year at Jazz Fest. Yet more often than not, when we run into our friends on the Fair Grounds, what we really talk about is what we have eaten!

Preparation is all fresh and in accordance with local traditions. There are a number of high-quality fried offerings including crawfish and shrimp, many of them consistent with the New Orleans Program when enjoyed occasionally. A Jazz Fest favorite, Crawfish Monica, attracts big crowds. Here are some of our Jazz Fest-inspired dishes, streamlined for home preparation.

CHICKEN BREAST SAUTE SUPREME
Serves 1.

¹/₂ large boneless chicken breast
Few drops light soy sauce
Few drops Louisiana hot sauce
Paprika (not hot) to taste

Sea salt and black pepper to taste
2 tbsp. extra-virgin olive oil
1 clove garlic, pressed
¼ cup decent medium-dry white wine
1 tsp. sliced green onion (optional)
1 tsp. chopped red bell pepper (optional)

Pat chicken dry. Sprinkle soy and hot sauces on each side and rub to coat evenly. Sprinkle each side generously with paprika, salt, and pepper.

Heat oil in a skillet over medium-high heat. Press garlic into center of skillet, and immediately place chicken on garlic. Sauté on one side until golden brown, turn, and sauté until nicely browned. Turn again, add wine to skillet, and finish cooking a few more minutes. Serve immediately. Plate alone, sprinkled with green onion and red peppers, or with rice or pasta. This dish makes its own sauce, which should be delicious.

FAKE FRIED CHICKEN

1 medium free-range chicken, dressed for frying
Nonstick cooking spray
½ cup milk
2 egg whites
1-2 cups (depending on size of chicken) dry, whole-grain bread-
    crumbs
⅓-½ cup finely grated Parmesan cheese
1 tsp. black pepper
¼-½ tsp. cayenne pepper
½ tsp. dry mustard
½ tsp. paprika (not hot)

Preheat oven to 375 degrees. Be sure chicken pieces have excess skin and fat removed. Pat chicken dry. Spray large glass or ceramic baking dish with cooking spray.

Mix milk and egg whites thoroughly in medium bowl. Mix bread-crumbs, cheese, and spices in another medium bowl. Toss dried chicken in egg wash. Then toss in coating.

Arrange in baking dish. Bake 45-50 minutes, turning twice (once after about 20 minutes and once again after about another 20 minutes). Chicken is done when nicely browned. Serve at least warm.

LOST AMONG THE DIET BOOKS

We have many Jazz Fest temptations, both traditional and world class. With a revved-up metabolism and a good lean-muscle-mass-to-fat ratio, you can party hearty and splurge on food at Jazz Fest without derailing your fitness. Etouffées and gumbos feature high vegetable content. Crawfish, shrimp, or vegetarian macque choux (a corn-based dish) is a Louisiana tradition passed from the local Native American population to French settlers. It offers richness and flavor as well as vitamins and minerals, good protein, and high fiber content.

Jazz Fest can pose dilemmas, with great players like Pete Fountain and Beau Soleil appearing at the same time. The winding grounds encourage strolling at an enjoyable pace, but a printed schedule becomes indispensable. It's easy to find such a guide for Jazz Fest, but it's much harder to find a guide for enjoying our present and future years through good eating, healthy exercising, and caring for our inner selves.

We are all looking for the diet, exercise, or self-help guide that will "beeline" us to where we know we need to be. Since over half of the United States is overweight, this quest applies to most of us. We can envision our individual goals in our minds and hearts—and our mirrors. Yet unlike the delightful winding paths of Jazz Fest, the routes offered to us by most diet books can be complex and painful. If you're unaware of the number of diet books available, you can surprise yourself by checking the shelves at your local bookstore or the virtual shelves at Amazon.com and barnesandnoble.com. Since the late twentieth century, most of the superfad diets, and all the well-meaning and "are-they-really-telling-me-to-eat-that?" diet books, have failed to deliver. These diets can be not only false prophets but also dangerous lures.

Recent Superfad Diets

Atkins, the High-Fat/Low-Carb Champ of the Dueling Diets: *Dr. Atkins' New Diet Revolution,* by Robert C. Atkins, M.D., Avon, 1999; and *Atkins for Life,* by Robert C. Atkins, M.D., St. Martin's, 2003.

- A restrictive diet that does cause weight loss.
- Many negative bodily experiences (such as headaches) from this unbalanced diet.
- Original diet is very micronutrient poor. Dr. Atkins recommended and sold megadose vitamin/mineral supplements.
- With the emergence of commercial Atkins-brand products, and the weight of scientific evidence, Atkins' recent versions have added more vegetable, fruit, and exercise recommendations.
- Concern persists over high-saturated-fat intake and recommendations that ignore pitfalls in our twenty-first-century food supply.
- It's still just a diet, and a very complex one, if you take it seriously. Just what is a "net carb" anyway? If you don't know, then you don't have to worry about counting them. (Actually, it is just subtracting fiber, an "inert" carb.)

Atkins-Like Diets: *The South Beach Diet: The Delicious, Doctor-Designed, Foolproof Plan for Fast and Healthy Weight Loss,* by Arthur Agatston, M.D., Rodale, 2003.
- Warmed-over Atkins: tight on the "first phase" and looser in later "phases."
- Still just a diet.
- How can a cardiologist give the impression that exercise is so unimportant? (See page 14.)

High-Fat Variation Diets: *The Zone: A Dietary Roadmap,* by Barry Sears, Ph.D., Magus, 1995.
- Attributes serious health risks to spikes in insulin that he says stimulate disease-producing inflammatory hormones.
- Recommends a 30:30:40 balance "zone" of protein, fat, and carbs to reduce insulin swings.
- Castigates the Ornish diet (see below) as possibly heart *un*healthy, while advocating a high animal protein, fat diet with low nutrients (especially plant derived).
- Strong reliance on the glycemic index "litmus test" slights many nutritious foods, such as carrots.

- Contention that insulin spikes create weight gain flies in the face of the true cause: eating too many calories of *any* kind.
- Do athletes *really* perform better on a high-fat diet, as Dr. Sears suggests?

Ornish, the Low-Fat/High-Carb Champ: *Eat More, Weigh Less: Dr. Dean Ornish's Life Choice Program for Losing Weight Safely While Eating Abundantly,* by Dean Ornish, M.D., Harper Perennial, 1997.
- Tightly focused on reducing cardiac disease.
- Stresses a radical shift to ultralow fat (under 10 percent of what you eat).
- Demands dramatic shifts in food preparation (very few prepared foods, even from organic market kitchens, meet Dr. Ornish's standard).
- Challenges and possibly harms diabetics because of the low-density carb load.
- Ignores the evidence that some fats are good for life, and also heart health (e.g., extra-virgin olive oil). Definitely not for growing children, who need appropriate fats.
- Still just a diet. And who has time to meditate and prepare fat-free stock for poaching veggies, anyway?

Ornish-Like Diets: *Eat to Live: The Revolutionary Formula for Fast and Sustained Weight Loss,* by Joel Fuhrman, M.D., Little, Brown, 2003.
- A plant-fiber, nutrient-rich diet that, like all others, relies in great part on low calories to work. We agree with his emphasis on whole foods as more nutritious, and benefits of fiber, but like most very-low-fat diets, much of the allowed fare is *low* on flavor.
- We wonder about Dr. Fuhrman's claim that "research scientists" can actually take fat biopsies off your hips or waist and tell you where it came from—pig fat, dairy fat, chicken fat, or olive-oil fat. What about crawfish fat, cher? Dr. Pamela Martin, the most attractive pathologist at Touro Infirmary, labels this claim "impossible."

CRITIQUES OF CURRENT DIETS

The Atkins Diet, controversial since its original publication in 1980, is the vanguard and exemplary high-high-fat, low-evil-carb diet. Several later diet programs have followed its lead. Shortly after Dr. Atkins' recent untimely death, his program—revised in some versions to include some carbohydrates such as fruit—exploded all over bookstands, *Time* magazine, and the Internet. After decades of vilification by several medical establishment groups, Dr. Atkins' "diet revolution" has scored a virtual coup.

The Atkins Diet encourages eating saturated fats, a known health risk, and sodium intake can also be very high on the diet. High fat consumption opens the door to clogged arteries and other results of eating too much of the fat available to twenty-first-century Americans. Animal fat bears many of the chemicals used to ready animals for market. Fat fails to signal our brains that we "have had enough." It lures us to overeat. Yet portion control takes a backseat in the Atkins Diet—you are encouraged to eat as much of the recommended food as you wish. Unbalanced intake of this sort can throw your metabolism into the production of body-breakdown elements called ketones. These small molecules burn muscle and cause dehydration, fatigue, and nausea. Ketones can damage fetal brains. Pregnant women especially, beware!

The carbohydrate restrictions in the Atkins Diet prompt initial weight loss through loss of body fluid. Yet along with the water, micronutrients such as calcium are also lost, raising the chance of osteoporosis. The insufficiency of micronutrients, including important antioxidants, is perhaps the most pernicious risk of the Atkins plan. Dr. Atkins recognized this danger and recommended megasupplements, especially the ones he created.

Another popular program is Dr. Agatston's South Beach Diet. This diet avoids giving the reader many facts and claims to be neither "low carb" nor "low fat." It identifies "good" and "bad" fats and carbs, letting protein more or less take care of itself. Dr. Agatston recommends three "phases" of dieting, the first being the strictest. In balance, it is a low-carb approach, and much attention goes to the glycemic index, which has little practical application besides imparting a few generalities that we cover further on.

Yet the South Beach Diet recommends eating combinations that can pack a high-sodium punch. Unfortunately, many of its recipes call for the use of prepared and processed materials such as gingersnaps, which are loaded with trans fats. It also fails to take up the micronutrient slack its dos and don'ts can create. Perhaps worse, the South Beach Diet was designed to be "effective regardless of exercise habits" (page 14). This gross blind spot should encourage readers to approach this diet and its attendant philosophy with caution.

The Sugar Busters! diet, a New Orleans product, echoes Atkins and suffers from some of the same problems. For instance, this popular low-carb diet also encourages eating as much of the "approved" items as one wants.

Another program that has appeared in recent years is the Carbohydrate Addicts Life Span, a low-carb, high-protein, and potentially high fat diet. Unlike the diets just discussed, this does not emphasize fat but actually protein. The authors claim that overweight people are "addicted" to carbs. A true addiction, however, would be a genetic condition not dictated by choice. The fact is that insulin—the hormone that ushers sugar into cells, among many other functions—causes a carbohydrate lover to crave even more carbohydrates, creating dangerously low blood sugars or hypoglycemia, and finally triggering insulin resistance.

High protein and high saturated-fat intake may increase the risk of cardiovascular disease and cancer, stress kidneys, and worsen existing kidney and liver diseases. As with other diets of this type, low carbohydrate intake produces fatigue, water loss, and attendant calcium loss, as well as possible micronutrient deficiencies.

These high-fat and protein, low-carbohydrate diets can work initially when their rules are obeyed, but do not work in the long run for most people. Perhaps the most discouraging part of all of these diets is that the initial weight loss from dehydration crouches out there, just waiting to jump back into your body the moment you change to a higher-carb eating pattern.

A friend who struggled with these low carb plans, enduring headaches and malaise to lose about ten pounds, fell off the wagon with a Tastee Donuts meal. "They were so good—better than sex—and I got rid of my headache."

The polar opposite of these diets, the Dr. Dean Ornish and Dr. Pritikin diets, require low fat and high carbohydrate intake. Dr. Ornish's hypothesis is that high complex carbohydrate intake combined with very low fat consumption will boost metabolism and the hormone thyroxin to increase the body's caloric burn rate. The extremely low fat intake helps to reduce—or even reverse—the risk of cardiovascular disease.

To Dr. Ornish's credit, evidence does exist that an extremely low fat diet can reverse cardiovascular clogging. However, his own data from dieters on his plan showed no benefits to blood triglycerides or to the HDL good cholesterol, though his extreme imbalance of intake did lower bad cholesterol. This selected benefit may not alter cardiovascular disease risk significantly. Further, there is some question whether the diet alters thyroxin so as to actually change metabolism for the better.

The Ornish/Pritikin type of diet program may throw diabetic persons out of blood-sugar control due to the carbohydrate load, even if the carbohydrate intake features a lower glycemic index. These very low fat diets ban many foods that are healthful, such as fish and extra-virgin olive oil, and may lead to micronutrient deficiency. We would especially caution the use of such diets for children and adolescents. Good fat is necessary for all people, and in particular for growing children.

The Mediterranean Diet and its champions, such as Dr. Walter C. Willett of the Harvard School of Public Health, have received a lot of attention. The Mediterranean Diet, which arose from the pioneering work of Dr. Ansel Keys, seems to be middle of the road in many ways. The "French paradox" of rich food consumption with low cardiovascular disease rates has stimulated interest in this diet. The adherence to the true Mediterranean Diet requires significant changes in some food ingredients and has several drawbacks including micronutrient deficiency.

Why does a country notorious for rich food have a very small incidence of obesity? This so-called French paradox may not be so paradoxical after all. A new study has compared eating habits in France and the United States. It was discovered that the average portion size in Paris was 25 percent smaller than that in Philadelphia, that Chinese restaurants in Philly served meals that were 72 percent bigger than in Parisian Chinese restaurants, and that a candy bar, a soft drink, and a hot dog in Philadelphia were respectively 41 percent, 52 percent, and 63 percent larger than their counterparts in Paris. Interestingly, Parisians spent twenty-two minutes on average dining at their McDonald's, compared with the fourteen minutes that Philadelphians spent.

The Mediterranean Diet has been challenged by the Okinawa Program, a twenty-five-year study of long-lived Okinawans. The authors, associated with the Harvard School of Public Health, chose the Okinawans to study their longevity. Their findings indicate that even elderly Okinawans have "young arteries" with low cholesterol and low blood homocystein. Their rates of cardiovascular disease and stroke are low in comparison with ours in the United States. The Okinawa Program emphasizes lifestyle, including diet, regular exercise, moderate alcohol use, avoidance of tobacco, social integration, and spiritual life. The Okinawan data suggests that genes are less important than environment: Okinawans who have moved away from home and adopted the eating habits of their new homelands have also developed their homelands' levels of cardiovascular disease and stroke. The Okinawa Program emphasizes pork consumption and permits a significant amount of fat consumption. Yet actually practicing the program, as indicated in the book, requires changing a lot of kitchen utensils and habits and is impractical overall for the average twenty-first-century American.

The Okinawa Program does support a complete and balanced picture, including improved food choices, the correct type and amount of exercise, and attention to the spiritual side of life. God has given all of his creatures a soul. It is up to us to nourish our spirits by remaining active in the community, being faithful to a religion of our choice, using private meditative techniques—or combining all of these.

PUZZLING OVER GOVERNMENT GUIDELINES FOR 2005

We might think that we can avoid the confusion of diet books simply by trusting our government's advice. If so, we would be wrong. Governmental guidelines have a history of being unreliable and misleading. The Dietary Guidelines for Americans 2005 (healthierus.gov/dietaryguidelines) are the latest version of these, published jointly by the USDA and the Department of Health and Human Services. We do agree with what seem to be their three chief tenets: eat fewer calories, be more active, and make smart food choices. Yet these Guidelines for 2005 are flawed by a limited scope of information. For example, they highlight the importance of fiber, while leaving to our imaginations how to consume their recommended amount. They suggest a "balanced" eating pattern without explaining what "balanced" means. Many of their suggestions are simply not practicable. The authors seem also to have yielded to pressure from the bread, beef, and dairy industries.

Calories. The Dietary Guidelines 2005 feature weight control and exercise, and they advise attention to daily calories. However, there are problems and inconsistencies. The new guidelines advise three glasses of low-fat milk every day, almost 400 calories. They allow six ounces of "fruit juice" as a serving of fruits, while failing to warn us of the high load of empty calories in most commercial fruit juices. Overall, it would seem enormously difficult to cram their definition of adequate nutrition into the calories-per-day eating patterns recommended in their appendix. They caution us to eat "sufficient amounts of fruits and vegetables while staying within energy needs." But how?

Bread. The Dietary Guidelines 2005 say that whole grains should make up half our grain intake, while the rest can be from "enriched or whole grain products." This advice benefits only those who bake with refined flour. We are left to assume that "regular" bread is nutritious. We're not taught how to distinguish between mass-produced "whole wheat" shelf bread (which provides empty calories) and a true whole-wheat product. The New Orleans Program, by contrast, does not recommend any refined-flour products.

Vegetables. The Dietary Guidelines 2005 advise four to five servings of vegetables per day, or about two and a half cups. This might be, for example, two cups of raw leafy vegetables (do they mean packed or loose?) and half a cup of cooked vegetables. For the cooked vegetables one can substitute six ounces of vegetable juice—which would seem to contradict the guidelines' emphasis on low sodium intake, since most vegetable juices are high in sodium. Vegetables are categorized as (1) dark green, (2) orange, (3) legumes, (4) starchy, and (5) other.

We applaud this attention to vegetable nutrients, with a few caveats. We're left feeling a little sorry for the red, yellow, and light green vegetables, which also have important nutrients. The meaning of "legume" is not clearly explained. And the calorie load of one serving can vary greatly, according to the particular vegetable (or legume!) one chooses. Overcooked vegetables supply more simple than whole carbohydrates, not a good thing. Unfortunately, the Guidelines 2005 also equate cooked with raw vegetables, when we now know that lightly cooked, crispy vegetables will yield many more micronutrients than vegetables left completely raw. In fact, the whole question of bioavailability, or the relationship between intake and nutrition, is ignored by this government report. Bioavailability is crucial when we consider the choice of supplements, which are acknowledged only grudgingly in the report as useful in "limited circumstances."

The nutritional content of our food supply in the twenty-first century holds certain perils, and the Dietary Guidelines 2005 fail to acknowledge that fact. They don't take into account the incidence of methyl-mercury-contaminated fish and milk, nor the presence of antibiotics and hormones in our beef and poultry. One can imagine the authors have been pressured by the beef industry not to discriminate among protein sources, even though several recent studies favor poultry, fish, and beans over red meat. The guidelines equate all protein sources. This lack of distinction among different types of proteins misses some important points. Some proteins carry more toxic "baggage," for example, than others.

Fats and Oils. The Dietary Guidelines 2005 wisely recommend that growing children and teens should consume a little more fat than usual until they are past their teenage years. And they wisely caution against extremely low fat intake (less than 20 percent of total calories), which they admit may deprive a person of vitamin E and essential fatty acids. We would add that low-fat diets also may reduce high-density cholesterol and increase triglycerides. In spite of their correct observations, and in spite of their accurately reported differences between good and bad fats, these guidelines do seem to restrict fats and oils extremely, down to two or three servings per week. A serving is one teaspoon of vegetable oil or "soft margarine" without trans fats. This tiny bit of oil, presumably including extra-virgin olive oil—our recommendation, not theirs—will hardly be enough to dress the salad needed to meet the two to four cups of raw, leafy vegetables the guidelines say we should consume every day.

What were these scientific experts thinking by recommending "light salad dressing"? Have they looked at the chemical and artificial ingredients in commercial light salad dressing? The guidelines also tap dance around the allowable amount of trans fats. They create a loophole to permit snacks within the recommended calorie allowances, when almost every snack on American grocery shelves contains trans fats. We recommend eliminating such snacks entirely. This will work to minimize trans fats, as well as refined sugar.

Milk and Dairy Products. We find it astounding that the Dietary Guidelines 2005 call for three cups daily of "fat-free or low-fat milk or equivalent milk products." We may see the fingerprints of the dairy industry here. Increasing numbers of adults are lactose intolerant, especially among certain ethnic groups, including African-Americans.

Removing the fat from milk does not remove the lactose, and the report is silent about lactose-reduced products and adjunctive enzymes. This recommendation is at best ethnically insensitive, and at worst scientifically unsound. Do the "scientific experts" who produced these guidelines not understand that the absorption of calcium from most dairy products is only 15 percent? Other foods, especially those with elements that aid calcium absorption, have a much higher rate of absorption per milligram of calcium. We have excellent calcium supplements available with an absorption rate of over 55 percent. Calcium is vital to developing and maintaining body and skeletal health. We suggest that unless you really like the taste of low-fat milk, you consider other calcium sources and high-absorption supplements.

The calorie recommendations for older persons seem stringent, and in many cases they provide an odd assortment of foods. For example, here is the daily regimen the new pyramid (available at www.mypyramid.gov) advises if you are a sixty-year old woman who weighs 125 pounds and exercises (but not vigorously) less than thirty minutes a day.

- total calories per day—1,600
- milk—3 cups
- fruit—1.5 cups
- vegetables—2 cups
- grains—5 oz.
- meat (lean) or beans—5 oz.
- oils—5 tsp.
- discretionary calories—130 (approximately one small bag of potato chips)

RETROSPECTIVE: A CENTURY OF FLAWED GOVERNMENT GUIDELINES

It is no surprise that the Dietary Guidelines 2005 are full of puzzling and contradictory recommendations. The USDA has been giving us questionable dietary advice for more than a century. Their advice is designed to be broad and inoffensive, and it routinely capitulates to commercial interests. That's why many themes pushed by government and government-related experts since the last part of the nineteenth century are echoed by themes in the Dietary Guidelines 2005. Nutritional knowledge is often muted by governmental and commercial concerns. Over the last century, our government's eager-to-please advice may have done us more harm than good.

The history of governmental dietary guidelines shows that commercial, political, and social forces have heavily influenced our government's advice. The earliest experts suggested we eat large amounts of a wide selection of foods, with a high-carbohydrate, moderate-fat (30 percent), and lesser-protein intake. Then in 1917 the USDA published its first Dietary Guidelines, categorizing foods into what became our "Four Major Food Groups" for most of the century: (1) meats, poultry, and fish; (2) fruits and vegetables; (3) grains, cereals, starches, and sugars; and (4) fats and oils. This advice was hardly specific or user friendly, but no food industries were offended.

During World War II, when butter was rationed, margarine and lard were the main fats available for cooking. In the 1950s the well-intentioned Dr. Ansel Keys, building on earlier medical literature, worked in association with government agencies on studies linking cholesterol consumption with heart disease. The result was a tremendous industry effort to demonize cholesterol. As substitutes for butter and saturated fats, both margarine and partially hydrogenated vegetable oils were promoted as "healthful" to the public. Ironically, olive oil was widely dismissed as "foreign" and smelly, a product for immigrants and poor people. As fast foods, frozen foods, and TV dinners grew in popularity through the 1950s and 1960s, Americans were consuming large amounts of unhealthy fats and refined carbohydrates in response to both governmental advice and "enriched bread" marketing efforts. The results for the public are in retrospect understandable: a rise in obesity, cardiovascular disease, Type II diabetes, and cancer.

One cultural response to this overeating climate was helpful, at least for women. Jean Nidtech, a New York City housewife, began to assemble women in parlor meetings to share weight-loss strategies and mutual encouragement. Weight Watchers grew out of these meetings. It continues today, with arguably the best track record of helping people lose weight and keep it off of any for-pay diet business.

Governmental responses were less helpful, by contrast. In reaction to the nation's growing obesity and related illnesses, Sen. George McGovern chaired a Senate select committee on nutrition and human needs in the early 1970s. The McGovern report in 1977 urged

Americans to eat more carbohydrates and avoid animal fats, cholesterol, saturated fats, sugar, and salt. It did not distinguish between
"good" and "bad" carbohydrates. In what would become a political
pattern for the future, this 1977 report stirred up a tempest among the
affected food industries and was revised a year later, under commercial pressures. In the new report, the suggestion that Americans eat
less meat was transformed to advice that we choose "meat, poultry, and
fish which will reduce saturated fat intake." Cautions against eggs and
salt were softened, as well.

A few years later, Congress instructed the USDA and the U.S.
Department of Health and Human Services jointly to prepare "Dietary
Guidelines for Americans." These appeared in 1980 and provoked no
protests from food industries because they had few specifics. They
advised, for example, that we should eat a variety of foods; maintain
ideal weight; avoid fat, saturated fat, and cholesterol; eat enough fiber
and starch; avoid too much sugar and salt; and drink alcohol only in
moderation.

These guidelines were hardly courageous leadership. Their inoffensive and nondetailed suggestions did not serve us well. Our obesity epidemic picked up steam, and the weight of the general population
increased. Doctors became more strident about saturated fat and cholesterol. Finally, in 1992, the USDA published the Food Guide
Pyramid. Why, we may ask, did they not publish this document on
schedule, in 1990? Because the meat and dairy industries delayed the
report, pleading their economic causes. The official government cover
story was that the original Food Guide Pyramid would "confuse children." We believe that the 1992 Food Guide Pyramid has confused not
just children but anyone who has looked at it.

The dangers of the pyramid are many. It encourages snacking, for
one thing. Snacking! This advice defies common sense. Growing children might need snacks after athletic activities. Diabetics may need
healthful snacks for blood sugar management. But the rest of us? Does
our government really want us to eat commercial snacks while we
watch TV and lose track of how full we are? Who benefits from our
"snacking culture," besides the snack industry? Snacks are not popular
in Europe. The French don't snack. Here is what Chef Greg Sonnier
has to say about snacks.

You know, I think that we always have to go back to what our ancestors did.

Looking in France and in Europe alone, obviously they have fried foods all around. . . . The French . . . only eat three meals a day. They don't eat snacks and they don't eat all this other junk or garbage. The don't really watch their fat that much at all, but that's what they do. They really take pride in each of their meals, their lunches, their dinners. So I always think, even when it comes to fried food, . . . anything in moderation is the way to go. . . . I find especially when I visited France recently, . . . the Europeans enjoy their plate of food and their glass of red wine . . . and that's it. They don't go on and keep on eating.

Participants in the New Orleans Program don't snack. We simply do not need to snack—not in front of the TV, not before bedtime. We should kick the snack habit.

We suggest that snacks be limited to parties. When we need a healthful snack for a football-game party, for example, here are some good snacks with protein.

CHILI, NO BEANS

2 lb. good-quality very lean beef, coarse ground by butcher or shaved and chopped at home
Sea salt and black pepper to taste
3 celery stalks with leaves, destringed and chopped
2 medium yellow onions, chopped
1 green bell pepper, seeded and chopped
2 small fresh jalapeño peppers, seeded and chopped fine
4 medium cloves garlic, pressed
4 tbsp. chili powder
1 tbsp. cumin
1 tbsp. oregano
1 tsp. cayenne pepper
16 oz. Rotel diced tomatoes
Beef stock *or* water

Heat a large skillet (or pot) that has a cover. Toss in beef. While the bottom is searing, sprinkle on a little salt and pepper. When browned on bottom, stir to turn and brown nicely without burning. Drain off any rendered fat.

Add celery, onions, peppers, and garlic, and sauté on medium high until onions are clear. Add spices and tomatoes; mix well. Add beef stock (or water) to cover chili. Cover pot and cook *slowly* 2 hours.

Check occasionally and adjust seasonings towards end of cooking if needed. (It probably won't need adjustment unless you want to increase heat by adding more cayenne. Be cautious!)

BLACKENED TUNA WRAP

Serves 6.

The idea of this wrap is to combine a nice hot piece of tuna with cold salad ingredients to create a contrast of flavors, textures, and temperatures. You may use other salad ingredients such as avocado, sliced mushrooms or peppers, or even a light cheddar cheese.

6 soft tortillas
2 tbsp. low- or nonfat mayonnaise
1 cup thinly sliced romaine or curly loose-leaf lettuce
2 cups bean sprouts
2 cups alfalfa sprouts
2 large tomatoes
Salt and black pepper to taste
12 1-oz. pieces tuna
Creole spice

Spread tortillas with mayonnaise. Distribute lettuce and sprouts over tortillas. Slice tomatoes into 12 thin slices and place 2 slices on each tortilla. Add any other ingredients you wish, such as avocado slices. Add salt and pepper.

Rub tuna with spice. Sear in very hot pan that is nicely oiled until it is crispy on the outside and medium rare on the inside. Add 2 pieces tuna to each tortilla. Roll and secure with toothpicks. Slice and serve immediately.

The 1992 Food Guide Pyramid is also based on carbohydrates, and it treats all carbohydrates as equal. The pyramid has been extremely kind to the "ordinary bread" industry, lending them a platform to push their products as healthy. No wonder that America's caloric consumption rose in the late 1990s! As government figures show, Americans were not eating more meat and animal fats; they were eating more carbohydrates. They were doing exactly what the pyramid recommended.

We agree that the 1992 pyramid is "actually dangerous," as declared by Dr. Walter C. Willett, from the Harvard School of Public Health, in his 2001 book *Eat, Drink, and Be Healthy: The Harvard Medical School Guide to Healthy Eating.* One could easily have remained within the triangular walls of this pyramid and consumed more than 5,000 calories a day, a guarantee of obesity for everyone except (perhaps) lumberjacks.

We have all been confused by paying attention to our multitude of "experts." Chef Besh and I have battled this confusion in our own lives. The New Orleans Program is our response. It has proved to be our path out of confusion, and we want to share it with you in this book.

WATER: HOW MUCH? WHAT KIND?

Water is an essential nutrient. Our bodies are made up primarily of water. We can't manufacture water in our bodies, except in minute quantities, yet we lose water every day through sweat, breath vapor, and urine. Depending on exercise, weather, and the diuretic properties of what we eat and drink, we lose about 72 oz. water a day.

Water Keeps Us Going

- Water creates the environment in our bodies that allows our life processes—all those enzymes, hormones, DNA, repair mechanisms—to work properly.
- Water provides the tides of life that rise and fall in our tissues, bringing in nutrients and hormones and carrying out waste and toxins.
- Water provides disease protection by promoting mucus flow in our eyes, noses, throats, and lung airways, an effective barrier to bacteria and other bad agents.

We know to drink when we're thirsty. But why wait until then?

Although some people feel thirsty with as little as 2 percent dehydration, others aren't thirsty until their level of water loss is much higher. Many things can dehydrate us, from heat to dry air to plain old time. An airplane cabin's humidity is about 11 percent, worse than the Sahara Desert. When I sit on an airplane for two hours or more, my skin changes texture. It wrinkles and flakes. It leaves me much more vulnerable to sun than I am in the moist climate of New Orleans. When I realize that the changes I'm seeing in my skin are the same changes that dehydration causes in my kidneys or my brain, I'm instantly convinced that a good water balance is vital to my life. We should drink water actively, and we should eat fruits and vegetables with a high water content. After all, we need constantly to replace the 72 oz. we lose each day.

Results of Acute and Chronic Dehydration

- In young children and elderly persons, rapid deterioration of bodily functions, and eventual death if untreated
- Heatstroke
- Kidney stones, kidney failure
- Heart vessel disease
- Gingivitis and tooth problems
- Cancer of the bladder, colon
- Decreased athletic performance
- Premature aging with repeated dehydration

How can we take in enough water? We might, for example, drink two 10-oz. glasses water at lunch and another two at dinner, while eating such water-rich foods as cucumbers and melons. We might drink five to nine 8-oz. glasses water per day, depending on our food consumption, our exertion, and the climate where we live. Many people drink bottled water, which may be naturally flavored with small amounts of minerals.

We offer some cautions about bottled water. The Natural Resources Defense Council has shown that 30 percent of 103 tested brands of bottled water were contaminated with organic chemicals such as plasticizers (some of which can have hormonal or cancer-promoting effects), bacteria, and toxic metals such as arsenic. The Web site for more information is www.nrds.org\water\drinking. There is also a "backwash" effect from a person's drinking. Sharing bottled water is not a good idea.

There is also a recent warning that too much water can be dangerous—that is, if you are exercising very strenuously. In a recent university study, athletes who drank too much water during or just after extreme exertion risked lowering the balance of sodium and electrolytes in their blood to dangerous levels. Low enough levels have been known to cause death.

Do commercial fruit juices count as water? What about carbonated drinks? Coffee? Beer? The short answer is simply *no*. Most of these drinks encourage water loss, each in its own way. Nothing works as well as water itself. Granted, there may be the odd individual who has a net water gain from an Oca Choca Mocha Latte or a cup of New Orleans-style French roast coffee with chicory served "black, cher." Yet you or I may not be that particular individual. We're better off drinking water. To quote Prof. Ed Maumenee, the late, great, past chairman of the Wilmer Eye Institute at Johns Hopkins and an avid tennis player: "Only water truly satisfies thirst."

Water has no calories, and it makes us feel fuller faster. These facts alone should motivate us to have water on the table for all meals. If we eat slowly and drink water along with our food, we naturally feel more satisfied. To purify our tap water inexpensively, without risking fluoride deprivation, we can buy a quality in-line home water filter.

Personally, I have hoped for one small exception to the mantra that "only water truly satisfies thirst." We of Southern heritage do enjoy our brewed iced tea, called "sweet tea" in Georgia and most of the Southeast. I prefer mine in a large glass, unsweetened, with lots of ice. Does iced tea provide as much hydration as water? My own hypothesis is this: well, almost. And yes, I've self-tested my hypothesis, comparing the effects of two 12-oz. glasses ice water and two 12-oz. glasses iced tea. For me, iced tea supplies only 10 percent less hydration—not that this is your usual double-blind study!

There are many types of tea: caffeinated (thus diuretic) teas, decaffeinated teas, herbal teas, green teas. Teas have antioxidants and other goodies. In the next chapter we'll discuss antioxidants and micronutrients, which can help to maintain our tissues and strengthen our immune systems.

Coffee continues to garner all kinds of health news. On the positive side, one research study in women concluded that up to four cups a day of caffeinated coffee lowered high-blood-pressure risk by 12 percent. Using Magnetic Resonance Imaging (MRI), another study demonstrated that caffeinated coffee activates a brain area that serves short-term memory. On the negative side, in persons with tinnitus (ringing in the ears) and true vertigo (or Meunier's disease, another ear problem), the conditions can be aggravated by caffeine consumption, particularly in coffee.

PLEASURABLE EATING

We offer a couple of tips on pleasurable eating here. Reconnect with your food. Most of us have lost a real connection with food. We do not savor it by eye, nose, or tongue. If we can't savor, we miss out on much of the pleasure that food offers us. Our reconnection can begin with "making groceries," when we actively appreciate the colors, forms, textures, and smells of fresh produce in an artful grocery-store display, or in the more casual atmosphere of the farmers' market. Later, preparing food for cooking can be a delight. Translucent onions, rich red and bright green bell peppers, jade-colored celery, and dark green parsley, laid out on the chopping board or in prep bowls for an étouffée, will please the eye and promise more pleasure to come. Visual pleasure enhances taste. Good fresh food, well prepared, can be nicely presented at home without a lot of fuss. The recipes by Chef Besh throughout this book are there to enhance your pleasure in shopping, preparing, and presenting our flavorful local cuisine. Some may choose to bless the food as it comes to the table, which can be a means of thankful connection with the appearance, the aromas, and the sources of our food.

Eat slowly and chew well. Slow eating can complete the experience of savoring and can help your digestion. When the body signals "enough," that is the time to stop, gently and pleasurably.

PAN-ROASTED BASS OVER CELERY-ROOT PUREE AND CELERY SALAD

Serves 6.

6 6-oz. seabass filets

Salt to taste
Extra-virgin olive oil

Season fish with salt and oil. Sear in a hot pan until flesh side is golden and crispy. Flip over and finish in 400-degree oven until medium rare, about 8 minutes.

Celery-Root Puree
1 cup large-diced celery root
1 cup large-diced Yukon gold potatoes
1 cup julienned onion
Sachet of 1 sprig thyme and 1 head garlic cloves
1 cup hot cream

Combine vegetables and sachet in a large pot. Fill with water to cover by 2 inches. Salt water to taste and simmer about 45 minutes or until celery and potatoes are fully cooked but not waterlogged.

Drain well and puree while still very hot in a food processor. Add hot cream to finish. Pass through fine-mesh sieve and season.

Celery Salad
3 tsp. extra-virgin olive oil
1 tsp. rice-wine vinegar
1 shallot, minced
Pinch salt
½ cup yellow celery leaves
½ cup cleaned parsley leaves

Whisk oil, vinegar, shallot, and salt together. Toss with celery and parsley leaves. Plate bass over celery puree on individual plates and top each with celery salad.

You'll need plenty of good (nonalcoholic) hydration to make your way through the Fair Grounds at Jazz Fest! At Jazz Fest you can savor fresh food, dance for exercise, and nurture your spirit. Leave those misleading diets and flawed government guidelines behind. Bring along your own version of healthful hydration, and dance with us into the New Orleans Program.

CHAPTER 8

Fruits of the Earth:
Harvests and Festivals

In Southern Louisiana, we have a colorful array of local festivals, many of them honoring traditions more than a hundred years old. For current information, consult www.louisianatravel.com/calendar.

Small-town festivals are more likely to be unpretentious, slower paced, and uncomplicated. They sound a refreshing attitudinal counterpoint to the busyness and sensory overload of contemporary life. Festivals like the Tomato Festival in New Orleans bring us closer to the earth as our basic source of food. We are reminded just how many micronutrients, many derived from natural foods, are vital to our well-being. We have a great variety of natural foods available in Louisiana. For example, here are some seasonal offerings at New Orleans farmers' markets.

Spring: strawberries, blueberries, artichokes, arugula, beets, broccoli, carrots, cauliflower, cilantro, fava beans, bulb fennel, garlic, green onions, lettuces, new potatoes, radishes, snap beans, spinach, mustard greens, turnip greens, collard greens, turnips, along with wild caught catfish, hard- and soft-shell blue crabs, oysters, red snapper, drum, sheepshead, white and brown shrimp, crawfish, and trout.

Summer: blackberries, blueberries, cantaloupes, figs, muscadine grapes, Asian pears, cooking pears, peaches, watermelon, basil, butter beans, cucumbers, mustard greens, collard greens, turnip greens, eggplant, field peas, garlic, green onions, white onions, yellow onions, okra (both spiny and Creole), peppers of all varieties, potatoes, snap beans, yellow squash, zucchini, corn, Creole tomatoes, red snapper, brown shrimp, and flounder.

Autumn: satsumas, oranges, muscadine grapes, persimmons, basil, butter beans, cucumbers, eggplant, field peas, garlic, mustard greens, collard greens, turnip greens, green onions, lettuces, okras, peppers, pumpkins, snap beans, butternut squash, sweet potatoes, Creole tomatoes, heirloom tomatoes, turnips, alligator, oysters, red snapper, sheepshead, white shrimp, and trout.

Winter: grapefruit, kumquats, Meyer lemons, oranges, pumpkins,

mandarins, tangelos, early season strawberries, arugula, beets, broccoli, cabbage, cauliflower, mustard greens, turnip greens, collards, lettuces, tomatoes, turnips, oysters, red snapper, sheepshead, white
shrimp, and trout.

Community Supported Agriculture (CSA) is on the rise in popularity in New Orleans and many areas of the country. CSA offers another
way to get low-toxic-"baggage" produce. It relies on subscription service. Consumers pay a standard monthly fee and receive weekly deliver-
ies of just-harvested seasonal crops. You know it's organic, you know it's
fresh, but you don't know what you'll get until you get it. The Center
for Integrated Agricultural Systems at the University of Wisconsin
recently estimated that there are over 1,500 CSA farms with over
100,000 subscribers. New York City has seen CSA farms grow from one
in 1995 to thirty-seven in 2005, according to the Just Food organization.

Some subscribers enjoy the surprises that weekly CSA bags contain.
Others feel overwhelmed when tomatoes come in large numbers.
Father Christopher McLaren, rector of St. George's Episcopal Church
in New Orleans, describes his family's CSA experience.

*Being involved in a CSA has helped us to realize that tomatoes can actually
have taste—what a novel idea! It is a proven fact that tomatoes do not actually acquire any additional taste or nutritional value by being transported
halfway across the country on refrigerated trucks. Our new household policy is
simple: eat fresh local produce when possible. It is delicious. It is good for the
earth, good for us, and good for the development of sustainable agriculture in
the place where we have chosen to live.*

MICRONUTRIENTS: WHY?

Natural foods lead us to the subject of micronutrients: vitamins,
minerals, and plant nutrients such as bioflavonoids and isoflavones.
We include micronutrients as a basic food group. They are essential to
our life processes. Without necessary minerals, such as zinc or man-
ganese, the enzymes that drive our tissue engines won't fire. Without
the right vitamins, the toxic byproducts of our metabolism—we call
them "oxidative free radicals"—will snatch more electrons from our
bodies, damaging or killing our cells. Micronutrients like vitamins C
and E can help protect us from these free radicals. Vitamin E has

received some negative attention lately, but at 200 IU (international units) it can be both safe and helpful. I have stopped regularly taking supplemental vitamin E, since I eat a large amount of vitamin E sources. I may use a 200-IU supplement daily for particular stress, such as helping wound healing. Here are some of the things that micronutrients can do.

What Micronutrients Can Do

- Quench oxidative free radicals, protecting tissues and DNA and cell membranes from damage
- Enhance hormonal activity
- Promote reparative enzyme activities
- Promote immune system function
- Reduce inflammation

Here's another reason to keep up your antioxidants, every day: they help protect the nitrous oxide, naturally generated in our tissues. Nitrous oxide works to dilate our blood vessels and keep the vessel lining (the endothelium) healthy. A healthy endothelium keeps down the formation of blood clots and plaque. Over 80 percent of those who die suddenly of cardiovascular disease have evidence of plaque inflammation in their artery walls. To help prevent formation and inflammation of plaque in your blood vessels, keep those vessel linings healthy—protect your body's nitrous oxide from oxidative free radicals. Take enough micronutrients to fight your oxidative free radicals.

Cardiovascular Disease Facts

- It is the number-one killer in the U.S., the Americas, and Europe.
- It is the number-one killer of American women.
- 50 percent of heart attacks occur with normal cholesterol.
- 25 million in the U.S. are at risk, despite low LDL cholesterol.
- 80 percent of it is preventable, yet less than 5 percent is prevented.

Where can we find these micronutrients? They must come from what we eat. Whole fruits and vegetables contain some, such as the B vitamins, vitamin C, and trace minerals. Some come from other sources: zinc is abundant in red meat, and walnuts and fish oil provide vitamin E. Plants contain other micronutrient molecules.

The amount of micronutrients can depend on the quality of your food. According to one study, for example, our local Creole tomatoes have eight times the nutritional value of mass-produced, chemical-goosed tomatoes, and our local produce is generally rich in micronutrients. Processing can reduce plant nutrients like bioflavonoids, whereas quick boiling can bring them out. (See chapter 1.) Whole foods are best. When you eat a whole piece of fruit, like an orange, the bioflavonoids will enhance the absorption of vitamin C. That's better than taking the same amount of vitamin C in a pill.

Only absorbed micronutrients count, and no one can absorb all the nutrients in a given food. For example, less than 15 percent of the calcium in dairy foods can be absorbed by our blood for bone building. When we age, our absorption rate for micronutrients decreases, even if we are healthy. Here is one big flaw in the government's Dietary Guidelines 2005: they depend solely upon food as the source of micronutrients.

SUPPLEMENTS

We believe that food is not enough. People today need supplements. Supplements can make up for the reduced micronutrients in our current food supply. Many micronutrients are poorly available even in a varied eating pattern, such as chromium, which is critical for our metabolism balance. Supplements can also help us as we age. They can increase our absorption rate, because their high concentrations can drive micronutrients through the intestinal lining and into the bloodstream.

With supplements, you can even teach an old dog new tricks! In one study, older dogs who received dietary supplements and regular exercise learned new tricks much faster and better than those who got standard food and no exercise. These results, typical of many other studies and observations in human beings, pose an important question. Can micronutrients in food and supplements retard the signs of aging? We believe so.

Like other parts of the body, the eye undergoes different types of aging. When we study how the eye develops and ages, we can learn something about aging throughout the entire body. Long-term observations of the eye suggest that micronutrients, through both food and supplements, are crucial to our health. They can even help us turn back the aging clock. My own scientific research has given me the experience and confidence required to make this claim.

THE LIFE CYCLE OF A SCIENTIFIC IDEA: MY PERSONAL JOURNEY

In the early 1980s, I observed older patients at the National Institutes of Health (NIH) who had macular degeneration. The were losing the ability to read, recognize faces, decipher prices at the grocery story, and drive safely. Why? I looked for a hypothesis.

The macula is the specialized center of focus in the back of the eye. It has a little dip in the middle, shaped like a satellite dish. Right there, the vision cells are tightly packed, more so than in other parts of the retina. We might compare the dense vision cells to a monitor with a huge number pixels, for the sharpest possible resolution. The macula also allows us to see in full color. If we pause to consider what our eyes give us, we begin to realize how miraculous it is that we can see full-color, three-dimensional, texture-rich, moving images. This everyday miracle, however, requires real energy. The tissues of the macula have an extremely high metabolic rate—perhaps the highest in the body—and that high metabolism generates those dangerous oxidative free radicals that can hurt or destroy cells. The macula is supplied with a fund of protective enzymes, but these enzymes in turn depend on our intake of micronutrients.

When I was studying older patients with macular degeneration in the early 1980s, it was already known that relatively high amounts of zinc, one of our micronutrients, were present in the macula. In women, zinc is more densely concentrated in the macula than in any other body part; in men, only the prostate has more. At the same time, abnormally low concentrations of zinc had been found by Dr. Anan Prasad in the tissues of certain men who lived along the banks of the Nile. These men were short, their hair was thin, and they had incomplete penile development. They were also night blind. Yet when they were given zinc for several months, these men grew. Their hair thickened, and their penile development increased. Their vision also improved. Dr. Prasad had demonstrated the vital importance of zinc for life processes.

My hypothesis became clear to me. I noticed that eyes with macular degeneration have usually served a person well for decades, with no signs of disease. I noticed also that in these older patients I was studying at the NIH, a predictor of macular degeneration was the accumulation of metabolic deposits, or "trash heaps," in the center of vision. This suggested to me that the "wear and tear" life processes were winning over the repair processes. I knew that zinc gives vital support to many repair processes. It seemed reasonable, then, to formulate the scientific hypothesis that zinc supplementation could help people with early macular degeneration, by slowing their loss of vision.

For this idea, I obtained private research support. Our team carefully documented typical macular disease in significant numbers of patients for a clinical trial. Then we randomly divided our subjects and gave one group a zinc supplement and the other group a placebo (an inactive pill). After two years of collecting information, we analyzed our data. Surprise—zinc worked! Our results showed, for the first time, how to slow down vision loss from macular degeneration. This discovery was groundbreaking, since macular degeneration is the major cause of severe and untreatable vision loss in older Americans.

Working from our data, I wrote a manuscript describing our ideas, our experiments, and our results. Our conclusions were simple. Obtaining a fair response from our top peer-reviewed journal was more difficult. After a year of answering reviewers' queries and sharing raw data, we had our manuscript accepted for publication. It appeared in the *Archives of Ophthalmology* in 1988.

The immediate reaction was disbelief. The medical establishment in those days was skeptical of any claims involving nutritional supplementation. In ophthalmology, especially, it was unheard of to claim health benefits from nutrients. The eye community could not seem to believe that anything as simple as zinc could help the eye—much less affect a previously untreatable public health vision problem.

In reaction to our work, the National Eye Institute mounted a decade-long, multimillion-dollar clinical trial designed—at least in part—to disprove what was widely referred to as "Newsome's Zinc Hypothesis." During this study, the laughs continued. Yet the clinical evidence mounted. Many factors were found to increase the risk of vision loss from macular degeneration: high blood pressure, sun exposure, and eating only small amounts of leafy green vegetables. Among these factors? Not taking enough zinc. Surprise again—zinc worked! After the National Eye Institute study (A.R.E.D.S.) was concluded, their results supported "Newsome's Zinc Hypothesis." Their article appeared in October 2001 in the *Archives of Ophthalmology*.

The zinc hypothesis had undergone the full life cycle of new ideas in science: (1) the first demonstration that the idea is correct; (2) disbelief; (3) ridicule; (4) the accumulation of supporting evidence; (5) the realization among peers and others that the new idea was valid all along.

MICRONUTRIENTS AND THE EYE

Our original work spawned the whole business of nutritional eye supplements, which now includes over a dozen products. The disbelievers now believe. Many types of eye aging can be delayed and sometimes reversed by eye nutrients. For example:

Cataracts. A cataract is a clouding of the eye's natural lens, right behind the pupil. In younger persons, the lens is a bag of structured proteins; in older people or those with diabetes, these proteins can become disordered and cloudy. The results include blurred vision, difficulty driving at night, and pain in bright sunlight. Two large national studies have now revealed that enough antioxidants, consumed through food and supplements, can delay cataract formation. Likewise, insufficient micronutrients can allow cataracts to form more rapidly, according to the National Cataract Study Group.

Dry eyes. Tears are not just water. They are a complex structure, essential to the sparkling, clear, comfortable eyes we all value. The tear film itself has chemicals, hormones, and growth factors that keep the eye surface healthy. This film also traps bacteria and other intruders and moves them away, maintaining our eye comfort. Supporting our tears is a mucous layer that anchors the tear film to the eye tissue. Another fatty layer covers our tear film and keeps our tears from evaporating too fast. When this balance of mucous layer, tear film, and fatty layer is upset, dry eyes result. People with dry eyes can have a range of problems, from occasional discomfort to life-altering struggles with pain and light sensitivity. Antihistamines or eye drops can unfortunately make a dryness problem worse.

Micronutrients can help dry eyes. We need Omega-3 fatty acids for our bodies to manufacture tear films, but these are often not plentiful in our food. When we add such Omega-3 supplements as soy nuts or good fish oil capsules, we help relieve dry eyes. With enough oral antioxidants among our nutrients, we can protect our tear glands from oxidative free radicals. There are also medications that reduce the tear gland inflammation caused in part by free radicals. All these improvements—reducing inflammation, boosting free radical protection, and supplying critical ingredients for tears—can turn back the clock and reverse aging in our tear-production mechanism.

"Wet" macular degeneration. When abnormal blood vessels appear beneath the macula, they tend to leak fluid, cause bleeding, and otherwise disrupt the tissues near the center of vision. This is a devastating turn of events, complicating the damage of ordinary macular degeneration. An interplay of factors can lower the risk of developing this progressive or "wet" type of macular degeneration. Adequate nutritional supplementation, especially with zinc, is associated with a lower risk. Consuming many green leafy vegetables, and with them a lot of fruits and vegetables in general, is linked to a much lower risk. Obesity and high fat intake are joined to a higher risk.

Supplements for eye health. Many of the dietary supplements on the market retain the limited old formula used in an NIH study. In place of this old formula, we recommend the broader spectrum supplements. We've been excited to learn that some people, who have taken the broadest spectrum eye supplements available for a year or so, have decreased those "wear and tear" deposits in the back of the eye—deposits we associate with patients older than fifty-five, deposits that can forecast macular degeneration. In one study of patients with early macular degeneration, those who took the limited old NIH narrow spectrum supplement fared worse than those taking a broad spectrum approach, with additional antioxidants and other nutrients, to boost more parts of the eye repair system.

Dr. Mark Siverd has witnessed the link between healthy food and eye health:

Patients . . . will tell me that . . . their eyes aren't dry and irritated all the time but intermittently; they are problematic. When I counsel them and tell them what the source of this problem could be, they'll come back a year later and [say,]"Oh yeah. Now I notice that if I eat a cheeseburger or a lot of pizza one day, then the next my contacts are dried out and my eyes are inflamed. I wake up the next morning and they're kind of red." Once they start to make the connection, they realize the impact that this has on their contact lens wear.

Important Micronutrients for Eye Health

Name	*Function*	*Daily Amount (Bioavailable)*
Zinc	Supports repair in vision tissues; supports visual cell functions	40 mg
Lutein/ Zeaxanthine	Builds protective pigment; slows vision loss and may help reverse wear and tear	16 mg
Beta-Carotene	Antioxidant; converted to vitamin A if deficiency exists	5,000 IU
Vitamin C	Antioxidant; protects all eye tissues; reduces cataract	250-500 mg
Vitamin E	Antioxidant	200 IU
Cysteine	Stimulates major protective antioxidant pathway	100-120 mg
Selenium	Antioxidant	100 micrograms
Taurine	Promotes visual function	200 mg
Bilberry	Antioxidant; promotes visual function	150-250 mg
Omega-3 fatty acids	Antioxidant; promotes tears, tissue integrity	1 fish oil capsule, 1 handful soy nuts

MICRONUTRIENTS AND THE BODY

If micronutrients can turn back the clock in the eye, they may be able to do the same for other organs and tissues in our bodies. We present this concept not as an absolute guarantee but as a well-informed hunch that we ourselves believe in. Micronutrients can make us healthier and better able to function.

When we're looking for advice on micronutrient amounts, we are more than skeptical about government recommendations. The government sets itself up as expert on some trace minerals and vitamins, giving us recommended daily amounts (RDAs). Yet to determine these numbers, the government's method is to inquire what amount of a nutrient would be necessary to prevent nutritional deficiency. This has been its method since 1935. It was derived from knowing, since the 1700s, that nutritional deficiency diseases can be prevented by providing certain amounts of the missing nutrient—like providing limes with vitamin C to English sailors, or "Limeys."

We disagree with the government's minimalist, deficiency-supplementation approach. We are seeking best health, not merely the prevention of deficiency diseases. The government's thinking has led to surprisingly picayune amounts of crucial nutrients on their RDA list, far short of what may be needed for best health. In most instances, vitamin A being one exception, the RDA reflects a safety factor of ten. We believe that ten times these recommended amounts would still be safe. We have a large safety margin for eating more fruits and vegetables and taking quality supplements.

Not all supplements are of equal quality, though. Vitamins and minerals face less regulation by the Food and Drug Administration than do pharmaceutical manufacturers. According to Dr. Peter Verdigem, testing supplements is much harder than testing pharmaceuticals, anyway.

It's difficult to observe an effect from a nutritional. If you compare pharmaceuticals and nutritionals, pharmaceuticals have a lot more chances to be shown to be beneficial. Why? Because it's a strong, nonnatural component which works on one receptor and typically blocks it completely. That kind of effect is achieved, whereas nutrition in food is much milder; the effects are not so much pronounced; [they] take longer to become apparent. So, it takes a larger group for analysis and a longer study period. These studies are just more difficult to do.

On the shelf, two bottles labeled with the same amounts of a micronutrient may in fact have different amounts. It's important to know the source of a supplement so that we can select for quality, even if it costs a little more. Poor-quality supplements with extraneous material may not be absorbed well and may give you a false sense of security. Here are some general suggestions.

Tips for Safe Use of Dietary Supplements and Herbals

- Buy products from quality manufacturers.
- Read the product label to distinguish the active ingredients from the nonactive additives. Choose the fewest number of additives.
- Tell your doctor what nutritional supplements you use. Include quantities and frequencies.
- Be aware of the multiplicity of vague side effects that can occur with many nutritional supplements and at least discuss any perceived problems with your healthcare giver.

Many sources provide advice about micronutrients. We've chosen some key micronutrients and teamed these with an overview of their effects in the body, their primary food sources, and our advice on supplement amounts.

Top Seven Vitamins for Best Health and Long Life

Vitamin	Top Functions	Food Source	Suggested Daily Supplement
Beta-Carotene	Antioxidant; promotes eye and liver health		5,000 IU
B6	Supports "building block" metabolism and combats bad chemicals, especially homocysteine; boosts nervous and immune systems	Many foods especially oatmeal, baked potato with a serving of chicken, pork; bananas, beans	10 mg
B12	Energy; memory	Beef; chicken	50 micrograms

C	Antioxidant; promotes immunity and collagen, folate metabolism; reduces stroke risk	Citrus fruits, red fruits such as strawberries, numerous other fruits, red and green peppers, Brussels sprouts, broccoli	500 mg
D	Makes calcium work	Dairy; sunlight	400 IU
E	Antioxidant; reduces heart disease, cancer; reduces stroke risk by 20 percent in smokers	Greens; other veggies; nuts	200 IU
Folate	Combats homocysteine		800 micrograms

Vitamin B12 is essential to maintaining health. Less than enough B12 can create fatigue, tingling or numbness in the hands and feet, reduced vision, arthritis-like symptoms, and memory problems. As we age, our supply of stomach acid to digest B12 diminishes. By age fifty, there will likely be a vitamin B12 deficiency in 25 percent of Americans; by age seventy, in 50 percent of Americans.

Vitamin C can lower blood pressure and protect against stroke. It improves the function of cells that line blood vessels. In a recent six-year study of people over fifty-five, those who took 130 mg of vitamin C daily (twice the RDA) reduced their stroke risk by 70 percent, even if they smoked, were obese, or had high blood pressure. Those taking 90 mg of vitamin C daily did not have this protective effect.

Vitamin D synthesis can be stimulated by sunlight. According to dermatologist Dr. George Farber, ten to fifteen minutes of sun exposure (before 10:00 A.M. or after 4:00 P.M.), three to four days a week, will provide what's needed for health without damaging your skin. Those with sensitive skin may use a sun block of at least SPF 15, especially during other times of the day. Vitamin D aids calcium metabolism. Vitamin D reduces the risk of rheumatoid arthritis by a third.

Vitamin B6 and folate are known to lower homocysteine levels in the blood, and as a result they reduce the risk of bone fractures. Especially for older people, a daily B-complex supplement is a good protective measure. It also helps maintain healthy skin.

Top Eight Minerals for Best Health and Long Life

Mineral	Top Functions	Food Source	Suggested Daily Supplement
Boron	Builds muscles; promotes bone and brain health		1 mg
Calcium	Promotes bone and tooth health; regulates vision, blood vessel tone, muscle contraction, blood clotting; helps with weight control	Dairy; green veggies like kale, broccoli, Brussels sprouts; shellfish; calcium-set tofu; nuts	1,000 mg
Chromium	Helps sugar metabolism; promotes sugar entry into cells	4 oz. liver, apples, bell peppers	50-200 micrograms
Glucosamine	Stimulates production of collagen, which builds cartilage and joint supporting tissues		1,000 mg
Magnesium	Promotes muscle, heart function, bone health; reduces PMS	Nuts, beans, peas	400 mg
Manganese	Supports nerve and brain function, muscle function/repair		2 mg
Selenium	Antioxidant; promotes eye health; reduces cancer, heart disease; boosts immunse system and prostate function	Veggies	200 micrograms
Zinc	Boosts immune system; protects eyes, taste; improves mental and muscular performance; wound healing; reduces wrinkling; promotes joint health; helps over 200 enzymes, plus DNA; improves communication within cells	Oysters, beef, pork, lamb, nuts	40 mg

Glucosamine helps renew our joints, especially as we age, and can reduce the discomforts of osteoarthritis. Some diabetics feel that glucosamine, an amino sugar, may raise blood sugar.

Calcium supplements have variable absorption rates. Calcium carbonate has at best a 20 percent absorption rate, and as little as 4 percent if you are taking Prilosec or another stomach-acid-reducing drug. Calcium citrate has a 45 percent calcium absorption rate, and Malate has a calcium bioavailability of 55 percent. After age thirty, we begin to lose calcium from our bones. Calcium supplements, along with vitamin D and weight-bearing exercise, can combat this loss. Calcium also helps reduce the risk of colon cancer.

Zinc, in a North Dakota study, was found in a 20-mg dose to increase performance in visual perception, memory, and reasoning in a group of teens.

Top Nine Other Supplements for Best Health and Long Life

Supplement	Top Functions	Food Source	Suggested Daily Supplement
Choline	Improves mental function (I.Q.); supports memory		1,000 mg
Fish oil (Omega-3 fatty acids)	Supports memory; protects heart; reduces inflammation (arthritis), cancer, Alzheimer's; promotes learning	Cold-water fish (sardines, mackerel)	1,000 mg
Garlic	Protects heart	Garlic	1 clove
Lutein	Protects eyesight; reduces cancer risk	Green, leafy veggies; flower petals	16-20 mg
Lycopene	Promotes prostate and heart health	Tomato products	6 mg
Soy protein (phyto-estrogen, isoflavone source)	Reduces cholesterol; promotes breast, prostate, heart, bone health; reduces menopause symptoms	Soybeans	1 handful roasted (and maybe lightly salted) soy nuts or edamame
Tea, green and black	Antioxidant; bioflavonoid source; promotes heart health	Tea leaves in water	1 cup

| Zeaxanthine | Promotes visual health; reduces macular degeneration | Red, yellow, orange, green vegetables | 16 mg |
| Chondroitin | Stimulates action of glucosamine | | 500-600 mg |

One clove of garlic a day can lower heart disease risk by 25 percent. With the New Orleans Program recipes, consuming this much garlic is easy.

We should also remember that many pharmaceuticals can rob the body of micronutrients. For instance, high blood pressure medications can reduce the availability of zinc. The cholesterol-lowering statins seriously deplete coenzyme Q10 from heart muscle.

LET'S NOT FORGET FOOD

As much as we need supplements, let's not forget our wider context of healthful eating through the New Orleans Program. For micronutrients and nutrition in general, our bodies require a wide variety of fresh food.

Should diabetics or obese persons eat fresh fruit? The glycemic index approach would scare them away, but we've found that a moderate amount of whole fruit has little practical negative effect on blood-sugar balance. The water content of fruit contributes to hydration and makes losing weight easier. And eating whole fruits does correlate with better heart health. Remember, we mean whole fruit—*not* sugar-laden processed fruit drinks, and *not* those sugary canned fruits allowed by the Dietary Guidelines 2005.

Collard greens and cabbage give us excellent micronutrients for our eyes and our entire bodies. Collards happen to be one of my favorite vegetables. Maybe when you've tried these vegetables, they haven't been well prepared. Overcooked cabbage, for example, releases stinky chemicals. Cooked just a little, both cabbage and collard greens can have a delicious, sophisticated taste. My friend Dr. Michael Francis introduced me to the use of collards in local soups.

CREOLE COLLARD, BLACK BEAN, AND ANDOUILLE SOUP
Serves 4 to 6.

This quickly prepared, fragrant dish was inspired by Dr. Michael Francis, anesthesiologist and creative amateur cook. Dr. Francis's version, reportedly a favorite of his father, Dr. Norman Francis, president of Xavier University in New Orleans, uses twice the sausage in this recipe and, served over rice, can be a meal in itself. To lighten the soup, you can omit the sausage altogether.

2 cups chicken stock
10-oz. can black beans, washed
10-oz. can salt-free tomatoes, drained, or 2 ripe medium tomatoes,
    cored, seeded, and chopped
¼ lb. andouille or other sausage, chopped
¾ cup collard greens, stemmed and chopped
1 tsp. salt-free Creole spice
1-2 dashes cayenne pepper or to taste
Sea salt and white pepper to taste
2 tbsp. green onion tops, sliced thin

Heat stock to a slow boil. Add beans, tomatoes, and sausage. Boil about 10 minutes.

Add collards and seasonings. Boil 10 more minutes. Add green onion, stir, adjust seasonings, and serve.

We believe in eating the fruits—and vegetables—of the earth, during all four seasons. That's the spirit of the New Orleans Program, helping us take in all the micronutrients our bodies need, all year long.

Speaking of year-long health, remember those old dogs who learned new tricks? Well, they exercised. On we go, to the next chapter.

CHAPTER 9

Independence Day:
A Melting Pot Celebrates

You never find yourself until you face the truth.   —Pearl Bailey

"You could barbecue shrimp on the banquette, it's so hot." New Orleans' semitropical climate is the focus of many conversations. Yet our weather is also misunderstood. We are often targeted by the cliché "it's not the heat, it's the humidity." But more often than not it's neither one. New Orleans enjoys at least six out of twelve months of clear, sunny days with relatively low humidity. During this time we have absolutely delightful weather, on a par with anywhere else. Of the other six months, some are cooler but crystal clear. I have to take the orchids in off of the fence in the backyard only one or two nights a year because of low temperatures. The lake effect from that large water-filled saucer, Lake Pontchartrain, keeps our temperature here on the south shore considerably higher than even just across the lake on the north shore. We do have rain, and during our days of tropical showers there's always the threat of a hurricane.

The infamous hot-and-humid New Orleans weather can last as few as three weeks in a row but never, in my experience, more than five. When New Orleanians speak about a "cold front coming through" it often means that cooler air, sweeping in from the northwest, will drop the temperature from a high of eighty-two degrees to a high of seventy-four. New Orleans nights have a sensual texture in spring, summer, and fall, alive with the scents of abundant flowers. As we walk the streets of the French Quarter, we smell the fragrances that come from secret sources behind patio walls. No wonder our nights are famous for thoughts of romance!

After Easter, the French Quarter Festival, and Jazz Fest, we have our summer traditions. School's out. Many area schools have much-appreciated graduations, festive beyond the usual cap and gown. At Ursuline Academy, founded in 1727 by nuns from France, graduates are given delicate early-summer nosegays by the nuns. At the Louise S.

McGehee School, graduates appear in ladylike pink, looking quite different from today's teenage girls in their bare-belly miniskirts. Since the 1850s, New Orleanians have continued to put their houses "in summer dress" as they leave for gulf beaches, placing loose white covers over all the furniture and sometimes even the chandeliers.

Summer is our backdrop for newer celebrations. In August, the Satchmo Summer Fest honors the legacy of New Orleans native Louis Armstrong with exhibits, music by local musicians, and—of course— food. (By the way, this great man pronounced his name "Looiss," as in St. "Louis" Cathedral. He wouldn't recognize the common mispronunciation "Looie.") In early July we have the Essence Freedom Fest, created by *Essence* magazine. Over two hundred thousand people come to hear big-name entertainers and attend empowerment lectures, seminars, and workshops on personal improvement and issues of the day. Essence Fest adds to our celebration of diversity on the Fourth of July.

Essence Fest attendees, like our millions of yearly visitors, come for the whole New Orleans experience. We are a special place, made and kept so in no small measure thanks to the African-American influences on our food, music, and culture. Essence Fest thrives on our diversity. (For more information on African-Americans in New Orleans, check our "Resources" chapter.)

Other ethnic groups such as Italians and Germans have contributed to building New Orleans. We also have large Latino groups, with Hondurans prominent, and a vibrant Vietnamese community. Some cutting-edge chefs, blending our traditional fresh foods and Creole heritage with international sensibilities, have added to our local food scene.

And of course, we like to eat. Many traditional picnic foods offer both New Orleans flavor and a New Orleans Program flair. On the Fourth of July, or any nice day, try a quick, satisfying New Orleans Program picnic. You can adjust the quantities below depending on the number of people joining in. Don't forget the picnic chest with plates, napkins, straws, ice, etc.!

CREOLE EGG SALAD SANDWICHES
Serves 2.

2 large eggs

2 tbsp. low- or nonfat mayonnaise
¼ tsp. Creole mustard
Sea salt and black pepper to taste
Dash paprika
Dash cayenne pepper
4 slices whole-grain bread, crusts trimmed

Hard-boil eggs 7-8 minutes, peel, and finely chop. Combine eggs, mayonnaise, mustard, and seasonings. Spread on 2 bread slices, cover with other 2 slices, cut in half, and wrap in plastic wrap for picnic.

QUICK BROILED CHICKEN FINGERS
Serves 2.

6 strips chicken breast
Sea salt, white pepper, and salt-free Creole spice to taste

Wash and dry chicken. Rub with seasonings. Place under hot broiler on heavy-duty foil, and cook 10-12 minutes, turning 2-3 times. Do not overcook. Wrap in plastic wrap when cool.

CREOLE LOW-SALT BARBECUE SAUCE
Makes about 2½ cups.

This sauce keeps well in the refrigerator. You can use it as a dipping sauce for grilled chicken, to dress up grilled chops, or as a regular mop-it-on barbecue sauce.

Extra-virgin olive oil
1 large clove garlic, chopped
1 medium sweet yellow onion, chopped
1 large celery stalk, chopped
1 green bell pepper, stemmed, seeded, and chopped
1 cup low-sodium tomato sauce
2 tbsp. satsuma or orange juice (fresh preferred)
2 tbsp. lemon juice (fresh preferred)
4 tbsp. apple-cider vinegar

2 tsp. hot sauce (not Tabasco)
4 tbsp. dark brown sugar
2 tbsp. Creole mustard
1 tbsp. salt-free Creole spice
1 tsp. paprika (not hot)
½ tsp. sea salt
½ tsp. black pepper

Coat large skillet with oil. Sauté garlic, onion, celery, and bell pepper until onion is clear (about 5 minutes). Add tomato sauce, citrus juices, vinegar, hot sauce, sugar, mustard, Creole spice, and paprika. Stir and bring to a boil.

Add salt and pepper, stir well, and adjust seasonings. Simmer on medium, stirring, until thickened. If more liquid is needed, add water or more satsuma/orange juice. When thickened (about 10-20 minutes), adjust to taste by adding more sugar, vinegar, or other Creole seasonings. When cool, puree in blender.

PICNIC SNACKS

Serves 2.

1 small cucumber
6 radishes
6 celery stalks
3 strings low-fat mozzarella
Grapes or other seasonal fruit of choice

Wash cucumber, peel, slice, and wrap in plastic. Wash radishes, trim, halve, and wrap. Clean celery. Cut mozzarella in half lengthwise. Place cheese strings in celery stalks and wrap. Pack grapes or fruit in bag for picnic.

POMEGRANATE ARNOLD PALMER

The revered golf pro Arnold Palmer enjoyed a half-and-half mixture of lemonade and iced tea (sweet tea, as is said in the South) for his preferred rehydration drink. This recipe adds the juice of pomegranates, which have very high antioxidant levels. For the tea in this recipe, use a "regular" pekoe blend such as Luzianne brand.

2 parts tea
Sugar
2 parts fresh lemonade
1 part commercial pomegranate juice
Ice

Sweeten tea with sugar if desired. Sweeten lemonade with sugar to taste. Mix liquids. Serve over ice.

COOL STRAWBERRY SAUCE

Fresh fruits of the season can be chosen, mixed in color and texture, and "dressed up" for a Fourth-of-July picnic, or any occasion. This cool summery sauce makes fruit flavors sing.

7 oz. cream-style farmers' cheese (or mascarpone, if you can get it)
¼ cup plain low-fat yogurt
1½ cups cleaned fresh strawberries
1 tsp. lemon juice
2 tbsp. light brown sugar

Process all ingredients in a food processor until smooth. Refrigerate 1 hour. Serve with fresh fruit.

EXERCISE: JUST DO IT

Go Fourth on the River is the name of the Fourth-of-July picnic organized by New Orleans along the river batture in the French Quarter. The event includes our annual Fourth-of-July run or walk. The uninitiated might be worried about running in the New Orleans summer heat! Yet July jogging in New Orleans holds little anxiety for our regular runners. They know how to handle the warmer temperatures by staying well hydrated before and during their exercise.

"I hate exercise," says Maryflynn Thomas, a trim New Orleans businesswoman, playwright, and actress. "But I know I have to do it. I may not do it for a while—a short while, I might add—but then I get right back."

We agree with Maryflynn. Most of us don't enjoy exercise and yet believe, rightly, that we have to do it. The benefits of exercise are manifold, and the risks of not exercising are ominous. To explain our exercise recommendations for the New Orleans Program, we begin with three basic questions:

- How is exercise good for us?
- How much exercise do we really need?
- Is too much exercise dangerous?

All experts agree that exercise is good for us. We know that in children, regular exercise increases muscle strength, agility and flexibility, and bone density. For both boys and girls who exercise, the stage is set for a lifetime of lower osteoporosis risk. Researchers recently reported 7 percent more bone density in children who played soccer twice a week than in other control groups.

Here is our all-purpose reduction sauce for children's exercise, boiled down from the professional literature and the experts.

- All children should be as active as possible daily. Walking up and down stairs, doing active chores, and bicycling or walking rather than being driven—all should be encouraged whenever safe.
- Children and teens should be encouraged to engage in sports activities within their capabilities. Coaches and physical education instructors have access to a large body of information on safe exercises. Parents should ask whether their children's coaches are well versed in these matters.
- All teens should perform at least thirty to forty-five minutes of moderately vigorous, heart-rate-raising physical exercise three times a week.

Some teens might want an exercise plan to follow. The New Orleans Program first-level plan has been proven to work nicely, especially for the overweight, and it has a low-joint-stress regimen (see Appendix B). These exercises can be done entirely at home with minimal equipment. Teens can also increase the activity level.

Children should exercise vigorously, and most of them will exercise naturally if we can lure them away from video games. Younger and older adults need to understand the benefits of exercise if they're expected to make time for it among work and family commitments.

Neither TV nor the Internet nor cell phones are going to go away, and children may feel that using them is their right. Some experts believe that electronic games and media improve eye-hand coordination. But children need *limits,* for their own health, and it's up to parents to control the use of these electronic devices in their children's lives.

While most parents say they are vigilant, studies have demonstrated the opposite. Children spend more time at their various screens than parents suspect, and the American Academy of Pediatrics believes this exposure can pose "a significant risk to the health of children and adolescents." Here we'll pass over the debate about whether TV, Internet, and video-game content can provoke aggressive behavior and irrational fears in children, and we'll pass over the risks of exposure to chat rooms, Web sites, and spam. We'll simply say that too much of these various electronic pursuits can steal our children's time and weaken their health, mesmerizing them for long periods and making them chronically inactive.

We will not debate author Steven Johnson (*Everything Bad Is Good for You: How Today's Popular Culture Is Actually Making Us Smarter*), who maintains that "the most debased forms of mass diversion—video games and violent television dramas and juvenile sitcoms—turn out to be nutritional after all." He feels, without solid supporting evidence, that the "training" from games and reality TV exercises the brain's decision-making process. He completely ignores the erosion factor of TV and electronic game time on real human interaction, exercise, and proper eating and the inappropriate influence of many kid-directed TV ads.

HOW IS EXERCISE GOOD FOR US?

Immediate benefits. The benefits of a single workout happen right away. A ripple effect of body chemicals throughout our tissues helps lower our blood pressure, improve our sense of well-being, reduce blood sugar, enhance blood flow, and stimulate hormones and other substances that build and preserve our tissues instead of breaking them down. A study in the *American Journal of Cardiology* showed that men in their fifties who exercised the previous day had 25 percent less fatty substances in their blood than those who had not exercised. When we exercise, we feel better, our metabolism is revved up, and our stress level is reduced—benefits that will increase over time.

Long-term benefits. For adults, exercise can help maintain our lean muscle mass, which is our chief metabolic engine. It keeps the weight-control train chugging along, even while we sleep. Lean muscle mass consumes energy in the form of sugar around the clock, helping to prevent insulin resistance. So lean muscle mass is a vital asset for health. Studies show that adults over fifty tend to lose 5 percent of their lean muscle mass each year, but this process can be virtually halted or even reversed by exercise and resistance training.

Dr. Anthony Capps has personally experienced the "metabolic switch" that regular exercise brings.

I notice when I don't exercise for about five days . . . I feel like something's not right. When I don't eat right, it's the same thing. I'll notice that if I eat too much of something that's not good for me, it will affect my whole being and I'm just not feeling myself all of a sudden. The fatty foods . . . are exquisitely tasty. But I think once we've switched over our lifestyle, . . . we can prime other taste buds . . . where these other foods that are fresh vegetables and protein foods can become really tasty. . . . I have to have nuts now. I never ate nuts before. I can eat as many nuts as I want, different kinds of nuts, and I don't gain an ounce because of the good fat that's in them and of course because I'm working out.

A study of 2,000 retired men, ages seventy to ninety-three, showed that walking two miles a day reduced by half the risk of Alzheimer's. The Harvard Nurses Study of 16,000 retired women, ages seventy to eighty-one, revealed that those who walked as little as ninety minutes a week had much better mental capacity than those who did no exercise. Brisk walking can provide aerobic benefits and burn calories, and it's much easier than jogging on your bones, joints, tendons, and feet. So don't feel inferior to those who might be jogging past you. For more information, consult the Web site www.walking.about.com.

Dr. Richard Meyer, a New Orleans orthopedist, recommends bicycling.

It is absolutely the best exercise for the knees. Unlike the treadmill, it actually builds strength, especially in the quadriceps. You can do it at your own pace.

The one secret is to make sure that at the bottom of its travel, the pedal nearly extends your leg completely. With this one precaution, bicycling is very safe and has little likelihood of causing any injury.

Weight-bearing exercise (this excludes swimming) can preserve our bone density, which can diminish with age. Along with calcium supplementation, exercise that includes strength training is the best thing we can do to protect our bones.

If we exercise regularly, we can reward ourselves with an occasional Fourth-of-July indulgence. Once our metabolism is revved up, we can eat that special treat once in a while without gaining weight or derailing our health.

As a lovely bit of lagniappe, we find that exercising regularly just makes us feel good. Gov. Mike Huckabee of Arkansas, who relates his personal triumph over the metabolic syndrome in his recent book *Quit Digging Your Grave with a Knife and Fork: A 12-Stop Program to End Bad Habits and Begin a Healthy Lifestyle,* gradually learned to enjoy exercise. He says, "It's not about what goes in your mouth but what goes on in your mind."

Stopping exercise temporarily. On the New Orleans Program, achieving a level of physical best health may take two to three months. Once we're there, what happens if we stop exercising? Sadly, we lose that best-health level, little by little. It takes two or three weeks to lose it completely, according to exercise physiologist Dr. Melinda Sothern. This observation fits my personal experience. Yet if we resume exercising within that time, we can regain our best health faster than it took us to achieve it initially. So we should all "get right back," like Maryflynn Thomas, even if our exercise pattern has been temporarily derailed by illness, pressing events, or travel.

Brain function. It has been suspected all along that complex exercise improves brain function. McGill University researchers very recently reported that of three groups of older people—nonexercisers, walkers, and tango dancers—only the tango group showed improvements in complex brain function. As expected, the walkers showed better function than nonexercisers. But the walkers did not improve in complex function as did the tangoers. This observation confirms my own experience with my late-eighty- to ninety-year-old dancing patients.

HOW MUCH EXERCISE DO WE REALLY NEED?

In the Dietary Guidelines 2005, our government urges us to include exercise.

Exercise Specifics: Government Expert Panel Recommendations in the Dietary Guidelines 2005

- For general health benefits: 30 minutes, moderate intensity, 4 days a week.
- For weight loss and prevention of weight gain: 60 minutes, moderate to vigorous intensity, 4 days a week.
- For sustained weight loss: 60 to 90 minutes, moderate intensity, 7 days a week.
- For older adults: What the panel means by "older" is not specified, and neither is the duration, intensity, or frequency of the "regular activity" it recommends. This is among the many hazy recommendations in the Dietary Guidelines 2005.

Neither Chef Besh nor I are exercise physiologists, but we have studied what various experts recommend. We believe that ninety minutes a day of vigorous exercise is not necessary for best health. Studies since 1995 have compared the benefits of moderate and vigorous exercise, and the results show that moderate exercise confers just as many health benefits, if not more. We recommend for the New Orleans Program that all adults engage in thirty to forty-five minutes of moderate exercise, three times a week. If you want to do it more often, that's fine. Within reasonable limits, more exercise will not hurt you but will simply burn more calories. No-exercise days allow muscles to repair and grow.

Our exercise program expends a good amount of calories for someone of average adult male weight, about 170 pounds. If you are interested in customizing a program for yourself to meet a certain level of calorie expenditure per week, information is available at www.caloriecontrol.org\exercalc.html (see "Resources" chapter).

By moderate exercise, we mean exercise to the point of breaking a light sweat and increasing breathing and heart rates but not to the point that it's impossible to carry on a brief conversation while exercising. We're talking about exercising for best health, not preparing for a marathon or the Olympics.

The New Orleans Program includes exercise as a necessary component. We recommend that anyone with known health problems, especially heart or breathing problems or severe obesity, consult a doctor before starting exercise. For some individuals who are simply overweight without obvious heart, lung, or joint problems, such a checkup is optional, since our Phase I exercise program (the first six months) provides the muscular effort needed to obtain the benefits of exercise without placing undue strain on joints or tissues.

**The New Orleans Program Exercise Recommendations
Phase I, Adults**

- 30 to 45 minutes, moderate intensity, 3 days a week.
- Combine cardiopulmonary exercise, stretching, and resistance exercises.
- Utilize every opportunity to walk, use the stairs, and keep moving whenever possible.

After reviewing the evidence, we are convinced that combining cardiopulmonary exercise (walking, biking, using the treadmill) with stretching and resistance exercises will give the best results.

Walking as cardiopulmonary exercise. Walking has long been recognized as good for our health. George Cheyne in his sixteenth-century *Essay of Health and Long Life* praised walking as a "most natural and most useful exercise." Cristobel Mendez of Spain in *The Book of Bodily Exercise* (1553) warned that "inactivity hurts." Both were physicians.

Several recent books enumerate the virtues of walking. We agree. Walking works either in your own home, on a treadmill, at a mall, or outside. It is easy on the joints. It provides a cardiopulmonary workout that you can adjust to your own pace. When done in proper form, walking can improve posture and prevent some of the stooping that can come with age. The participants in Phase I of the New Orleans Program walked briskly for twenty minutes. By then, they had broken a light sweat and started breathing more rapidly. You may also be comfortable increasing the exercise level by carrying weights of one or two pounds in each hand and/or adding the arm-swing strength component. Some experts caution against weights. Unless used correctly, they can damage muscles and tendons. Light weights are OK but not necessary when the important resistance exercises are done.

After the first six months of entry-level exercise, we recommend a somewhat more strenuous thirty- to forty-five-minute group of exercises be done three times a week. Many find that a regular, nonchanging sequence of exercise works best: walking, then aerobic exercise that is challenging enough to make you sweat. Others find that varying the aerobic exercises from session to session works best: walking, then upper-body exercises; next session walking, then lower-body exercises.

Magazines and Internet sites scream headlines like "Perfect Spring Workout for the Best Abs Ever on the Beach This Summer!" Can you really "spot focus" exercise? Not entirely, and not with moderate exercise. We are recommending a "body maintenance" program, not a bodybuilding program. You cannot, for example, exercise away a double chin. You can reduce it by losing weight overall. Performing our aerobics naturally exercises the neck muscles. Weight loss and exercised neck muscles together can reduce a double chin.

We recommend, after losing some weight and doing our Phase I exercises for about six months, that you consider advancing to the Phase II exercises we suggest. The menu of Phase II exercises we offer can be found on our Web site. If you have any health concerns, consult your doctor before moving on to Phase II aerobic activities, which, although not strenuous, do involve more weight bearing.

For Phase II, we definitely suggest adding the power-walk component with one- to five-pound weights in each hand, using rhythmic arm swings. Don't start with the heaviest weights! As you move into strength building, you should build up gradually and comfortably—as with all parts of the New Orleans Program.

Walking requires healthy feet. All too often we don't pay enough attention to foot health. Diabetes can damage the circulation and the peripheral nerves in the feet, and other vascular problems can even make amputation necessary. We take our feet for granted, as we do our thumbs, until they're injured or not functioning. Here we offer a number of common-sense suggestions to help us remember our feet, before it's too late.

Maintaining Foot Health

- Make sure regular and sports shoes fit well, providing good support and toe room.
- Alternate shoes you wear daily.
- Diabetics with neuropathy or others with any problems: get prompt medical attention or regular checkups.
- Massages help.
- Remember, if your feet are in trouble, so is your mobility and ability to exercise.

Of course, many of these complications, including diabetes itself, can be prevented by embarking early in life on the New Orleans Program for best health.

Stretching. Even though walking is an excellent cardiopulmonary workout, it is not enough exercise. By itself, it does relatively little to build muscle strength. We use stretching, practiced with good form, to complement the muscle and joint benefits of walking. Stretching should occupy four to five minutes of every workout session. If we stretch, we are less likely to injure ourselves, which is possible even with moderate exercise. Stretching also encourages flexibility and helps us get back in touch with our physical selves. You may be surprised how enjoyable it is to stretch.

Resistance exercises. These exercises are the last of the three components to help you reach your best-health level. We've already seen one small resistance exercise in the use of weights while walking. There are many other kinds of resistance exercises: free weights, resistance devices, and machines. If you are sufficiently overweight, you may be able to use your own body parts for resistance exercises, as we recommend in the Phase I resistance component of the New Orleans Program. When you inspect these exercises in Appendix B, don't be fooled. They're harder than they look. The Chair Rise exercise is actually a modified squat exercise that provides a big metabolic boost.

Even having done these exercises many times, I still feel the stretch. Feeling this stretch should be pleasant. And I still sweat a little when I perform these exercises with correct form and the specified repetitions.

These resistance exercises are based on the advice of certified fitness trainers, a review of the scientific literature, and the success of our clinical testing. They are meant to increase your bodily awareness. Moderate exercise, with some increased breathing and a little sweat, should be a sensual and rewarding experience.

Resistance exercises do what a regular cardiopulmonary workout alone cannot do. They strengthen the major muscle groups—lower back, buttocks, and abdominals—that help us maintain our posture and stability, reduce the risk of falling, and give us the ability to do everyday tasks such as lifting sacks of groceries. They increase bone density as well as muscle strength. Their simple but vital functions led us to include resistance exercises in our thirty- to forty-five-minute workout. Your best health requires *some regular resistance exercise.*

IS TOO MUCH EXERCISE DANGEROUS?

Vigorous and prolonged exercise is hard to sell, and for good reason. First, it can be unpleasant; the average person does not want to work this hard. Second, it is inordinately time-consuming; the average person does not have the time. Finally, we are skeptical: too much exercise may not be good for us. In fact, studies have told us that strong muscle exertion creates potentially damaging oxidative free radicals. As we know, these can damage tissues and promote the wear and tear of aging. Too much exercise may even suppress the immune system.

Several epidemiological studies since the 1990s have examined the post-retirement health of National Football League players. They found that former linemen for the NFL have 50 percent more heart disease than the average American male. They also suffer more from depression, bursitis, and tendonitis than the general population. We do not know whether these are the results of too much exercise while playing, or too little after the playing career is over. We see televised images of the once-trim "Sir" Charles Barkley and other ex-players who act as color commentators, and we wonder.

For the New Orleans Program, we do not recommend running— not even in Phase II. Running has a long history. Its popularity in the United States blossomed after the governmental emphasis on fitness that began in the 1950s. Commercial product lines, books, magazines, and careers have been built on running. One of the best-known morality tales about running revolves around Jim Fixx, a convert from the obese and cigarette-smoking lifestyle who published a best-selling book in 1978. He ran many miles every day between lectures and appearances. Yet his running career came to an abrupt end. As we was jogging along a rural road not far from his home, he was felled by a heart attack. Statistically, he had converted himself into a healthy person, after years of putting his health at risk by lifestyle choices. So what killed him? Was it the antioxidants from over-exercise, which damaged his previously stressed tissues? His untimely death will remain a mystery. However, it was around this period that experts began to question the value of strenuous exercise.

We do suggest maintaining hydration, or rehydrating after exercise, with water or, if you have burned a good amount of calories, with a sports beverage that contains good-quality minerals (electrolytes) as well as antioxidants. Muscle efficiency goes down over 12 percent with as little as 3 percent dehydration. However, as we have learned, rapid rehydration with plain water can be dangerous unless we replenish sodium and electrolytes also, which are available in sports drinks.

OUR EXERCISES WON'T KILL YOU OR BANKRUPT YOU

The mighty voices of our government have preached about exercise for a long time, to no avail. Today's ideas about exercise began with the attention-grabbing headlines of the 1950s. These headlines informed us that American children were in miserable physical shape, compared with children in other countries, and Pres. Dwight D. Eisenhower therefore established the first Presidential Council on Physical Fitness. Exercise programs became big business. Yet Americans did not get up and get moving. They have remained on the couch. Two-thirds of Americans still do not exercise regularly. This state of affairs is great for our cardiovascular, pharmaceutical, and osteoporosis industries, but not good for our population. Why aren't we on the move?

Maybe we still think that healthy exercise has to be difficult, overexerting, "killing" exercise. It doesn't, as the New Orleans Program shows. Or maybe we believe that we have to "pay a lot of money and join a gym" to get the right kind of exercise. Millions of Americans do belong to gyms and use personal trainers. In one professional organization, the members who had personal trainers grew from 1,000 to 10,000 in fifteen years. Athletes have personal trainers, after all. Must we all have personal trainers in order to maintain our best health? Absolutely not, as the New Orleans Program shows us again. Personal trainers may be fashionable to some people, or motivating to others, but they are not necessary. All we need are a supportive pair of shoes for walking, some inexpensive dumbbells, and a good straight chair.

Connie, a fifty-year-old patient, continued to have trouble controlling diabetes. I asked what exercises she did. She replied, "I belong to a gym, but I never got a dime's worth, it was so inconvenient." We discussed a doable three-times-a-week thirty-minute-session plan. "I have a nice driveway. I can walk that for twenty minutes, then exercise in my bedroom," she concluded. After three months on the New Orleans Program, and with daily soluble fiber and micronutrients, she had lost nine pounds, achieving good blood-sugar control and stablizing her eye problems.

I have exercised regularly at the rate we recommend. I have belonged to gyms, but I gave it up as unnecessary and inconvenient. Now I exercise regularly as the New Orleans Program recommends. And we've tried to make our exercise suggestions completely convenient. In short, we're trying to tell you that exercising makes you feel good. It will increase your sense of well-being. It will reduce your stress.

EXERCISE CAN'T DO EVERYTHING

Lifelong moderate exercise can work wonders for maintaining your health and weight. Yet exercise is not a magic route to a "perfect" body, in this culture obsessed with appearances. In the real world, single "spot" exercises for flattening abs or reducing thighs are not worth your time and money. And what about cellulite? If you begin moderate exercise early in life, you may help prevent cellulite, but no amount of exercise, wraps, creams, lotions, or gels can cure it. Cellulite plagues women, especially, and its cause eludes consensus. It may be that women's particular tissue structure, right below the skin, makes fat cells more likely to lodge between the skin and the muscle tissue. Women who exercise heavily and then gain weight are especially prone to developing cellulite, which seems quite unfair. Yet there are no cure-alls—not even exercise.

I learned about cure-alls when I was introduced to comic books as a child. We took the train from North Carolina to Mississippi to visit my cousins when I was seven. It was great. The countryside flew by. Eventually I ran out of things to read, though, and some uniformed servicemen (grand adults to me, but probably in their early twenties) offered me some comic books. I was hooked fast. After fighting the bad guys with Batman and Robin or saving the world with Superman, I read about how to treat the heartbreak of psoriasis, how to collect better stamps and coins, and even how to create a manly chest! The comic-book ads promised that anyone could transform himself from the object of a bully's attack to a Charles Atlas figure that no one else on the beach would mess with. Here was a cure-all for "weaklings"! But like most exercise champions in the last century, these ads didn't mention the heart or lungs or blood sugar of that Charles Atlas guy—just his appearance. That guaranteed muscular chest was where the money was.

FOR A LONG LIFE, AN ACTIVE LIFE

Some studies do show a correlation between adequate exercise and longer life. Perhaps exercise does promote longevity. Yet unquestionably, exercise enhances the quality of the life you have. We encourage you to increase your exercise beyond your maintenance workouts. Park far away from the store in the parking lot. Use the stairs instead of the elevator. Carry your own packages, even if it takes several trips. Play volleyball in your backyard. Dance. Garden. Have fun.

Meeting the residents of the French Quarter ought to convince anyone that exercise both lengthens life and improves its quality. The French Quarter has one of the highest concentrations in the United States of independently living and active people in their nineties. Even when they are elderly, French Quarter residents walk nearly everywhere. They walk with packages. They walk to meetings. They walk to dinners. They walk to social engagements and cultural events. They may go to bed at 9:00, but four hours earlier they are at a local wateringhole having a cocktail and visiting with friends. Our observations here agree with other anecdotal evidence. For instance, why do those who live in two-story houses live longer than their neighbors in one-story houses? More exercise from climbing stairs, presumably. And exercise lowers the risk of serious injuries as time goes by.

By exercising throughout their long lives, residents of the French Quarter don't need the Fourth of July in order to celebrate their independence. If we follow their example, we too can have more "independence days" of our own, even as we grow older.

We must not forget our minds and spirits, however. Especially in the new millennium, we need to reduce our anxiety levels. Our suggestions in the next chapter for stress reduction are healthful, pleasant, and even fun. They "grow on you."

CHAPTER 10

All Saints' Day:
Wake and Repast

Virtually every organ and every chemical constituent of the human
body is involved in the general stress reaction.
—Dr. Hans Selye, human stress-reaction
pioneer and author of *The Stress of Life*

Schoen's Funeral Home—a pastel, stuccoed fantasy of a Spanish-
colonial building on a lovely landscaped corner of Canal Street—has
sent off many New Orleanians in style over the last century. As I pulled
into Schoen's parking lot several years ago, I knew the wake I had come
for would be no ordinary one. Sadly, Kay Heinrichs Prudhomme, the
Kay of the renowned K-Paul's Louisiana Kitchen, had passed away. Kay's
husband, Chef Paul, was upstairs to receive.

The spirit of a New Orleans wake combines mourning with celebration.
This combination is true to our New Orleans vision of life. We believe
that life is to be enjoyed, even though we all die eventually. It's not simply that we love to party (and we do). Our vision is broader than that. We
cherish our whole lives, complete with their ups and downs. Whatever life
brings us, we accept. We can find ways to laugh, to heal, to hope, and to
be content. We recognize and treasure our *joie de vivre,* and we also know
when we need to seek peace of mind. This is the New Orleans attitude.

True to our New Orleans way, an amazing feast was presented at
Schoen's for the wake of Kay Heinrichs Prudhomme. The dishes available in the undercroft included Kay's Pasta, beef debris, Chef Paul's
incomparable étouffée, and melt-in-your-mouth pralines.

New Orleans wakes do not have to be this spectacular to embody
the New Orleans attitude. The typical wake in such Creole enclaves as
the Seventh Ward will include the family and a few close friends who
are invited to the family home for "repast."

Leah Chase, internationally known queen of Creole chefs, explains.

Repasts are not prepared by one person—it's a bring-a-dish thing. That's how they pay homage, how they show respect—by bringing a dish. Even after death, you have the food. I make jambalaya, baked macaroni, and baked chicken.

Here is Leah's own low-sodium chicken recipe.

LOW-SODIUM CREOLE OVEN-FRIED CHICKEN
Serves 2.

½ **frying chicken**
White pepper to taste
1 cup flour
¼ **tsp. ground thyme**
½ **tsp. paprika**
¼ **tsp. granulated garlic**

Preheat oven to 375 degrees. Remove skin from chicken, cut chicken in pieces, and season with white pepper. Place flour in bag or bowl. Mix in last three ingredients. Shake chicken in bag in flour mixture. Remove chicken and shake off excess flour. Spray pan with nonstick cooking spray. Place chicken in pan. Bake 45 minutes.

Good food brings us together at New Orleans gatherings, even wakes. With traditional dishes and ample libations, family and friends can remember the life of the loved one now gone. Here is a dish that would fit right in at such a gathering.

FREE-RANGE CHICKEN POT PIE
Serves 6.

Some people may be shocked at the inclusion of a recipe for a two-crust pie here, since those are notoriously high in calories. This preparation reduces the calories but retains the knockout, "I remember this Sunday dinner at Grandma's" taste. You won't believe it! When cooking, be sure that the bottom crust, which you can see through the glass pie dish, has browned nicely. As a bonus, you'll be making chicken stock, which can be refrigerated or frozen.

Pastry for 2-crust 9-inch pie
2½ lb. free-range chicken, cut up
1 small to medium yellow onion, chopped
2 celery stalks with tops, coarsely chopped
1 medium carrot, chopped
6 sprigs parsley
2 hard-boiled eggs
Sea salt and black pepper to taste
Paprika (not hot) to taste
¼ cup whole-grain flour
2 tbsp. butter

Preheat oven to 400 degrees. Line a glass pie dish with 1 crust pastry. In a large stockpot, place chicken, onion, celery, carrot, and parsley. Cover with water.

Bring to a medium boil and cook until chicken is tenderly done (about 25 minutes). Remove chicken and reserve stock. After chicken has cooled, remove skin, pick meat off bones, and chop chicken fine to make 2 cups.

Take whites of eggs and chop fine. Add to chicken with spices. Mix well. Place chicken filling in pastry-lined pie dish.

Defat stock in stockpot. Bring 1½ cups stock to a boil. Mix flour with enough water to form a thin, smooth paste. Add to stock and stir until thickened. Stir in 1 tbsp. butter.

Pour thickened stock evenly over chicken. Cover with remaining pastry, pinching edges together. Pierce top of pie with fork. Melt 1 tbsp. butter and brush or lightly rub on top of pie. Bake until beautifully brown, approximately 40 minutes.

Chef Besh shares here a family favorite.

GRANDMA'S ROASTED CHICKEN

2½ lb. whole fryer chicken
2 cloves garlic
Salt and black pepper to taste
1 bay leaf

Extra-virgin olive oil
Thyme
Rosemary
Tarragon
2 onions
1 carrot
1 celery stalk

Stuff chicken with garlic, salt, pepper, and bay leaf. Tie up bird. Rub with olive oil.

Chop herbs and rub all over chicken. Slice onions, carrot, and celery and place in bottom of a roasting pan. Place chicken on top and add water to avoid burning onions. Roast 1 hour at 400 degrees, rotating 180 degrees halfway through. Leftovers can make a great chicken salad for lunches, parties, or picnics.

The New Orleans attitude also sustains the jazz funeral and second-line customs. These traditions are carried on especially by jazz-community members, local leadership, and residents of Creole heritage. Most of the typical jazz funeral takes place in the street, where joyful songs are intermingled with mournful ones. The funeral procession walks from the funeral home to the cemetery, turning spectators into active second-line participants along the way. A jazz funeral involves the spirit of the community in that unique New Orleans mixture of mourning and celebration.

Second lines are popular throughout New Orleans, beyond jazz funerals. They can be sponsored by clubs, but they're often spontaneous. Second lines exemplify the New Orleans vision of life, and tourists love them. We all like the show: people dancing in the streets and keeping time with whatever they have handy—an umbrella, a handkerchief, a napkin.

THE NEW ORLEANS ATTITUDE AND YOUR HEALTH

We believe that our New Orleans attitude goes hand in hand with good health. A person cannot live by physical nutrients and exercise alone. To be fully healthy, we need to be able to enjoy life and nurture our spirits. We use the word "spirit" in the most inclusive sense possible, embracing similar meanings like psyche, essence, core, center, soul, chi, mind, emotional makeup, love, meaning, and happiness. We choose "spirit" because it is a holistic word, derived from the word "breath" and signifying "life force." With respect for both the religious and the nonreligious, this word "spirit" is our gesture towards whatever force makes our lives positive and meaningful, whatever gives us the will to live. *That's* what we believe should be nurtured, in each of us, for best health. The New Orleans attitude can help us nurture our spirits.

The three basic components of the New Orleans Program are good food, healthy exercise, and spiritual nurture. These enhance each other, of course. We've devoted several chapters to food, and the previous chapter to exercise.

Now we'd like to discuss the third component, spiritual nurture. We're dividing our discussion into two chapters. Chapter 10 will suggest some paths for self-nurture—that is, making positive connections with one's own spirit. Chapter 11 will deal with spiritual nurture through connectedness with others.

SELF-NURTURE: THE ATTITUDE

For spiritual self-nurture, we take our first cue from the New Orleans attitude—don't stress out; don't over-concentrate; don't take life (or yourself) too seriously. This is the Big Easy, remember? In a recent *New Yorker* cartoon, a newly arrived soul is escorted by an angel to the Pearly Gates. The caption reads: *So much for antioxidants.* This cartoon makes us laugh at our more serious selves, with our determination to figure everything out and do everything right all the time. We can't, of course! So let's relax.

We need to laugh. New Orleanians laugh a lot. That long-running *Reader's Digest* section called "Laughter—The Best Medicine" had it right. Laughter relieves stress, fear, and anger, and it provides these healthy results:

- Stress-chemical reduction
- Immune-system stimulation
- Heart stimulation (the good kind)
- Circulation improvement
- Improved pain tolerance

Of course, in the Big Easy, we're familiar with life's negatives, like everyone else. We live in everyday reality with all its pain, depression, disappointment, frustration, bigotry, racism, social injustice, rudeness, death, losses of all types, and just plain meanness. Yet we're "easy" here because we allow ourselves easy access to the antidotes for these negatives. We can "laugh it off" with love and respect for ourselves, with generous doses of giggles, belly laughs, pleasure, and good old silliness. We tap into the joy of our humanity—it's a New Orleans thing, maybe. Aristotle's definition of man as "the animal who laughs" is common wisdom with us.

Thoughts on Stress

- Repeated or continuous stress, not the quick "fight or flight" stress, causes disease.
- We are not educated to recognize stress, so it continues to attack.
- Life comes with stress factors for all of us, although they can vary.
- Twenty-first-century America creates stress in the overscheduled lifestyle: always busy, information overloaded, sensory overloaded, always competitive.
- The stress antidote: Recognize you have it, and practice personal recreation. Set aside a daily dose of (seemingly unproductive) quiet time. Have fun. Learn to laugh a lot, kidlike.

Jonathan Ferrara, gallery and bar owner at Royal and Kerlerec streets, refers to the New Orleans "way of life that is less stressful . . . more pleasant." He adds, "The flip side is, look at New York. You go down the street in New York and nobody says hello to anybody. Do you think that relieves any of the stress that happens in your normal day?" He says that "being happy, I firmly believe, adds to being healthy." We cultivate that genuinely easygoing attitude down here in the "City That Care Forgot."

So if you are on the New Orleans Program, and among the majority of Americans who are currently overweight, you should lose those pounds in a slow, non-stressful fashion. Don't beat up on yourself. Just avoid certain foods and choose a wide variety of others, in moderate portions. Don't let the scale add stress—don't weigh yourself, if it bothers you. Don't worry about counting calories. Simply notice how your clothes fit, and if you wish, take the tape measure to your waist once in a while. While you're losing weight, don't lose your sense of humor. It's an important part of your spirit.

We want to mention two physical methods that can help you nurture your own spirit: deep breathing and massage. Among the array of integrative medical approaches used by one-third to two-thirds of Americans today (others include meditation, yoga, prayer, and herbal medicines), we think these are the easiest to understand and do. We're encouraged that a growing body of literature supports the efficacy of integrative medicine as a whole.

Joyce Chifici, an advocate of yoga, has told us that her body has an appetite for this particular physical-spiritual approach.

I didn't go [to yoga class] last week for a couple of days for different reasons, and it's like there was something missing in my life. . . . I think that's one thing that is helping me now. I know it is [helping] with my sciatic nerve. I think I told you about that. My right hip got out of line, pinched off my sciatic nerve, and my chiropractor suggested and kept suggesting that I get into the yoga clinic, and that's what I finally did a little over two years ago, and as long as I practice yoga I have no problems with my back. It's unbelievable.

Joni Perell, Ph.D., social worker, therapist, and advocate of "alternative modalities" for healing, is encouraged that the Louisiana state practice board has recently been authorizing Eye Movement Desensitization Reprocessing and Thought Field Therapy, both of which have been practiced with some success in different, complex patients since the 1980s.

BREATHING EXERCISES

Quiet. That's the problem. Very little of twenty-first-century life is quiet. Try to remember the last time you were in a completely quiet place by yourself. Persons interested in self-nurture over the past 5,000 years have all emphasized the critical role of quiet in achieving that nurture. To use breathing exercises, we must make quiet time to nurture our own spirits. We recommend starting with five minutes of quiet time every day. I have found it helpful to carve quiet time from the early morning while all the others in the house, including the animals, are still asleep. I sit perfectly still, or I lie down and remain still.

The easiest way to clear the mind and make quiet time effective is to concentrate on your own breathing. Focus on the movement of air in and out of your body. Feel the internal rhythm of your breathing. As the days continue, you may be able to expand your quiet time to a full twenty minutes, the duration recommended by many regular practitioners of yoga meditation and other self-nurturing techniques. The goal is to clear the mind. Remain perfectly still and breath centered, as much as you can. Once clear, one can repeat a mantra or phrase, or just keep a quiet, blank mind. One can pray during this time, or think positive thoughts.

My personal preference has been to divide my quiet time into two segments. My morning quiet time occurs early. At first, I found meditating hard. My mind tends to be busy. Clearing the decks took some practice; once achieved, like physical exercise, subsequent sessions became easier. I have called this first part "the key." I usually practice the second part on the way home in the evening.

My quiet time technique involves deep, relaxing breaths. This technique has been a focus of human beings interested in self-nurturing for thousands of years. Once you get to know it, it is easy to understand why that focus has persisted. A deep, cleansing breath has great power. It can reduce your stress and relax your muscle tension immediately. It is a wonderful antidote to road rage. It provides an excellent technique for avoiding a confrontational comeback that may otherwise be forming in your brain.

Breath exercises can always come in handy. Science has now discovered the phenomenon of "Monday-morning mortality." This is indeed what it sounds like—we're more likely to die on Monday, from early morning to noon. Our chances of a heart attack or stroke from uncontrolled stress reactions and their blood-vessel-constricting chemicals are magnified then. The stress of a new work week, perhaps aggravated by road rage, creates chemical imbalances that are linked to acute coronary artery blockages, stroke, and death, according to researchers in the *Journal of the American Medical Association*. Driving to work on Monday would be a good time to practice our deep, cleansing breaths.

Harvard researchers, using MRI, very recently showed a physical change in the brains of a small number of Americans who meditate twenty minutes daily. The meditation employed brain "exercise" rather than any religiosity. The meditators performed better on brain function tests (memory and attention) than nonmeditators, even after sleep deprivation, a known enemy of brain function. So working breathing exercises and meditation into your routine can offer several kinds of benefits.

MASSAGE AND SELF-NURTURE

Therapeutic massage techniques can help you nurture your spirit. We realize that there are multifold types of massage work, and we are not attempting a complete description. We are simply suggesting that massage work that suits your needs can often help you get in touch with your own body, become one with your body, and listen to your body. Massage can help you nurture your spirit through your body. Consider the description by Ray Busmann, who practices the Integrated Somatics version of massage.

The client lies on the table in their clothes, comfortably clothed. They don't have to take their clothes off because the technique is to cradle, rock, gently move, float the body. So, what we're talking to mostly is the nervous system and the nervous system has a chance to experience something extremely beautiful, it's as simple as that. To experience one's body maybe in a way it was originally designed to be felt, in a floating stage just as we were floating in the mother's womb or as we float in a swimming pool or originally we floated in the ocean before we decided to move up the beach, to experience a state that brings us back to who we were supposed to be, who we really are. . . . In my experience, it is amazing how quickly, with focused intention, you can create a sensation . . . where this person feels itself, even just for a moment, relieved from the daily limitations of the body . . . and brought back to how it feels to be one with oneself. . . . That can be so profound. It's almost a spiritual experience.

This is a physical practice that can reach the spirit and nurture it. Massage can be one clear path to spiritual self-nurture, to feeling good about one's self or feeling liberated. These are feelings that will reduce stress and improve the circulation and immune systems. We can nourish our bodies and spirits through massage. We can learn the language of our bodies, so that we know when we've had enough food. We can learn to relax our bodies so that we can sleep without prescriptions. As Diana Panara, another massage therapist, says:

We're very out of touch with our bodies [and] we're very much out of touch with nature. I think it's also that tactile thing, being able to feel relief, being able to walk on the grass, being able to have that in your body, [being] able to connect to the earth. . . . There's a big advantage in New Orleans that we can see the weather. It's flat here so we can see the weather. I lived in New York City and you can't see the weather. The weather sees you but you can't see the weather. I reconnected when I came to New Orleans.

FEASTING WITH THE DEAD

Being at one with our bodies, and nurturing our spirits—these are ways of relaxing and enhancing our health. Making peace with our bodies, and even with our mortality, can help us live longer. We might as well relax and enjoy the Halloween activities and the voodoo references. Halloween has always meant fun and costumes in the French Quarter. Haunted houses are everywhere there, and of course the entire Quarter is near the grave of Marie Laveau, the Voodoo Queen of New Orleans.

For Halloween treats, my family offers very lightly salted plain popcorn, a whole food that children seem to like, tied up in an orange or black sack with a contrasting ribbon. We present these healthy treats in a large decorated bowl.

The day after Halloween, November 1, is All Saints' Day in the Christian calendar. On this day, the local tradition is to go with one's family to the graveyard for a visit with ancestors long gone. We give a new coat of whitewash to the family tomb, and then we have a picnic in the cemetery. For us, this is a comforting and affirming family ritual that nurtures our spirits.

The weather is usually pleasant then, with clear air, low humidity, and light breezes. Those with ties to Lafayette Cemetery in the Garden District, across the street from Commander's Palace Restaurant, may catch sight of popular author Anne Rice, whose vampire novels have made New Orleans a destination for her fans. Members of the preservation group Save Our Cemeteries will also be nearby, performing their own rituals.

We can leave care behind at our graveyard picnics on the first of November. We can be easy, and we can relax. We have the New Orleans attitude.

CHAPTER 11

Thanksgiving Down South: Saying Grace

Reality is something you rise above. —Liza Minnelli

Thanksgiving, the uniquely American holiday, takes the prize for travel in our country. Talk about staying connected! Americans travel more during Thanksgiving than at any other time, journeying to celebrate with family and friends. New Orleans family ties are especially strong, and many transplanted New Orleanians return home for this holiday. During this four-day weekend, we reconnect over food, liberally chased with the appropriate libations. The traditional Thanksgiving feast in Southern Louisiana, of course, acquires a special local flair. We have the Louisiana method of deep frying a whole turkey and the Cajun-injector method of spicing meat with a "shot" of flavor. Then we have the "tur-duck-en," a deboned chicken inside of a deboned duck inside of a turkey, often with three layers of different stuffings (oyster, sausage, and chestnut) dividing the birds. Here is a version with a healthier dressing, which may be made with homemade stock (recipe appears later in this chapter).

TUR-DUCK-EN
Serves many, many people!

1 chicken, deboned
Salt and black pepper to taste
Wild-Rice Dressing (see below)
1 whole duck, deboned
1 whole turkey

Lay out chicken and season it inside and out. Stuff with dressing and roll up. Season duck inside and out and stuff chicken into it. Tie up duck to keep in juices. Season turkey inside and out and stuff duck into it.

Roast 5 hours at 325 degrees, covered with foil until the last hour.

The doneness is very difficult to judge because of the density of the birds. Spend the money to buy a nice, long, thin thermometer and cook until 165 degrees in center of chicken.

Wild-Rice Dressing

1⅓ cups (8 oz.) raw wild rice, rinsed and drained
4 cups turkey or chicken stock, homemade or low-sodium canned
Kosher salt and fresh-ground black pepper to taste
2 tbsp. extra-virgin olive oil
1 cup minced onion
1 tbsp. minced fresh thyme leaves
3 tbsp. minced parsley (Italian flat leaf preferred)

In a large saucepan, combine rice, stock, and salt. Bring to a boil over high heat. Reduce heat to maintain a gentle simmer, cover, and cook until tender, about 1 hour.

Heat oil in a sauté pan and sauté onion and thyme. Let cool. Fluff rice and fold in onion and parsley. Season with pepper.

Louisiana is on the migratory flight path for various species of ducks. Some make involuntary detours to our tables. This preparation works well with non-wild ducks also.

ROAST DUCK

1 5-lb. duck
Sea salt and fresh-ground black pepper to taste
Cayenne pepper to taste
Paprika (not hot) to taste

Preheat oven to 450 degrees. Pat duck dry inside and out. Season cavity generously with salt and pepper, and add cayenne and paprika to taste. Rub skin with salt and pepper, and lightly season with cayenne and paprika.

Place on a rack in a roasting pan and cook 1 hour. Watch for browning. Reduce heat to 350 degrees. Check for doneness in 15-20 minutes by piercing; juice should be clear. Enjoy!

Roast turkey is still popular in New Orleans, although we recommend avoiding frozen turkeys with additives. We offer a quick roasting method for fresh turkeys up to 16 lb. that will guarantee a "juicy" turkey throughout. Some of us may regard white meat as too "dry" and dark meat as more succulent, but this difference is often caused by the particular roasting method. As with dark meat in cold-water fish, the dark meat in turkey has a few more calories. White meat has more pure muscle fiber, used for flight in birds and for "sprinting" to avoid predators in fish. Our quick roasting method yields a fragrant pan juice. Once the fat is separated out, this juice will make a tasty gravy.

Hot as the Gates of Hell "Quick" Turkey Technique
For fresh turkeys 10-16 lb., unstuffed

- Preheat oven to 525 degrees.
- Prepare bird and place in pan lined with enough foil to cover the bird securely. Add water, broth, satsuma juice, etc. (about 1 cup), around bird. Cover with foil and seal securely.
- Bake covered 1 hour 45 minutes.
- Open foil, and continue baking until nicely browned (varies up to thirty-five minutes or so, depending on size of turkey and oven).

CORNBREAD DRESSING
Serves 6.

$\frac{1}{2}$ **cup chopped onion**
$\frac{1}{4}$ **cup diced celery**
$\frac{1}{4}$ **cup diced green bell pepper**
$\frac{1}{4}$ **cup chopped green onions**
1 tbsp. minced garlic
1 tbsp. Creole spice
1 tsp. fresh thyme
1$\frac{1}{2}$ qt. crumbled Cornbread (see below)
1 pt. turkey-neck stock
3 eggs
Salt and black pepper to taste

Sauté vegetables, spice, and thyme until tender. Let cool. Fold in remaining ingredients.

Place in a 9x13-inch baking dish that has been coated with cooking spray. Bake 30 minutes at 325 degrees. It should have a golden, crispy crust.

Cornbread
1 cup buttermilk
¼ cup oil
1 egg
1 cup cornmeal
1 cup all-purpose flour
¼ cup sugar
1 tbsp. baking powder
½ tbsp. salt

Mix all wet ingredients. Mix all dry ingredients. Mix together and pour into a 9-inch buttered pie tin. Bake 20 minutes at 325 degrees.

OYSTER DRESSING

Serves 6.

1 cup chopped onion
2 tbsp. diced celery
2 tbsp. diced green bell pepper
1 tsp. minced garlic
2 tbsp. extra-virgin olive oil
3 cups small-diced French bread
1½ cups raw oysters, chopped
2 tbsp. oyster liquor
2 eggs
¼ cup chopped green onions
1 tbsp. chopped parsley
1 tsp. Creole spice
1 tsp. Louisiana hot sauce

Sauté onion, celery, bell pepper, and garlic in oil. Remove and place in a mixing bowl. Add remaining ingredients and fold together. Pour into a baking dish and bake at 350 degrees until golden brown, about 30 minutes.

The New Orleans seasonal harvest gives us many ingredients to choose from when we create a Thanksgiving feast Louisiana style. Southern Louisiana has its own variation of the Massachusetts Pilgrim story, when our new settlers were taught to appreciate the New World's bounty by Native Americans. Because the Native Americans connected and shared with the newcomers, we learned to gather fish and shellfish from the swamps and bayous, as well as corn and other vegetables from our rich soil. A number of Creole dishes still grace our Thanksgiving tables.

"COOL SNAP" AUTUMN SOUP

Serves 4.

Finely chopped cooked chicken or ham can be added for a heartier soup, perhaps for lunch with a salad. As is, this soup is light and flavorful enough to make a great dinner starter without being overly filling.

2 ears corn
$\frac{1}{2}$ cup peeled, seeded, chopped tomato
$\frac{1}{2}$ cup thin-sliced oyster mushrooms or cremini mushrooms
1 clove garlic, mashed
Sea salt and white or black pepper to taste
Dash cayenne pepper
$3\frac{1}{2}$ cups chicken stock or vegetable stock
$\frac{1}{2}$ cup medium-chopped collard greens
2 tbsp. thin-sliced green onion tops

Slice corn kernels off ears. Simmer corn, tomato, mushrooms, garlic, and seasonings in stock 15 minutes. Adjust seasonings. Add greens and onions. Simmer 3-4 more minutes. Serve hot with lightly toasted multigrain bread.

VEGETABLE SOUP WITH BASIL AND GARLIC
Serves 4.

You may use fresh beans for this recipe if available.

5 large tomatoes
10-oz. can red beans
10-oz. can white beans
10-oz. can black-eyed or field peas
3 small to medium yellow or zucchini squashes, peeled
3 medium potatoes, peeled
½ cup uncooked whole-wheat pasta shells
3 cups chicken stock
1-2 sprigs basil, washed leaves only
5 cloves garlic
⅓ cup extra-virgin olive oil
¼ cup grated cheese (Romano, Parmesan, or your choice)
Sea salt and black pepper to taste

Drop tomatoes into briskly boiling water (one at a time is easiest). Remove, peel skin, remove seeds, and crush roughly. Place with beans, peas, squash, potatoes, and pasta into a pot, cover with stock, and boil gently until cooked, about 1 hour, stirring occasionally.

Mince basil leaves and press garlic. Combine with oil, cheese, and seasonings. Pour the thick mixture into a tureen (or other bowl if you prefer).

Remove cooked potatoes and squash, mash well, and add to tureen. Add cooked tomatoes beans, peas, and pasta to tureen, mix, and adjust seasonings. Serve hot.

BUTTERNUT SQUASH SOUP
Serves 4.

1 medium-to-large butternut squash
2 dashes sea salt
¼ tsp. white pepper
⅛ tsp. cardamom
⅛ tsp. nutmeg

2 cups fat-free chicken stock
Minced parsley or red or green bell pepper
Plain yogurt or sour cream (optional)

Split squash in half (careful: it's tough!). Clean out seeds and strings. Place, cut sides down, in a glass dish. Add about 1 inch water. Microwave on high 16-18 minutes.

Remove squash from water. Let drain and get cool enough to handle. Scoop out flesh. Add with seasonings to a food processor. Process until smooth, adding stock a bit at a time.

Reheat to serve. Decorate with parsley or bell pepper. If you like, a small dollop of plain yogurt or sour cream goes nicely in this.

To make a bisque-type, heartier soup, add ¼ cup heavy cream after the stock. To serve, top with crumbled microwave-crisped, maple-smoked, sugar-cured bacon.

GREAT GREEN PEA SOUP

Serves 2-3.

1 cup fresh (or quick-frozen) green peas
½-¾ cup fat-free chicken stock
⅛ tsp. white pepper
1-2 dashes sea salt

Place peas in a pot. Add enough water to just cover. Cook over high heat, stirring, until almost all water is gone (about 10 minutes).

Place cooked peas into a food processor or blender with remaining ingredients. Blend until smooth. Return to pot to heat and serve hot. Or refrigerate to serve cool. Serve as is or decorate if you like with a little minced parsley (Italian leaf preferred), green onions, or red or yellow bell peppers.

PUMPKIN TRUFFLE SOUP

Serves 6.

1½ lb. pumpkin flesh
2 tbsp. extra-virgin olive oil

1 large onion, course chopped
2 leeks, chopped
1 celery stalk, chopped
3 cloves garlic
1½ qt. chicken stock
1 potato, peeled and chopped
1 sprig fresh thyme, leaves only
Salt and black pepper to taste
2 tbsp. shaved truffle
½ cup cream
1 tbsp. white truffle oil

Cut flesh (seeds removed) into large cubes. Place in a large sauce-pot with olive oil, onion, leeks, celery, and garlic. Over medium heat, cook until mixture is soft.

Add stock, potato, thyme, salt, and pepper and simmer 30 minutes. Add shaved truffle and puree in a blender. Pass through a chinoise or fine-mesh sieve.

Add cream. Bring back to a boil. Adjust seasonings. Serve in a bowl garnished with a drizzle of truffle oil.

CORN SOUP

Serves 6.

My favorite corn to use is a white corn called silver queen. It is grown throughout most of the coastal South and is sweet enough to eat raw.

10 ears corn
Salt and black pepper to taste
1 tbsp. sugar
Pinch cayenne pepper
1 onion, julienned
2 tbsp. butter
1 cup 2 percent milk
Chopped chives or parsley

Cover corn with water and add 1 tbsp. salt, the sugar, and cayenne.

Simmer 30 minutes. Remove corn and reserve stock. Cut corn kernels off ears.

Sauté onion in butter until limp. Add corn, reserving 1 cup. Strain corn stock and add sautéed mixture to stock. Simmer 30 minutes.

Puree soup and pass through chinoise. Return to stove to simmer briefly again. Season to taste.

Add milk. Strain once more before cooling. Garnish with reserved corn and chives or parsley.

Basic Stock Preparation

Remember:
- These stocks are easy to make, but they take time to cook.
- Good stocks make good cooking and good sauces.
- Never season a stock until use.
- Home preparation ensures low to no fat and sodium.
- What you make now can be frozen in a plastic-wrapped ice-cube tray or other container for future use. It will last 1-2 months frozen, 2-3 days refrigerated.

CHICKEN STOCK

Chicken parts (such as wing tips, necks, and/or carcasses)
2 small onions, peeled and halved
1-2 carrots, peeled and halved
3 cloves garlic, crushed
1 celery stalk with leaves, halved
2 bay leaves
1 tsp. whole peppercorns
Sprigs thyme, if available
6-8 sprigs parsley

Place chicken parts in a large pot. Cover with water and bring to a boil. Skim fat off, then add other ingredients. Boil gently 1-2 hours.

Skim fat off and strain stock to use immediately. Fat can be removed nearly completely using the "refrigerator trick": if there is time (3 hours or overnight), strain stock into a glass (or ceramic) bowl, cover, and refrigerate. The fat will float and congeal and can be easily and virtually completely removed. Another great way to separate fat, introduced to me by a friend and excellent cook, Carl Schwartz, uses a special glass vessel, a fat separator, with a spout at the bottom. You can pour out the stock free of fat.

BEEF STOCK

Beef bones with meat attached, fat removed
1 medium onion (or 2 if a lot of bones), coarsely chopped
1 carrot, diced
4-6 oz. tomato paste (commercial low sodium, no sugar added, if available)
1 boiled potato, halved
1 small onion, halved
1 carrot, peeled and halved
1-2 bay leaves
1 tsp. whole peppercorns

Preheat oven to 350 degrees. Place bones on a baking tray and sprinkle on onion and carrot. Bake about 1½ hours to "color." This greatly improves flavor of stock.

When bones are about half-done, spread tomato paste in a thick blob in the center of a small baking pan and add to oven. This will dry and reduce acidity of paste. Do not be afraid of darkened edges—this just adds more flavor.

When the bones are baked, add all ingredients to a pot, cover with water, and boil gently 2-3 hours, skimming fat off occasionally. Strain. Use as is or thicken by adding a mixture of 2-4 tbsp. Madeira wine and 2 tbsp. cornstarch. Cook 15-20 minutes to thicken and get rid of stocky taste. To ensure a virtually fat-free stock, use the "refrigerator trick" if skimming seems inadequate (see Chicken Stock recipe).

HAM STOCK

1 ham bone with meat attached
1 large onion, halved

2 celery stalks with leaves, halved
1 clove garlic, mashed
2-3 bay leaves
1 tsp. whole peppercorns
6-8 sprigs parsley

Place all ingredients into a large pot, cover with water, and boil gently 2 hours. Skim fat off and strain. Use immediately or freeze.

VEGETABLE STOCK

2 medium onions, halved
2 carrots, halved
3 celery stalks with leaves, halved
2 cloves garlic, mashed
8 sprigs parsley
1 sprig thyme
1 bay leaf
¼ tsp. sea salt

Place all ingredients in a large pot, cover with water, and boil gently 1 hour. Strain. Use immediately or freeze.

Variations:
1. Add broccoli stalks, split in half. Broccoli stalks give some complexity without overwhelming the flavor.
2. Add ½ small, medium-hot pepper. Adding a small amount of "heat" gives zing to the flavor without taking over.
3. Add ½ tsp. whole peppercorns.

EGGPLANT DELIGHT

1 large eggplant
Oil
1 large sweet onion, chopped fine
2 medium cloves garlic, pressed
1 tsp. sea salt

¼ tsp. cayenne pepper
½ tsp. white pepper
1 cup reduced-fat sour cream or plain yogurt

Preheat oven to 350 degrees. Bake eggplant, skin slit in a few spots, for 1½ hours. When cool enough to handle comfortably, peel and mince (a food processor does the job faster).

Heat small amount oil in a nonstick skillet over high heat. Sauté onion and garlic quickly, about 2 minutes. Add eggplant and cook; then add spices. Let cool. Taste for seasonings and adjust if needed.

Add sour cream or yogurt and mix. Place onto serving plate and refrigerate 1 hour or more. Serve with whole-grain bread or good crackers.

MARINATED MUSHROOMS

8 oz. small, very fresh button mushrooms or baby portobellos,
    brushed clean
1 medium sweet onion, sliced thin
⅔ cup extra-virgin olive oil or good vegetable oil
¼ cup rice-wine or other vinegar
2 tbsp. balsamic vinegar
½ tsp. white pepper
½ tsp. oregano (fresh, if you have it)
¼ tsp. cayenne pepper (optional)

Toss mushrooms and onion in a glass or glazed covered dish. Combine all other ingredients and pour over mushrooms and onion. Toss.

Cover. Refrigerate overnight. Serve without much liquid, using toothpicks. Enjoy!

APPLE OR PEACH CRISP

4 cups peeled, sliced apples or not-too-ripe peaches
¾ cup flour
½ cup dark brown sugar
½ cup sugar
1½ tsp. cinnamon

½ tsp. nutmeg
6 tbsp. cold butter

Preheat oven to 375 degrees. Place apples or peaches in a 9-inch-square ovenproof glass baking dish. Mix last remaining ingredients well. Sprinkle mixture on fruit and bake 40 minutes. Serve warm or cool. Does not keep well.

LOWER-FAT CARROT CAKE

1 cup dark brown sugar
½ cup good vegetable oil (not canola)
4 egg whites
2½ tsp. vanilla
1½ cups unbleached plain flour
1 tsp. baking powder
1 tsp. baking soda
½ tsp. sea salt
¼ tsp. white pepper
1½ tsp. cinnamon
½ tsp. allspice
½ tsp. nutmeg
2 cups grated carrots (washed but unpeeled)
Nonstick cooking spray

Preheat oven to 350 degrees. Mix sugar, oil, egg whites, and vanilla well. Mix flour, baking powder, baking soda, salt, pepper, and spices. Add bit by bit to liquid, blending well. Fold in carrots well.

Spray a 13-inch glass or nonstick baking pan with cooking spray. Pour in batter and bake about 35 minutes or until a toothpick inserted in middle comes out clean. Cool 15 minutes and turn out onto cake plate. This cake is fine uniced. If you want it iced, use the following recipe, remembering that it increases the calories and fat content.

Icing
12 oz. low-fat cream cheese
1 tsp. fresh lemon juice
1 tsp. vanilla
1 box 10X confectioners' sugar

Let cream cheese soften to room temperature. Whip with lemon juice and vanilla to fluff. Slowly add sugar, beating well after each addition. When icing reaches spreadable consistency, spread on cake top and sides. Now, have a smaller serving!

SWEET-POTATO SOUFFLE

Serves 6.

3 cups baked, skinned, mashed sweet potatoes
½ cup corn syrup
½ cup sugar
¼ lb. butter
1 tbsp. vanilla
3 eggs
¼ cup heavy cream
1 dash nutmeg
2 dashes cinnamon

Mix ingredients on high speed 3 minutes and pour into pie crust (see below). Bake 45 minutes at 350 degrees until set.

Pie Crust
1¼ cups flour
3 oz. butter
Pinch salt
1½ oz. ice water

Mix flour, butter, and salt in a bowl with a dough cutter until crumbly. Slowly add water until dough comes together. Refrigerate at least 30 minutes. Roll out and place in a pie dish.

SPIRITUAL NURTURE: CONNECTING WITH FAMILY AND FRIENDS

Thanksgiving recovers for us what really matters, as we gather with our dear ones to express gratitude for each other and for the blessings of life. We often mark this moment as a special event. In many

American homes, this moment is blessed by prayer—a quiet time when our thoughts are focused in the same direction and towards each other. There are many ways of saying grace.

In many other American homes, this moment is heightened by special toasts and good wishes. Cheers! Salut! Prayers and toasts have one purpose in common: both express our desire to give spiritual sustenance to our family and friends, and they to us. We seem to have a natural wish to nourish each other spiritually. Although we can and should give ourselves spiritual nurture, we need to reach out and be reached spiritually by others, as well.

Many studies have shown that we live longer and healthier lives when we feel connected to our families and friends. We are spiritually nurtured by these connections. Married people, especially men, live longer than single people. The existence of a connection with another human being seems to have a positive, nurturing effect. This kind of nurture seems to hold its strength even when we are at a distance, and even if we are strangers. Since ancient times, prayer has been thought to be a powerful means of healing. Since the 1970s, clinical studies have shown that sick people get better when groups use prayer intercessions on their behalf. The sick participants in these studies don't know they are receiving prayers, nor do they know those praying for them. They just get better. The control participants, who receive no prayers, show no medical improvements. This use of prayer for health and healing is now getting attention from the National Institutes of Health.

Of course, family connections are not always easy, not even in the Big Easy. Sometimes we must work to forge positive bonds. I find that just before saying grace around our Thanksgiving table, I will take a deep and cleansing breath. This is my self-nurture for reducing stress and dealing with whatever negative feelings might surface in the conversations ahead. In our small but meaningful family rituals, we can focus this way to increase our connectedness. We all have our quirks and foibles, and some people seem to be downright unpleasant. But we need each other. We need that positive connection, that spiritual nurture.

SPIRITUAL NURTURE: CONNECTING WITH A PARTNER

Sensuality and sex. What better ways to connect? Physical intimacy is pleasurable and natural. It relieves stress. Sexual activity burns up calories without formal exercise. Most of all, the intimacy of a relationship with your partner can nourish your spirit, your center, your essence. Yes, this kind of connectedness is good for your health.

If this view sounds strange to you, or if you are among those who believe that "soul" and "body" should be in essential opposition, consider the words of Ray Busmann, a therapeutic massage specialist. He's talking about different schools of massage therapy, including Western, Eastern, and others:

So if we have clinical as the first or Western part or department, and we have the Asian, . . . then there's a third part that is the least well known part. We in San Diego call it the Integrated Somatics part. "Somatics" [comes] from the Greek word "soma" for the body, and Integrated Somatics refers to the fact that the body is never the body by itself. There's always the mind and the soul, heart and spirit, connected. . . . This arena of body work really takes into consideration that whenever you touch a body, you touch more than the physical body. The moment you touch, you come so close, so intimate to a body, you cannot not touch that person's soul, that person's history, that person's spirit or spirituality.

We in the New Orleans Program also believe that "the body is never the body by itself." What we have called the "spirit" is right there with it, always, needing nurture through connectedness. In the Renaissance, John Donne referred to "that subtle knot that makes us man," that is, that makes us who we are. The "subtle knot" is the joining of body and soul into one, through the physical act of love, and Donne believed that this knot was formed by "spirits" in our blood that conveyed our souls to each other. We believe he's not far wrong.

Diana Panara, who practices deep-tissue massage, agrees that physical connectedness can also touch our spiritual selves: The laying on of hands goes back to the beginning of history Every religion and every culture has always practiced a hands-on kind of healing. Many of our modern professions are rediscovering or hooking into the spiritual potential of that connection.

Sometimes our physical condition can prevent us from enjoying sexual intimacy. Obesity ranks at the top of these conditions, especially for men, and diabetes correlates with obesity. Diabetes itself, in young men, can impair erectile function, and obesity can increase the risk of prostate cancer. Prostate surgery may result in impotence, although proton therapy spares this function.

Following the New Orleans Program can help protect us from obesity and diabetes, so that we can enjoy sex for many more years. For physical intimacy, we need to keep up our nutrients and micronutrients. We should also avoid those fat-laden Atkins meals that can deaden sexual appetite, especially in men. Some nutritional supplements for both men and women may enhance sexual performance.

SPIRITUAL NURTURE: CONNECTING WITH THE COMMUNITY

If ever New Orleanians get out and party, it's between Thanksgiving and Christmas. As the year comes full circle, the weather is a little cooler but still sunny. The sasanquas burst out around Thanksgiving, with their shiny, spearhead leaves almost obscured by white, pink, and magenta blossoms. This natural fanfare welcomes yet another festive season to the Big Easy.

Our ongoing rituals and celebrations always give us something wonderful to anticipate together, as a community. Here we feel connected not only with our family and friends but with the entire city. Our parades, our festivals, our food, our music—these contribute to our sense of camaraderie, our "joy of living . . . day to day," as Laura Tennyson, House of Blues executive, says. We have a lively culture in which everyone is connected, locals and tourists, and everyone gets into the act. Tony Green, of the musical group Tony Green and Gypsy Jazz, believes in the connection.

In a nutshell, it's great living in the Quarter. It's the closest thing to Europe I can find because you have the village atmosphere here. I can go down to the store—walking, of course—and I meet all the neighbors and we chat and talk. It's like the Old World. I love that. Of course, I love the architecture here—no strip malls, no suburban look about it. It's very much French colonial. It sort of suits my present lifestyle.

Here's what Jonathan Ferrara, owner of Jonathan Ferrara Gallery, has to say.

It is a very diverse group of people [who] support the arts . . . go to art auctions, go to theatre, . . . support musical art. . . . What you have here . . . is the participatory culture; people will participate. They may not buy anything but they still participate in being a part of the art happening. That's what still keeps it vibrant. For me especially in my gallery, just because you can't afford to buy it doesn't mean you can't come in. . . .

A lot of locals go to Jazz Fest. I think that's one of the things that people love about our city. It's not like Disneyworld, where the locals don't go. . . . What we do here, the tourists do. What the tourists do, locals do. There's a common thread, that the locals get as much joy out of . . . touristy things as tourists do. We value those things . . . it's a participatory culture because we participate and they want to participate in that too.

Even when we choose a restaurant, we base our decision on personality and community. In the words of Richard Shakespeare, of Ralph's on the Park:

I think in New Orleans when there's a group of people deciding to go out to dinner they don't think, well, let's go have Italian or let's go have German or let's go have Chinese. They just start thinking of destinations, whether it's Ralph's on the Park . . . or the French Quarter and the many restaurants down there. That's how they think. They're thinking of a personality, the restaurant and a personality. . . . Pascal's Manale has a certain kind of personality; all of these restaurants have a history and a personality.

As Shakespeare says, we like restaurants with "a warmth . . . rather than a showiness to them." Good food is very much a part of New Orleans' participatory culture. Mary Ann Octavio envisions a worldwide culture of those who share a passion for good food, with New Orleanians as part of this culture.

[It's] just wonderful to know that my recipes are finding their way into homes not just here in America but all over the world. That's what I'm finding, that good food and a passion about good food is shared worldwide. A gentleman came up—it turns out he was from Hong Kong, didn't speak a word of English—but he recognized that beautiful color of that sparkling peach jam and absolutely had to have it. It's wonderful to know that good food even transcends language.

A large number of healthy ninety-year-olds whom I know stay connected by dancing, a great form of exercise that can be done at your own pace. At our Wine and Food Experience, we have residents ranging from barely drinking age to seasoned nonagenarians with enough wine experience to write their own book. Our oldest citizens in the French Quarter belong to social and civic groups. They keep our community going strong, and they enjoy long lives.

Perhaps New Orleans has a strong sense of community because people here are genuinely friendly. We have no real agenda about status or class. We just enjoy connecting. We want to get to know each other as people.

Laura Tennyson comments on our egalitarian spirit that encourages connectedness.

You know what's really interesting here is that someone like a great musician in any other city is standing right next to you and you can just talk. It could be about the gumbo at the dinner table or it could be about their great artistry. There's no fear; there's no pretense; there's no agenda. [In] L.A. or New York or anywhere, people are afraid to talk to you because they're afraid of whatever agenda you may have. So you never get to really talk or get to know someone. . . . Even just going back to visit my family in Boston, people are so nervous about just interacting with each other. Nervousness makes you stressed out. That affects your health when you're nervous. . . . Because of . . . living in New Orleans, I've become totally this friendly person . . . different. It's just weird. But it's a great thing. It helps to deal with the poverty, with the crime, with the divisions. There are divisions here, you know. . . . Even if you're very wealthy and very poor, you still have proximity to each other, which is kind of unique. From a city layout perspective, you don't have these big divisions of segregation of people. . . . You can be very poor and you could be standing next to someone who's very rich and they still will talk to each other, which is really weird. I think that's another New Orleans unique thing.

This is a healthful vision: the barriers to human connectedness removed. In this view, money and race and fame don't matter, and people can speak to each other without stress or self-consciousness. To the extent this vision is our reality, New Orleans has achieved a wonderful spirit of community that can give spiritual nurture to anyone who lives or visits here.

Maryflynn Thomas observes that these easy, unselfconscious residents are the heart of New Orleans.

I guess you'd say I'm the Yankee [my husband] Brad brought down. Luckily for me I dropped into a city called New Orleans. I walked in and said these are my people. . . . The secret of New Orleans . . . is the people. The people are the fabric. They're the ones that make the city, and we . . . laugh at the outside world because they don't understand it. It's like this secret romance going on that nobody else is privy to. What else can I tell you? . . . Of course, it's the fun, but the fun is made by the people. They're friendly; they're outgoing; they're warm; they're kind. They're kind to a point of ridiculousness. I don't know of any other city in the world where you can be indicted in July and still be at a cocktail party the following month and everybody goes, "Oh, hi." And you become like a novelty.

No wonder visitors fall in love with New Orleans. They can sense a kind of spiritual nurture that residents share in our New Orleans community. Our city charms many people into moving here—people like Marty and David Speights, for example. David says:

We're both from Mississippi and I was born in a small town about two hours north of here in south Mississippi. . . . I told everybody in Washington and probably in New Orleans that the two most important cities in Mississippi are Memphis and New Orleans. You tend to gravitate to one or the other. . . . We just sensed that the Quarter is the place that is extremely friendly; you can walk everywhere. . . . If you wake up and need milk and eggs in the middle of the night, it's right there.

Something about our lifestyle seems to promote spiritual health. It's not only our beautiful architecture or the year-round flowers and trees. More likely, it's the care we take to remember both the living and the dead. It's the connectedness to others that sustains the spirits of our artists, like Harold Batiste and Pete Fountain, beyond a time in life when many would have retired and rusted out. It's our simple gestures in smoothing relationships that lead us to inner peace and happiness. New Orleans teaches a person to stop worrying, to get out and live life with others.

In that spirit, Mary Katherine Lonatro, captain of the Mystic Krewe of Shangri-La, tells us the story of a Mardi Gras parade adventure that could have resulted in lasting stress and conflict. Yet here in New Orleans even this has been transformed into a humorous anecdote, one of many stories to dine out on.

Blaine Kern delivered the wrong float. He is the float builder. He's been my friend and my enemy and I respect him dearly like family . . . and I think he's awesome. But the wrong float came out, and it was too late to get the other floats. . . . The ladies went on a float as Little Red Riding Hood and the float had nothing to do with Little Red Riding Hood. They were most distressed. They could not understand why I could not wiggle my nose and do something about it but it was just impossible. There were some very unhappy campers that day. When I look back, it's kind of funny. . . . I believe [the float was about] outer space. I believe it was. I'm sure if you asked Blaine, he'd remember because I screamed and hollered a lot.

Yes, down here we believe that "reality is something you rise above." In New Orleans we're thankful for a lifestyle that can help us cope with accidents and trials, even with setbacks on the scale of Hurricane Katrina. We may scream and holler a lot, but we'll get back to work and stay connected with each other, thanks to our New Orleans spirit.

CHAPTER 12

Reveillon: A Celebration of Cooking at Home

Everywhere I go, when people hear I'm from New Orleans, they smile. We will recover from this disaster and have that special fun again. Everyone needs some fun.   —Blaine Kern, Sr., "Mr. Mardi Gras," on CNN, September 15, 2005

In the mid-1800s, New Orleans Creole families celebrated Reveillon on Christmas Eve at home. After midnight mass in St. Louis Cathedral, they returned home for a meal that often lasted until dawn. Typical Reveillon home cooking might include oysters prepared in various styles, cream of celery soup, bouillabaisse, quail, sautéed shrimp on toast, cucumbers, tomatoes, and artichokes, with a dessert of bananas, soufflé, petits fours, Creole bonbons, and other delights. Other traditional Creole Reveillon dishes included court-bouillon and chicken pies, followed by apple pie and Louisiana orange sherbet.

These fabulous holiday feasts used to stretch through many courses, along with wines and champagne, music and dancing. Even 150 years ago, however, Reveillon had balance: serving more than ten courses was generally thought vulgar. Creole housewives were concerned about portion size. They practiced expert preparation with the freshest available ingredients, including the leanest quality meats affordable on their household budget.

Today, many of New Orleans finest restaurants offer a Reveillon menu throughout December as part of a citywide celebration— Christmas New Orleans Style. These feasts combine timeless Creole cuisine with more contemporary New Orleans dishes, but the spirit of the past remains. (For a description, analysis, and recipes from lists of menus, visit www.christmasneworleans.com/menus.html.)

The New Orleans Reveillon centers around the family table, a tradition rare in our over-busy days. Yet the family table can be recaptured with modest effort. Home cooking can be healthier and less costly than eating out. It can also be fun and creative, so that even the children will want to help prepare dinner. We offer a few simple suggestions here.

SOUPE DE POISSON WITH SPICY ROUILLE

Serves 6.

2 oz. extra-virgin olive oil
2 lb. gumbo crabs, crushed
1 leek, diced
2 onions, diced
$\frac{1}{2}$ lb. carrots, diced
1 celery stalk, diced
6 cloves garlic, crushed
1 tomato, crushed
1 tbsp. tomato paste
$1\frac{1}{2}$ lb. potatoes, peeled and diced
$1\frac{1}{2}$ cup white wine
1 bay leaf
1 sprig thyme
Pinch saffron
$2\frac{1}{2}$ qt. water
$\frac{1}{2}$ cup Herbsaint or Pernod
$\frac{1}{2}$ orange peel
6 2-3-oz. filets (skinless) speckled trout or other fresh
   local fish
Salt and black pepper to taste
Spicy Rouille

In a heavy 6-qt. sauce- or stockpot, heat oil over high heat. Add crabs and stir with a wooden spoon 5 minutes or until shells turn deep red. Reduce heat to medium high and add leek, onions, carrots, celery, and garlic, stirring.

Once vegetables have softened, add tomato, tomato paste, and potatoes. Cook 5 minutes. Add wine, bay leaf, thyme, and saffron. Bring to a simmer.

Cover shells with water. Add Herbsaint and orange peel. Simmer 45 minutes.

Remove peel and bay leaf and discard. Puree mixture (no shells) through a food mill. Then strain through a fine-mesh sieve. Return to pot, heat to slow boil, add fish filets, and poach until cooked, 3-4 minutes. Season to taste. Serve hot in bowls with rouille.

Spicy Rouille
2 roasted red bell peppers, peeled and seeded
5 cloves garlic
¼ tsp. salt
½ tsp. cayenne pepper
1 egg yolk
1 cup extra-virgin olive oil

Combine ingredients in food mill and puree. Spoon on top of soup.

OKRA A LA CREOLE

Serves 6.

1 large onion, diced
2 cups diced okra (fresh or frozen)
2 green bell peppers, diced
4 celery stalks, diced
4 cloves garlic, minced
1 tsp. dried thyme
1 tsp. crushed red pepper flakes
1 tbsp. salt
1 tsp. black pepper
2 cups crushed tomatoes
Smoked turkey-neck stock
2 cups uncooked Louisiana converted white rice
1 bunch green onions, sliced

Sauté ingredients, through tomatoes, in order listed, adding each one about 1 minute after the previous one. Add 4 cups stock and the rice. Bring to a simmer. Reduce heat as low as it can go and cover. Cook about 20 minutes until rice is cooked through. Thin with additional stock to your taste. Garnish with green onions.

GRILLED BOBWHITE QUAIL WITH WILD-RICE DRESSING AND PORT-FIG REDUCTION

Serves 6.

12 semi-boneless quail (bobwhite if possible)
Thyme
Minced garlic
½ cup sherry vinegar
2 cups extra-virgin olive oil
1 tsp. salt
1 tsp. black pepper
Wild-Rice Dressing (see index)
Port-Fig Reduction

Rub each bird with thyme, garlic, vinegar, oil, salt, and pepper. Grill 4 minutes on each side, turning to get nice grill marks. Serve quail with rice dressing. Spoon reduction around plate.

Port-Fig Reduction
1 bottle port wine
1 cup dried figs

Heat port and figs, reducing down to 2 cups. Strain out figs. Continue reducing liquid until it is 1 cup.

CRISPY CORNISH HENS

Serves 4.

These often underrated fowl make a light main course, can be a festive Reveillon course, or add a different touch to a holiday table—for example, as an addition to ham or lamb. This simple, quick preparation allows the garlic to infuse the meat delightfully.

4 cornish hens
¼ cup chopped parsley (Italian flat leaf preferred)
¼ cup minced celery leaves with small stalk pieces
12 cloves garlic
Sea salt and black pepper to taste
2 tbsp. unsalted butter, melted

Preheat oven to 500 degrees. Clean cavities of hens. Mix parsley and celery.

Smash garlic. Stuff 3 cloves in each bird cavity, and fill rest of cavity with parsley and celery mixture. Sprinkle on salt and pepper.

Place in foil-lined roasting pan. Reduce oven to 375 degrees. Cook 40 minutes (until juice runs clear when pierced).

Remove from oven. Raise heat to 500 degrees. Brush outside with butter. Return to oven for about 5 minutes, until skin is nicely browned and crispy. Remove any excess visible seasoning prior to serving.

DRIED FRUIT COMPOTE

1 bay leaf
Pinch mustard seed
Pinch coriander seed
Pinch black pepper
1 tsp. small-diced dried fig
1 tsp. small-diced dried apricot
1 tsp. small-diced dried cherry
1 tsp. small-diced fresh nectarine
1 tsp. tamarind paste
1 tsp. salt
3 tsp. sugar
3 tsp. rice-wine vinegar

Place bay leaf, mustard seed, coriander seed, and pepper in a cheesecloth. Combine all ingredients in a heavy saucepan and bring to a simmer. Then bake, covered, 15 minutes at 300 degrees or until compote is soft and sticky. Remove cheesecloth. Use as a condiment.

FILETS OF BEEF WITH ROASTED ROOT VEGETABLES AND MUSHROOM TEA

Serves 6.

6 6-oz. beef filets
Salt and black pepper to taste
6 red baby beets, peeled and quartered
6 yellow baby beets, peeled and quartered

6 pink baby beets, peeled and quartered
Extra-virgin olive oil
Mushroom Tea
Fresh chervil or chives

Season beef with salt and pepper. Sear to medium rare and set aside. Coat beets lightly with oil, salt, and pepper and roast in oven until fork tender.

Place small spoonfuls of each kind of beet in large individual serving bowls. Pour Mushroom Tea around beets. Place beef on top. Garnish with chervil or chives. Serve with spoons.

Mushroom Tea
½ lb. mushrooms
2 cups water
1 tsp. soy sauce
1 tsp. sherry vinegar
1 tsp. fresh thyme
1 tsp. sugar
1 tsp. salt

Simmer mushrooms in water 4 hours. Strain through chinoise lined with cheesecloth. Add remaining ingredients and bring to a boil. Strain and cool.

BALSAMIC BUTTERNUT SQUASH

2 cups chunked butternut squash
1 tbsp. extra-virgin olive oil
1 tbsp. butter (no substitutes)
1 tbsp. light brown sugar
¼ tsp. cardamom
¼ tsp. nutmeg
1-2 dashes sea salt
¼-½ tsp. white pepper
⅛ cup balsamic vinegar

In a large pot, boil squash until just fork done; do not overcook.

Drain immediately and cool a bit under running water, 30 seconds or so. Drain well. Pat dry if chunks seem too wet.

Heat oil and butter in a large skillet until hot but not smoking. Add squash, stir, and toss. Add spices, tossing 2-3 minutes. Add vinegar to deglaze skillet. Toss to coat; serve hot. Enjoy!

COOKING AT HOME

Let the kids help. My younger daughter enjoys cucumbers almost as much as the rest of our family. She has mastered the art of preparing traditional Creole cucumbers in vinegar.

CREOLE CUCUMBERS

Wash cucumbers. Peel to leave about half the skin (less if you must) and slice. Place cucumber slices in rice-wine vinegar diluted with water (2 parts vinegar mixed with 1 part water). Place in refrigerator about 30 minutes, to make "fresh pickles."

These can be tossed with coarse-chopped tomato and sweet onion in extra-virgin olive oil, vinegar, a little sea salt, and black pepper to taste (your choice of vinegar: balsamic—but not the oldest, rice wine, or apple cider).

Cooking at home can be simple and artful, like this recipe. With the guidance of parents, a child can build an appreciation of food, its colors, and its textures. If you appoint your children as "sous chefs" to help with the prepping, then cooking can become an active pleasure for all the family. The recipes in this book can be prepared speedily and efficiently.

Chef Besh and other chefs have begun a mentoring program for inner-city schoolchildren in New Orleans: "Pro Chef." Teams of kids enter an annual competition, and several chefs judge the culinary entries in a big "cook-off." It's possible that future chefs may be nurtured by this program, but at the least all children involved will learn the joy of making groceries and presenting their own creations. Ti Martin, proprietor of Commander's Palace, which has received multiple restaurant awards, shares with us the pleasure of shopping and cooking.

I think there s a lot of exciting food going around in town. . . . [There are about] four [farmers' markets] now in New Orleans. You have no excuse really to not at least occasionally shop in a farmers' market. They're . . . in a neighborhood near you. . . . I thought somebody would open these little things and then they'd go bust a few years later and that would be it. Wrong. They have really proliferated. . . . You go to the market once or twice a month and then your favorite grocery for your basics and you cook. You cook stuff that you can eat throughout the week. . . . You just cook in bigger amounts with fresh food that you freeze or refrigerate and eat it throughout the week. I love to do that.

Time, money, health. To any suggestion that they cook at home, many Americans might respond at once: "You expect me to cook more? I don't even have time to wait in line at the Burger King window!" And yet, stop and think for a minute. The takeout route itself steals our time and stresses us out: the deciding, the driving there and back, the inevitable complaints, the scattered bags and cartons. Takeout is on balance a low-quality experience.

By contrast, our New Orleans Program recipes are fast and easy to prepare, and we even have tips for a speedy cleanup. We've demonstrated in our first chapter that home meals actually save money. And here's the main thing: cooking at home can be a high-quality experience. As home cooks, we're in charge, and we can make it high quality. We can assure freshness and flavor; we can vary our foods and moderate our portions; we can control the salt and fat. Our recipes here are interesting, easy, flavorful, and healthful—those are our criteria.

We've heard that time is money. Well, time is also health. Healthy home-cooked meals will contribute to longer lives. Have you ever sat at dinner table after a takeout pizza, wondering what damage all that extra cheese is doing to you and your loved ones? After a delicious meal prepared by your whole family, you won't have that problem.

Food as art form. The creative ones among us will have a chance to express themselves in preparing meals. A home cook can connect essentially with food, immersing himself in the medium of his art, and then offer his creation to family and friends. People such as I—who cannot, for example, sing—can still perform. I've collaborated with Chef Besh in writing this book because I deeply appreciate how he selects the freshest ingredients, combines them with respect for Creole values, adds a subtle and seductive newness, and presents them in elegant, moderate portions. The first time I tasted his cooking, I thought, "Here is a foodie comrade par excellence." In this postmodern era, cooking at its best has escaped the encroachments of technology and become an artistic experience. Our many great chefs in Louisiana, as well as the growing number of terrific amateur chefs cooking at home, can attest to this truth.

Today we have celebrity chefs, such as New Orleans' Chef Paul Prudhomme and Chef Emeril Lagasse, who appear on the Food Network as stars of the culinary world. They reveal to us the excitement, the chances for creativity and individual expression, that cooking can bring to our own lives. In many other areas of the country, cooking may not be considered a manly art. Yet under the example of our native chefs, a surprising number of men in Southern Louisiana are the cooks of the house. In fact, the average twenty-first-century man or woman can become a fine home chef, with some advice on choosing ingredients and preparation tools. At home, we can create food that is, in Ti Martin's words, "cooked with the soul."

STOCKING THE KITCHEN

We don't need all the latest gadgets to create wonders in the kitchen. The best tools are those that make cooking enjoyable and fast and cleanup easier. The secret to an efficient kitchen is not overloading it with equipment. Holiday gifts can be a great way to build our selective supply of pots, pans, and knives. Today we have an unprecedented range of high-quality utensils and accessories to choose from. Because the choice can be bewildering, we offer here a list of our recommended basic kitchen equipment.

Knives
- 2 really good 4-5-inch paring knives
- 1 inexpensive serrated-edge knife
- 1 good-quality 8-10-inch serrated-edge knife
- 1 large chopping knife
- 1 8-10-inch slicer
- Knife holder or drawer divider
- Electric knife sharpener (3 stage)

Plastic chopping boards
- 1 large
- 1 small

Kitchen forks
- 1 with 5-inch tines
- 1 with 7-inch tines
- 1 grill size

Wooden spoons
- At least 2 long handle

Stainless-steel spoons
- 2 large nonslotted
- 2 large slotted

Cooking strainer
- 1 stainless steel, long handle

Ladles
- 1 large stainless steel, long handle
- 1 medium stainless steel, medium handle

Tongs
- 1 inexpensive triangular-head "bent-wire" type
- 1 large
- 1 grill size

Spatulas
- 1 wide, nonstick, cookware safe
- 1 mixing-bowl scraping type
- 1 grill size

Whisk
- 1 stainless steel, medium

Grater
- 1 stainless steel

Garlic press
- 1 large bowl

Scissors
- 1 good pair, kitchen type
- 1 regular desk type

Potato masher
- 1 sturdy

Measuring cups
- 1 1-cup measure
- 1 2-cup measure

Measuring spoons
- 1 set

Colanders
- 1 medium wire
- 1 large wire

Glass bowls
- Assorted, thick walled (e.g., Pyrex); *must include 1 bigger than you think you will ever need*

Skillets, preferably high-quality coated (not Teflon) with covers
- 1 12 inch
- 1 9 inch
- 1 5 inch

Heavy covered saucepans
- 1 8 quart
- 1 6 quart
- 1 1 quart

Covered heavy pots
- 1 very large
- 1 medium

Blender
- 1 industrial strength; can double as bar utensil

Electric mixer

Roasting pans, cookie sheets, cake pans

Paper towels or tea towels

Good potholders

Good knives are critical to quick and effective cooking. Once you have a core of quality knives, the most important accessory is an electric knife sharpener. This will make your work in the kitchen much easier. You also need at least one inexpensive knife—mine is a serrated-edge knife I bought years ago at a grocery-store promotion for ninety-eight cents. I use it to open packages, cut twine, and do other chores I wouldn't do with good knives. (Chef Besh may have his own inexpensive knife, whether he admits to it or not.)

I've tried the new ceramic-blade knife, and it's as sharp as they say. Nothing is better for slicing tomatoes thin. Recently passed editor of *The New Yorker*, Gardner Botsford, taught me the secret to full tomato enjoyment, "Slice 'em thin. Brings out the flavor," he observed with that characteristic grin. However, after a year, its somewhat fragile blade lost a bit of sharpness, so I'd regard this knife as an "extra."

It's true that wooden chopping boards are susceptible to bacterial contamination. Good, resilient, plastic chopping boards make better sense, and they can and should be replaced when their surface (inevitably) becomes scored.

Tongs are extremely useful. Most often, I find myself reaching for the inexpensive triangular-headed wire tongs available in most grocery stores for under four dollars.

We recommend buying a skillet with the heaviest possible coating. Contemporary, best-quality bonded, nonstick coatings are durable, and they speed cleanup immeasurably. Stainless-steel skillets, like most stainless-steel ware, tend to convert olive oil spatters to ugly brown coagulations that no amount of elbow grease can remove, despite the recommended paste of water and baking soda.

We don't recommend Teflon. Some believe it leaches bad chemicals, and often it is not well bonded to the pot or pan. My niece Tracy, when she was in that helpful preteen phase, volunteered to clean up after Thanksgiving dinner one year. The rest of us were enjoying our conversation when Tracy appeared with Mother's new Teflon skillet, asking for help with "getting all of that black stuff out of this pan." It's better to use cookware that is either uncoated or made with the best-quality bonded materials.

Heavy aluminum cookware performs well and is available at reasonable prices. It quickly develops an oxidized interior during use, and this natural coating prevents the aluminum metal from leaching into the food. We suggest cleaning all pots "as you go," especially aluminum. Cleanup is quicker, with less detergent and scrubbing, and preserves the healthful interior coating.

Aluminum pots are also safe. Some years ago, it was thought they could cause aluminum buildup in food, leading to Alzheimer's or other mental problems, but the research at the basis of this scare is highly questionable.

Like many home cooks in the South, Chef and I have black cast-iron skillets that have attained a wonderful "cure." These are kept off limits from anyone else. It is true that some cooks keep their personal black iron skillets under their beds.

BON APPETIT!

December holidays bring parties, with all their warmth and connectedness. Laughter and happiness promote good health. They will strengthen your immune system and reduce your stress chemicals. And after you've been on the New Orleans Program, you can withstand a bit of holiday partying without wrecking your metabolism.

Here are some tips for hosting your own holiday party.

Cooking Tips

- Prep everything ahead. Complicated recipes then become simpler, and cooking is faster and more fun.
- Sharp knives speed preparation.
- Clean up as you prepare and soon after the meal.

Kitchens Can Be Dangerous (and Not Just to Your Arteries)

- Steam has much more heat energy than boiling water. Be careful when opening foil and removing pot lids.
- Remember: hot glass looks just like cold glass.
- The best first aid for a minor burn is ice or cold water, and 2 aspirins or ibuprofen if you can take them.

Eat, drink, relate, and be merry.
Use common sense.
Live long.
Enjoy.

Appendix A

**RESULTS OF THE ORIGINAL NEW ORLEANS
PROGRAM AS CLINICALLY TESTED**

We devised a simple and readily usable manual to explain the food, exercise, and spirituality components of our program. We worked over a two-year period with five teens and their families, a total of thirteen people. We checked waist measurement, weight, blood pressure, and blood sugar on a periodic basis. We verified compliance with the program with a daily checklist, spot-checked by at least one parent or significant other.

Clinical Experience
Obese Teens and Their Parents After 6 Months on the New Orleans Program

	Teen	Mother	Father	Teen	Mother	Father	Teen	Mother	Teen	Mother	Teen	Mother	Father
Age	15	33	41	16	35	36	16	32	16	35	17	39	45
Sex	F	F	M	F	F	M	M	F	F	F	F	F	M
Height (inches)	64	65	70	67	66	71	71	65	68	69	65	66	72
Waist (inches), start	39	41	42	38	39	40	42	38	40	42	41	43	39
Waist (inches), 6 mos.	34	35	37	33	34	36	36	34	33	35	35	37	34
Weight (lb.), start	173	180	241	189	182	233	221	193	238	243	219	237	219
Weight (lb.), 6 mos.	149	158	206	141	153	201	179	161	182	209	178	204	197

	Teen	Mother	Father	Teen	Mother	Father	Teen	Mother	Teen	Mother	Teen	Mother	Father
Blood pressure, start	156/94	146/88	162/92	136/86	156/92	148/90	138/88	162/92	146/94	150/92	150/92	168/94	136/82
Blood pressure, 6 mos.	122/78	128/80	140/82	118/76	136/84	136/84	122/74	128/82	128/84	136/86	120/80	140/82	124/76
Blood sugar (fasting) start	131	142	129	124	134	121	136	146	153	138	142	138	111
Blood sugar (fasting) 6 mos.	92	103	97	99	101	96	104	116	102	111	96	103	94

Appendix B

EATING PROGRAM

This eating program has several goals.

- To remind you about a few key facts that will help you enjoy healthy eating New Orleans style.
- To lay out the strict no-nos that will get you started eating healthily.
- To help you reconnect with food in a healthy way.

Eating good food is necessary for health and provides a lot of pleasure.

- Family-style eating, especially the evening meal, is encouraged.
- If you eat alone, do so focusing on the food, perhaps with some music, but avoid the TV or reading if possible.
- It takes *at least 10 minutes* after you start eating for your brain to sense food.
- Eat slowly. Chew well.
- Learn to listen to your body. If you feel full, *stop eating!*

Specific No-nos (Phase I)

- No fast food except salads. Use as little dressing as possible; vinaigrette is best. "Subway" foods are OK.
- No French fries.
- No chips, snack foods, candy, donuts, commercial cookies, or pastries. Don't even ask!
- No fatty meats. Lean, trimmed meats such as roasts, cutlets, and chops are OK.
- No bread except *real whole-grain* bread or rolls and then only up to 1 piece twice a day. A *small* amount of real butter is OK.

- No ice cream.
- No desserts. Don't even ask!
- No more than 1 small glass fruit juice or sugary cold drink a day. *Sugar-free* drinks such as Coke, Sprite, or filtered coffee are OK.
- *Remember,* if you *don't buy no-nos to bring home,* you (and your children) are much less likely to eat a no-no!

Save money—cook more! If you take the money you would spend at a fast-food restaurant for four people to get burger combos and a pie and go to a grocery store instead, you would get better, fresh food and keep some money, too. Try this homemade menu, for example:

- Sliced boneless chicken breast, seasoned and sautéed in a little canola oil with a little butter (for flavor), *or* grilled
- Rice
- Red beans with small amount sausage
- Green vegetables
- Whole-grain roll
- Unsweetened tea, coffee, or diet drink

The following are good cooking oils:

- Canola
- Olive (*extra virgin* only)
- Real butter

Fresh vegetables are best, followed by flash frozen. If you use canned vegetables, drain the liquid and rinse them. *Avoid frozen, prepared foods, dinners, etc.* Some *"diet"* frozen foods can be eaten as "fallbacks," but even some of these have a lot of salt.

Healthy Rules to Live and Eat By (Phase I)

- Use salt in cooking in moderation. Get used to *no added salt* at the table.
- Eat a variety of foods with vegetables and salads twice a day.

- Eat one helping only. That's all you get, but it can be generous. Use common sense.
- You may eat cheese up to twice a week.
- You may have 1 small glass milk a day (but no more).
- You may have fried seafood once a week, in moderation (but no po' boys).

EXERCISE PROGRAM

This is an exercise program that you *can* do. You should spend a minimum of 30 minutes and up to 45 minutes three times a week exercising to break a little sweat. If all you are able to do is walk, that's fine. Ideally, you should combine walking, the warm-up stretches, and the simple exercises outlined below.

Here is an important point. If you include walking in your exercise, and we strongly suggest you do, you should walk at least 20 minutes and remain in constant motion. If you walk 20-25 minutes with constant motion and upper-body motion, you will achieve the goals.

This exercise program has several goals.

- To improve strength.
- To improve flexibility.
- To improve agility.
- To improve metabolism, with weight control.
- To improve appearance.

Now, let's do it! Remember throughout all of the exercises, watch your posture and watch your form.

Always begin with a *stretch* of your whole body, especially your lower back, which is your main support.

Each of these static stretches should be to your "pull point."

- Hold at your pull point, trying to focus on and enjoy the pull feeling, for a count of 5.
- This is a *slow* count to 5—no cheating here!
- Repeat the following series of 3 stretches 3 times.

First Static Stretch: Straight-Arm Pull

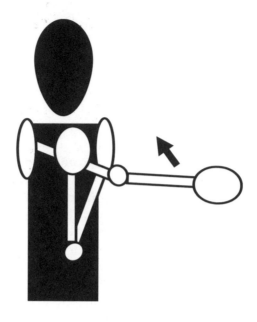

- Hold your right arm straight out in front of you.
- Place your left hand on your right arm at about the upper arm muscle.
- Bring your right arm straight across your chest, towards your left shoulder.
- Use your right arm muscles and the push of your left hand to bring your arm to the pull point, and hold there for a count of 5.
- Drop your left hand and, keeping your right arm straight, return it to the starting position.
- Drop your right arm and repeat with your left arm.

Second Static Stretch: Reach for the Sky

- Keeping good posture, with your feet flat on the floor, move both arms straight up and stretch your hands *as far towards the ceiling as they will go.*
- Remain at this pull point for a count of 5.
- Slowly relax down and place your hands and arms straight down by your sides.

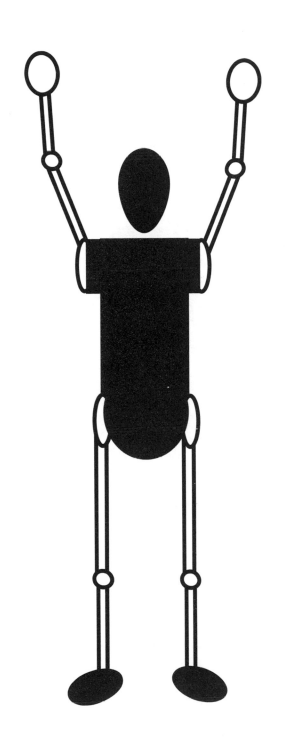

Third Static Stretch: Hang It All Out (or the "Rag-Doll" Stretch)

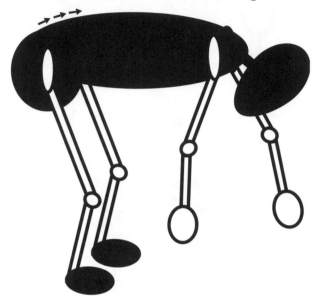

- With your feet flat on the floor, arms relaxed, and knees slightly bent, lean forwards *slowly* until you feel some pull in your lower back.
- Just "hang there" for a count of 5 to stretch out your lower back.

Now, you're ready to exercise 30-45 minutes!

Step 1: Walk with Upper-Body Motion

- Walk 20-25 minutes.
- Maintain constant motion.
- As you walk, pump your forearms up and down with your hands open or closed into fists.
- At the same time, move your arms rhythmically front and back from the shoulder.
- Walking to any kind of music can add pleasure to this exercise as well as the others.
- After you have finished walking, remember that you want to maintain steady motion to keep your heart rate up. Go directly into the next exercise.

Step 2: Straight-Arm Cross-Body Reach

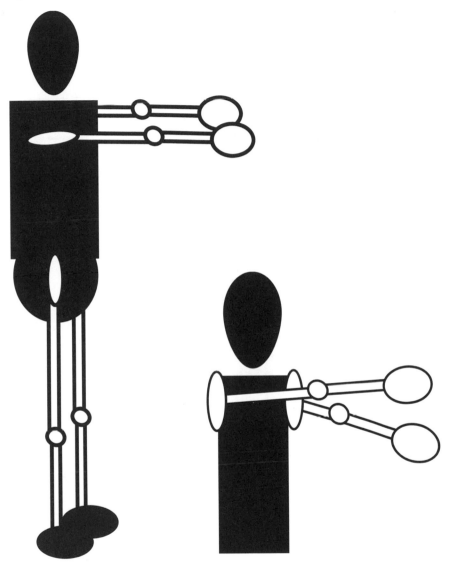

- Hold both arms straight in front of you and stretch first the right arm across your chest and back and then the left arm across your chest and back.
- Do at least 10 repetitions.

Step 3: Straight-Arm Butterfly

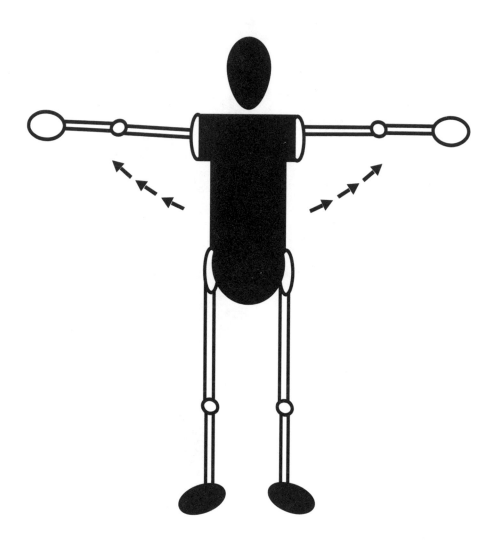

- With your feet flat on the floor and posture good, stretch your arms straight out in front of you with your palms touching.
- Keeping your arms straight at shoulder level, move your hands apart until you have reached your straight-out level and feel a pull point.
- Do at least 10 repetitions.

Step 4: The Chair Rise

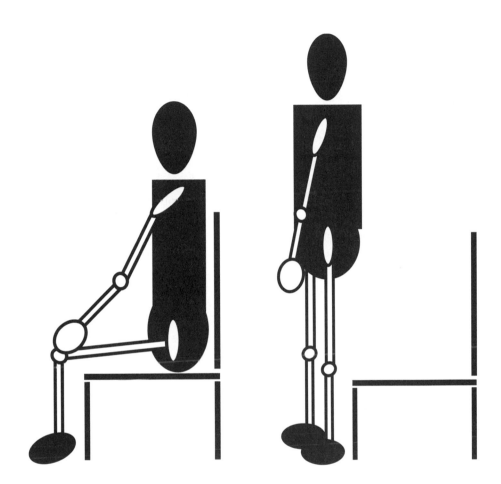

- You will need a straight, regular-height chair.
- Sitting in the chair, put your feet flat on the floor slightly in front of the chair.
- Hold your arms at your sides.
- Rise slowly, keeping good posture, from a sitting to a standing position.
- You can place your hands on your thighs for support.
- Sit back down slowly.
- Do at least 10 repetitions.

Step 5: Rhythmic Sidestep and Touch

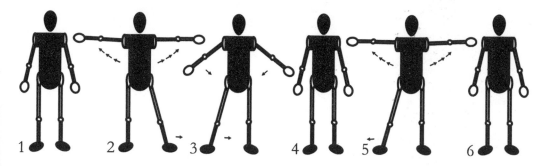

- Start from a standing position, feet flat on the floor, arms at your sides.
- Take a step to the left, stretching a little. As you bring your right foot over to its normal spot beside the left foot, raise your arms out from your sides to be level with your shoulders.
- As you bring your feet together, bring your arms back down, straight at your sides.
- Repeat this by stepping to the right.
- Do at least 20 repetitions. This exercise feels great, especially when you get into the rhythm!

Step 6: Standing Abdominal Tightener

- Start in the standing position with your knees slightly bent and hands on your hips.
- Slowly bend forwards as you breathe out, and contract your abdominal muscles towards your spine.
- As you feel the pull, count to 5.
- Begin to inhale as you raise yourself back up to the full upright position.
- Do at least 10 repetitions.

There, you've done it! You should feel as though you have had some exercise, even though you have used only your body. You should feel slightly sweaty, and most of all you should feel very good that you are stepping towards your own healthy lifestyle.

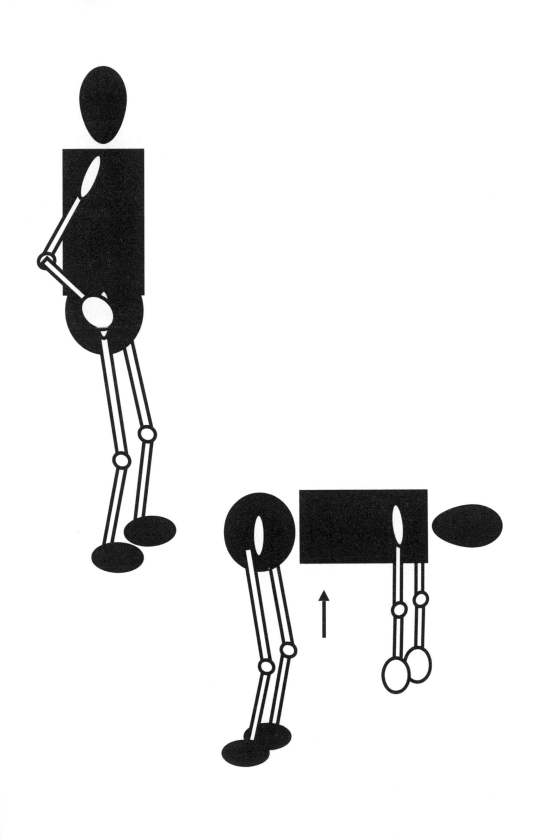

These are the Phase I exercises. For Phase II (see www.thenewor-leansprogram.com), we definitely suggest adding the power-walk component with one- to five-pound weights in each hand, using rhythmic arm swings. Don't start with the heaviest weights! As you move into strength building, you should build up gradually.

SPIRITUAL PROGRAM

Living a full, healthy lifestyle requires feeding and exercising not just our body but also our mind and spirit. As part of the New Orleans Program, we recommend a minimum of 5 minutes—if possible, 10 minutes—of quiet time each and every day. Even for the busiest of you, this goal is attainable. This part of the program requires no equipment. It can be done anywhere. It will provide you with surprising rewards.

- The ideal time for quiet time is anytime that you can make time.
- The ideal place for quiet time is a place that is quiet and private. Once you have learned and experienced some of the techniques for quiet time, you will find that the benefits can be achieved in less than perfect surroundings.
- Quiet time should be achieved and experienced in either the sitting or lying-down position.
- Be comfortable, whichever position you choose.
- First clear your mind by focusing calmly but intensely on your own breathing.
- Your mouth may be open or closed. Be relaxed.
- Breathe normally but deeply.
- Focus strictly on the physical experiences of breathing, especially in your upper and lower chest.
- After several minutes, your mind should be clear and focused and you should feel still and peaceful.
- When you have achieved this pleasant state, you may simply continue 5-10 minutes to focus on your calming breathing, or you may choose to pray to and focus on God. You will find what works best for you. Be open.

You will notice, when you end your quiet time, a feeling of refreshment and calm. In Phase II of the New Orleans Program (see www.the-neworleansprogram.com), this use of breathing can help with concentration, fear, and anger management.

Resources

African-American and other Louisiana ethnic events,
www.lsm.crt.state.la.us.
African-American business in New Orleans,
www.soulofneworleans.com.
American Association of Retired People, www.aarpmagazine.org.
American Diabetes Association, www.diabetes.org/home.jsp.
American Heart Association, www.americanheart.org/.
Calorie expenditure, www.caloriecontrol.org.
Cancer treatment information, 1-800-4-CANCER.
Center for Science in the Public Interest, www.cspinet.org.
Christmas in New Orleans, www.christmasneworleans.com.
Consumers Union, www.consumersunion.org.
Dietary Guidelines 2005, www.healthierus.gov/dietaryguidelines/.
Edible Schoolyard Program,
www.edibleschoolyard.org/homepage.html.
French Quarter Festival, www.frenchquarterfest.com.
Health assessments, www.healthstatus.com.
Healthweb2, www.healthweb2.com.
Horticulture specialist, Bobby Fletcher, Louisiana State University,
bfletcher@agctr.lsu.edu.
Infant feeding patterns, *European Journal of Clinical Nutrition*,
www.nature.com/ejcn/journal.
Jazz and Heritage Festival, www.nojazzfest.com.
Journal of the American Medical Association, www.jama.ama-assn.org/.
Louisiana Festivals and Fairs, www.laffnet.com.
McDonald's, www.mcdonalds.com.
Menopause information, www.menopausetype.com.
Men's health issues, www.menshealth.com.
New England Journal of Medicine, www.content.nejm.org.
New Orleans Program, www.theneworleansprogram.com.
Nutrients of food when dining away from home, www.ers.usda.gov.

Nutrition keys, www.washingtonpost.com.
Obesity information, www.obesity.com.
Seafood technology, Jon Bell, assistant professor, LSU,
    jbell@agctr.lsu.edu.
Shaking bad habits, www.unicitynetwork.com.
Soil fertility, J. Stevens, associate professor, LSU,
    jstevens@agctr.lsu.edu.
Specialty salts, ultimatespice2005.com.
Television Turn-Off Week, www.tvturnoff.org.
Toxins in food supply, www.environmentalnutrition.com.
Walking compared with vigorous physical activity,
    www.jama.ama-assn.org/.

Index